You're Out of Your Mind, Charlie Brown!

Other Titan Facsimile Editions by Charles M. Schulz

On sale now:
Peanuts
More Peanuts
Good Ol' Charlie Brown
Good Grief, More Peanuts!
Snoopy

Coming soon:
But We Love You, Charlie Brown
Peanuts Revisited
Go Fly a Kite, Charlie Brown
Peanuts Every Sunday

You're Out of Your Mind, Charlie Brown!

A New PEANUTS Book by CHARLES M. SCHULZ

TITAN COMICS

YOU'RE OUT OF YOUR MIND, CHARLIE BROWN!
ISBN: 9781782761600
PUBLISHED BY TITAN COMICS, A DIVISION OF TITAN PUBLISHING GROUP LTD,
144 SOUTHWARK ST, LONDON SE1 0UP. TCN 305.
COPYRIGHT © 2015 BY PEANUTS WORLDWIDE LLC.
PRINTED IN INDIA.
10 9 8 7 6 5 4 3 2 1

WWW.TITAN-COMICS.COM
WWW.PEANUTS.COM

ORIGINALLY PUBLISHED IN OCTOBER 1956 BY RINEHART & WINSTON
NEW YORK & TORONTO

A CIP CATALOGUE RECORD FOR THIS TITLE
IS AVAILABLE FROM THE BRITISH LIBRARY.
THIS EDITION FIRST PUBLISHED: OCTOBER 2015

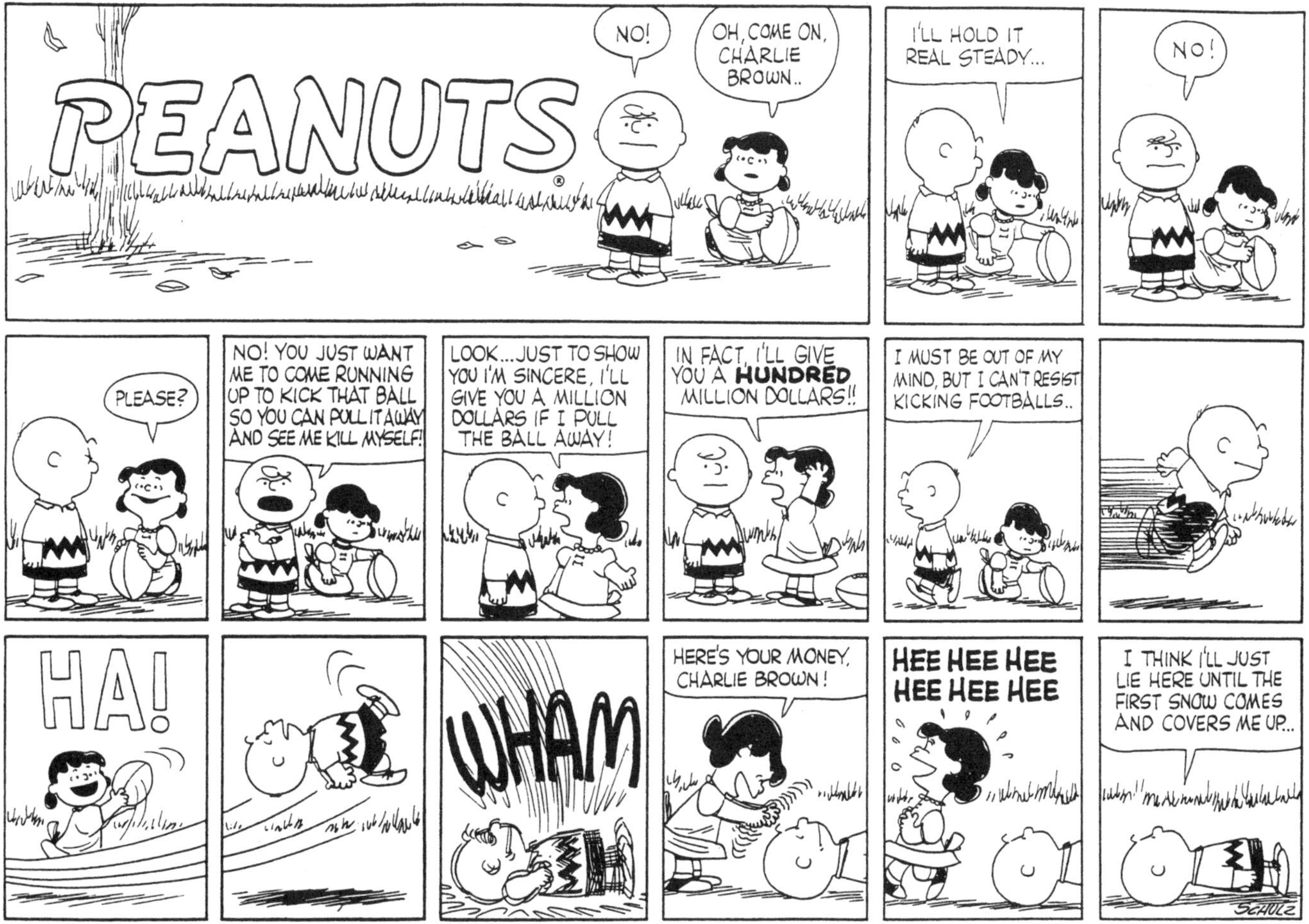
PEANUTS
NO!
OH, COME ON, CHARLIE BROWN..
I'LL HOLD IT REAL STEADY...
NO!
PLEASE?
NO! YOU JUST WANT ME TO COME RUNNING UP TO KICK THAT BALL SO YOU CAN PULL IT AWAY AND SEE ME KILL MYSELF!
LOOK...JUST TO SHOW YOU I'M SINCERE, I'LL GIVE YOU A MILLION DOLLARS IF I PULL THE BALL AWAY!
IN FACT, I'LL GIVE YOU A **HUNDRED** MILLION DOLLARS!!
I MUST BE OUT OF MY MIND, BUT I CAN'T RESIST KICKING FOOTBALLS..
HA!
WHAM
HERE'S YOUR MONEY, CHARLIE BROWN!
HEE HEE HEE HEE HEE HEE
I THINK I'LL JUST LIE HERE UNTIL THE FIRST SNOW COMES AND COVERS ME UP...
SCHULZ

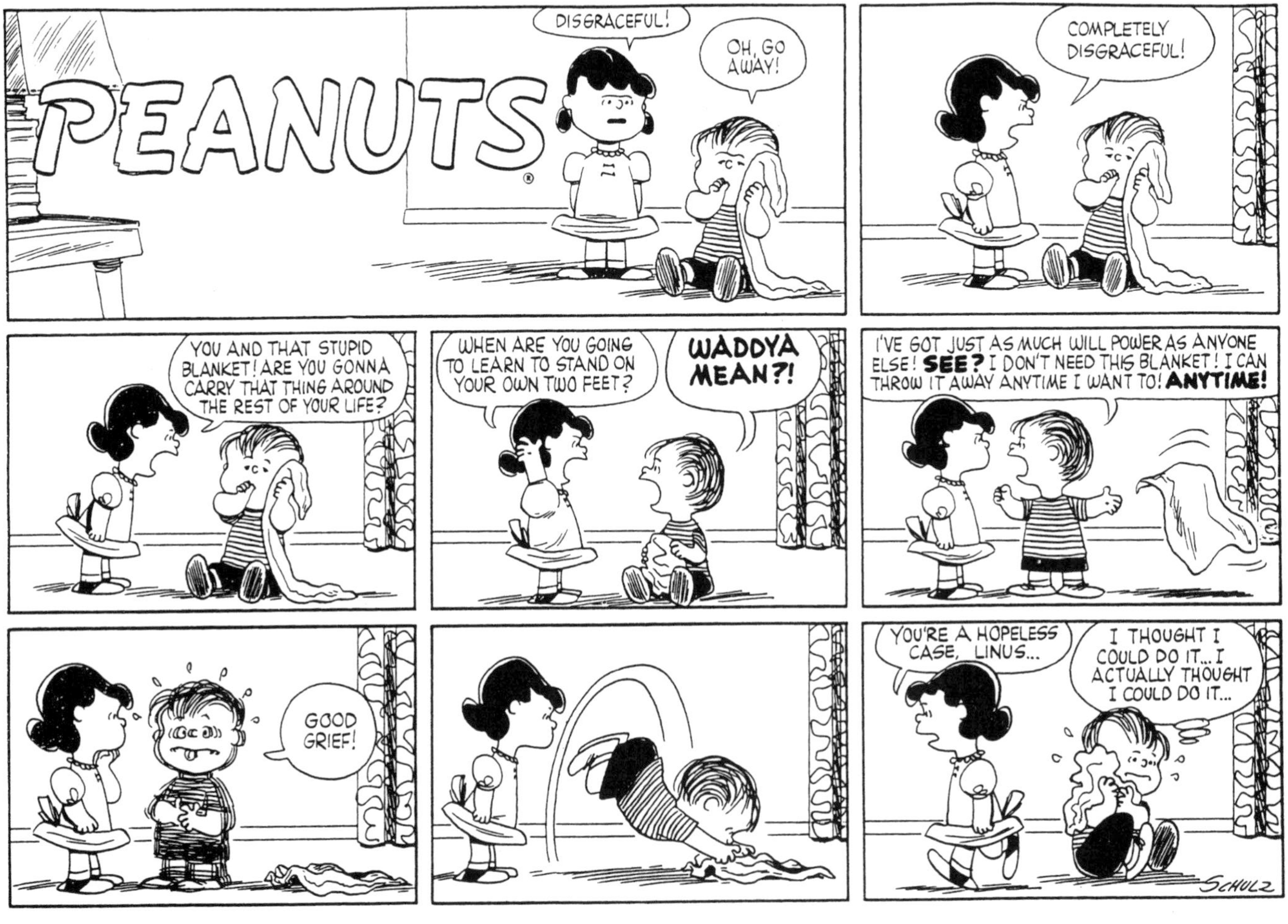
PEANUTS®
DISGRACEFUL!
OH, GO AWAY!
COMPLETELY DISGRACEFUL!
YOU AND THAT STUPID BLANKET! ARE YOU GONNA CARRY THAT THING AROUND THE REST OF YOUR LIFE?
WHEN ARE YOU GOING TO LEARN TO STAND ON YOUR OWN TWO FEET?
WADDYA MEAN?!
I'VE GOT JUST AS MUCH WILL POWER AS ANYONE ELSE! SEE? I DON'T NEED THIS BLANKET! I CAN THROW IT AWAY ANYTIME I WANT TO! ANYTIME!
GOOD GRIEF!
YOU'RE A HOPELESS CASE, LINUS...
I THOUGHT I COULD DO IT... I ACTUALLY THOUGHT I COULD DO IT...
SCHULZ

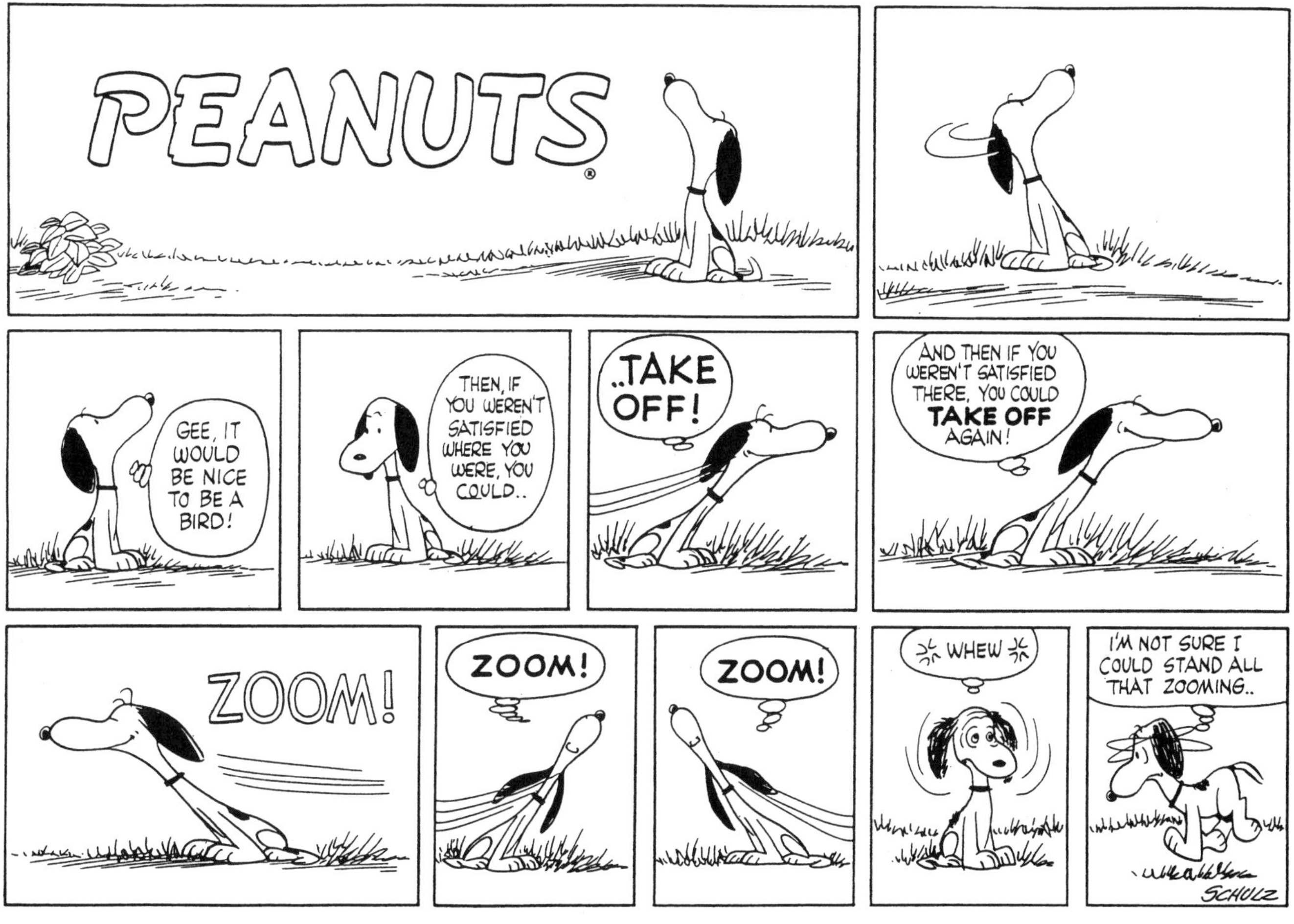
PEANUTS®
GEE, IT WOULD BE NICE TO BE A BIRD!
THEN, IF YOU WEREN'T SATISFIED WHERE YOU WERE, YOU COULD..
..TAKE OFF!
AND THEN IF YOU WEREN'T SATISFIED THERE, YOU COULD TAKE OFF AGAIN!
ZOOM!
ZOOM!
ZOOM!
WHEW
I'M NOT SURE I COULD STAND ALL THAT ZOOMING..
SCHULZ

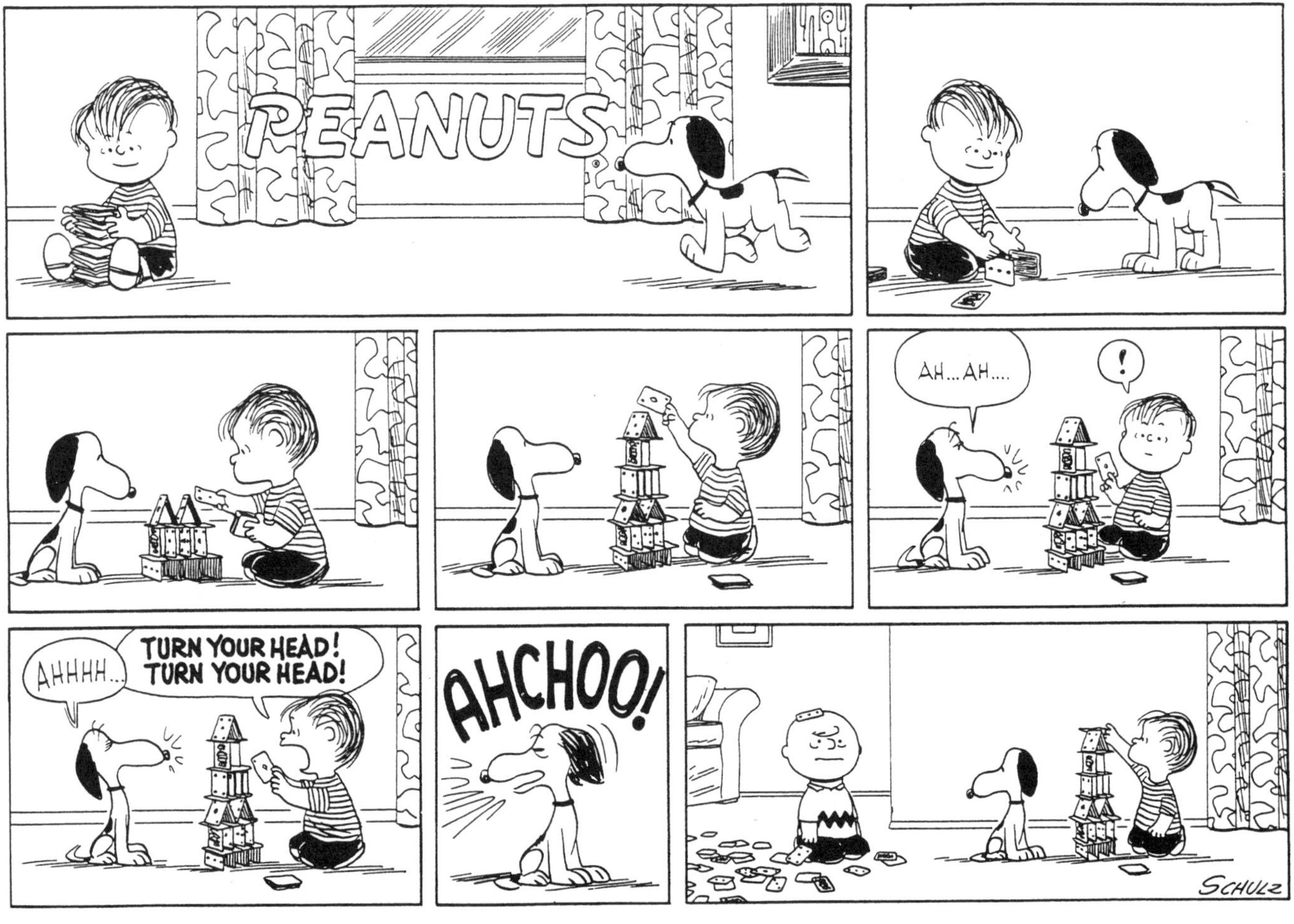
PEANUTS
AH...AH....
!
AHHHH...
TURN YOUR HEAD! TURN YOUR HEAD!
AHCHOO!
SCHULZ

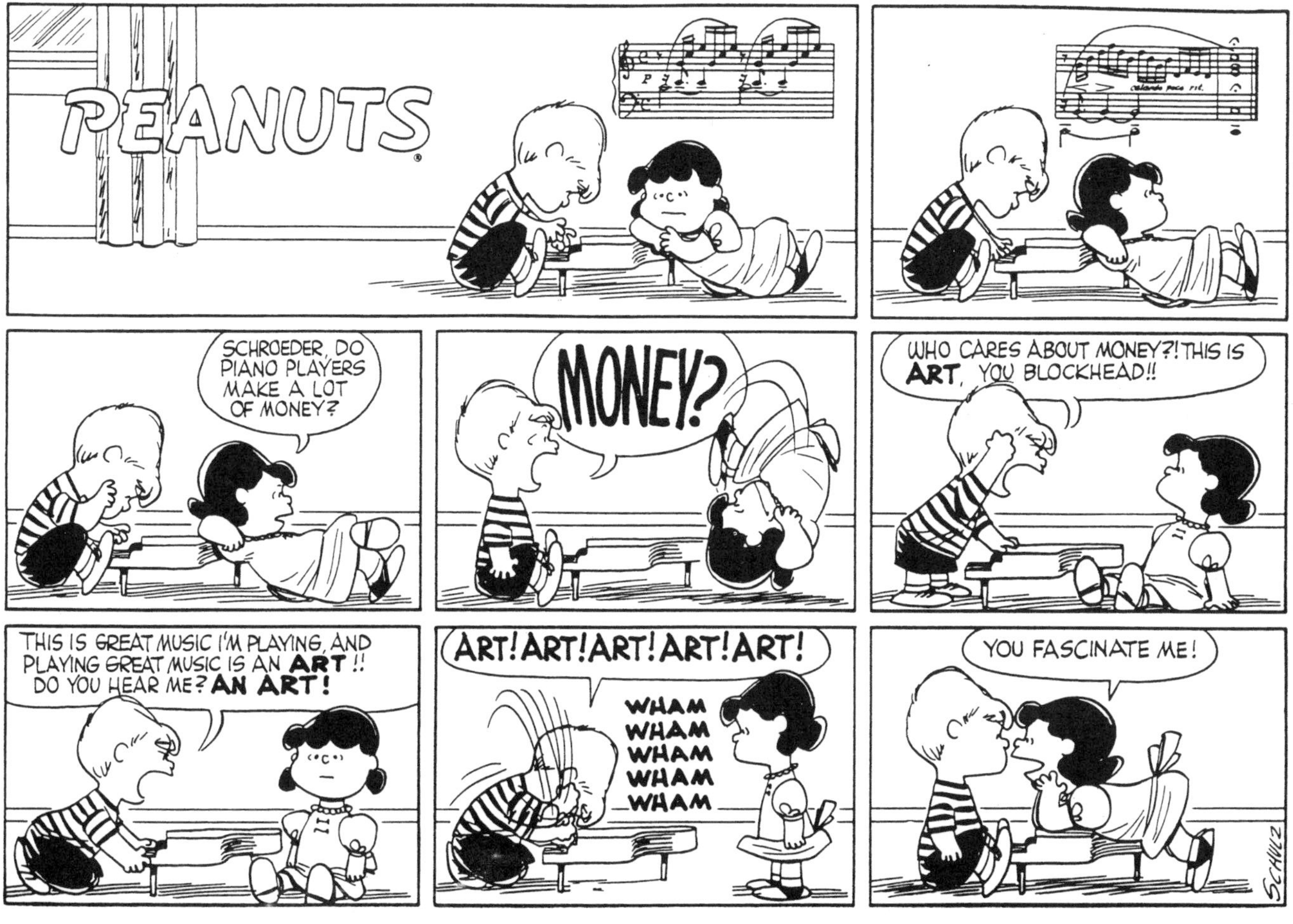
PEANUTS
SCHROEDER, DO PIANO PLAYERS MAKE A LOT OF MONEY?
MONEY?
WHO CARES ABOUT MONEY?! THIS IS **ART**, YOU BLOCKHEAD!!
THIS IS GREAT MUSIC I'M PLAYING, AND PLAYING GREAT MUSIC IS AN **ART**!! DO YOU HEAR ME? **AN ART**!
ART! ART! ART! ART! ART!
WHAM
WHAM
WHAM
WHAM
WHAM
WHAM
YOU FASCINATE ME!
SCHULZ

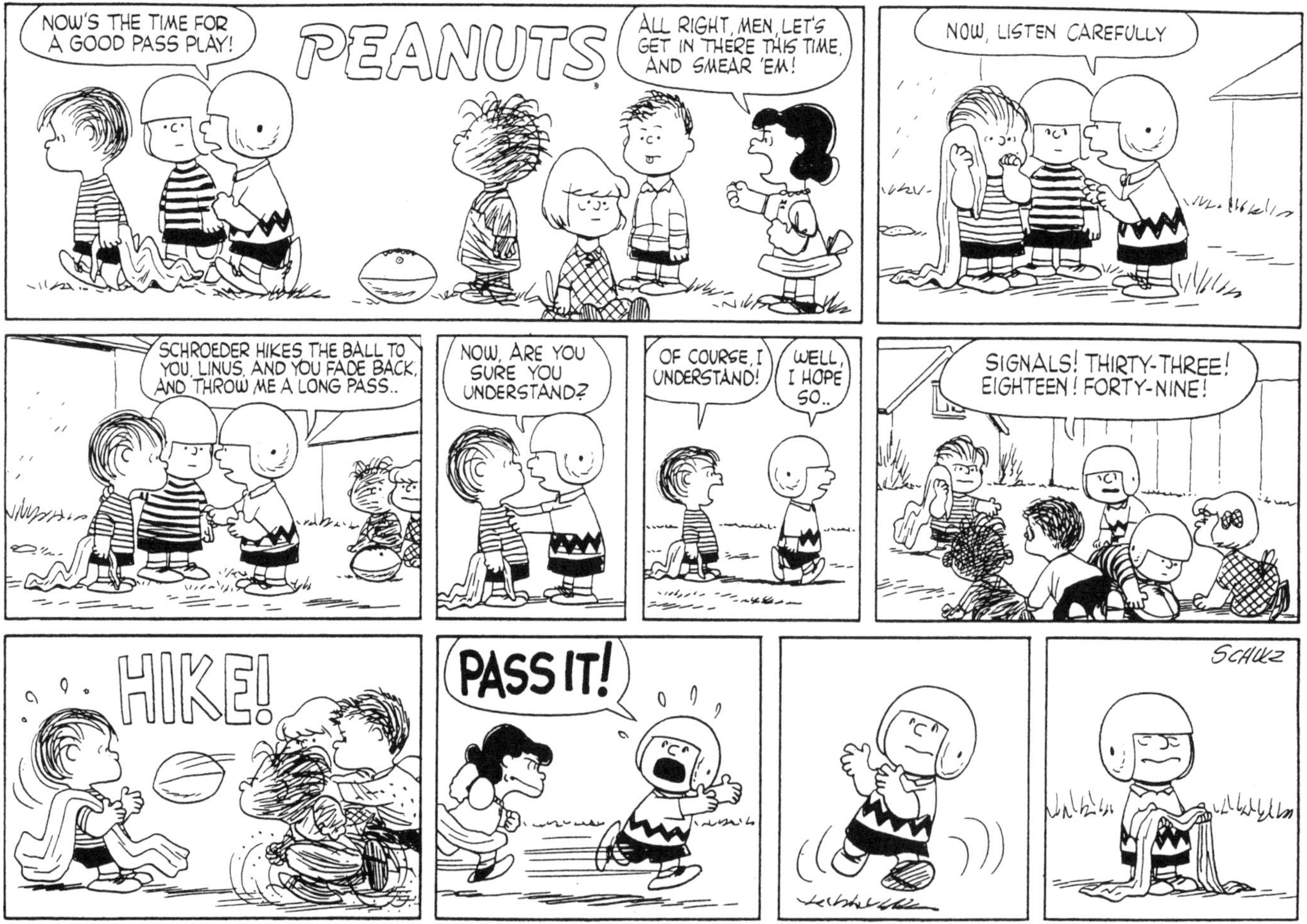
NOW'S THE TIME FOR A GOOD PASS PLAY!
PEANUTS
ALL RIGHT, MEN, LET'S GET IN THERE THIS TIME, AND SMEAR 'EM!
NOW, LISTEN CAREFULLY
SCHROEDER HIKES THE BALL TO YOU, LINUS, AND YOU FADE BACK, AND THROW ME A LONG PASS..
NOW, ARE YOU SURE YOU UNDERSTAND?
OF COURSE, I UNDERSTAND!
WELL, I HOPE SO..
SIGNALS! THIRTY-THREE! EIGHTEEN! FORTY-NINE!
HIKE!
PASS IT!
SCHULZ

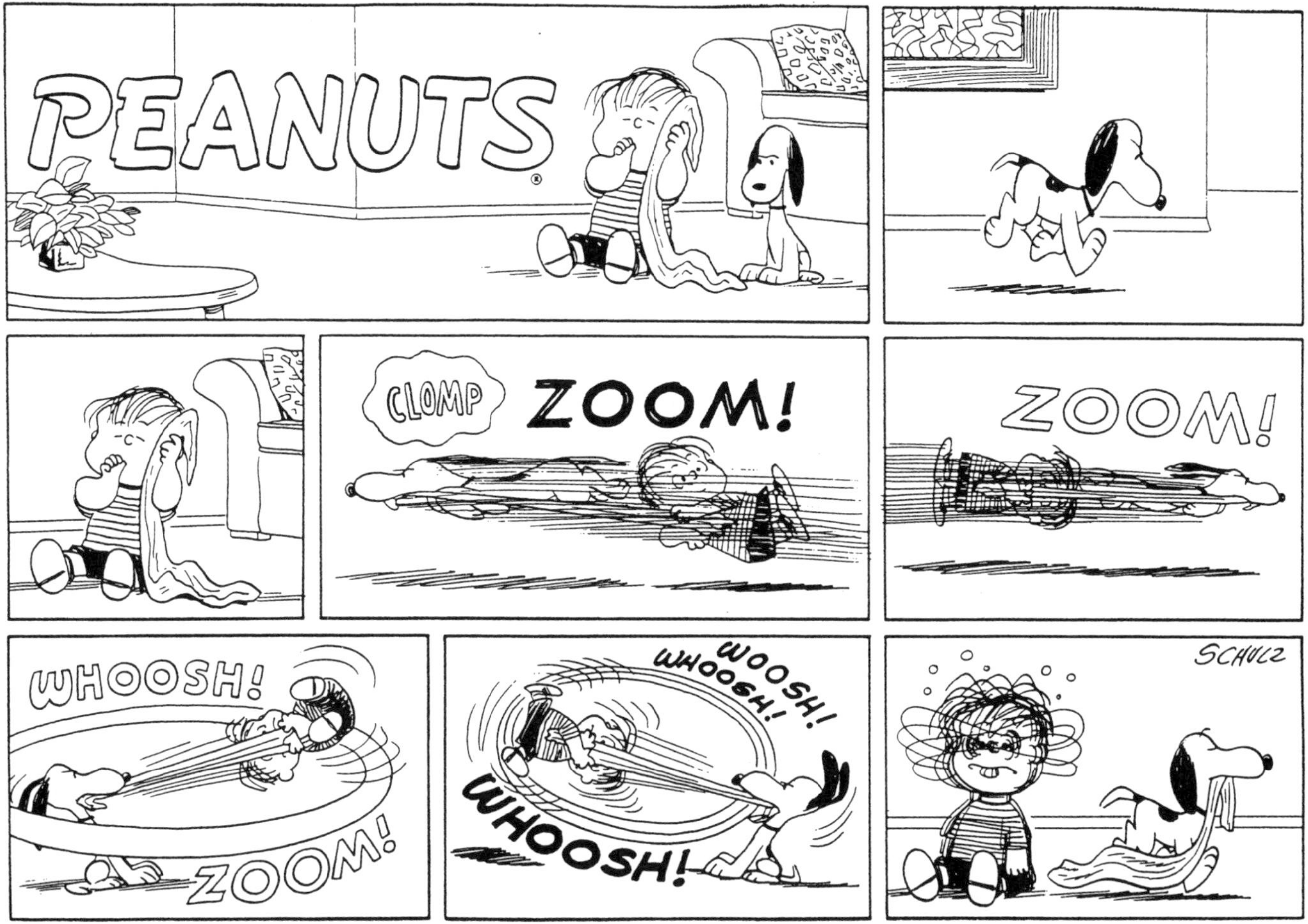
PEANUTS
CLOMP
ZOOM!
ZOOM!
WHOOSH!
ZOOM!
WOOSH!
WHOOSH!
WHOOSH!
SCHULZ

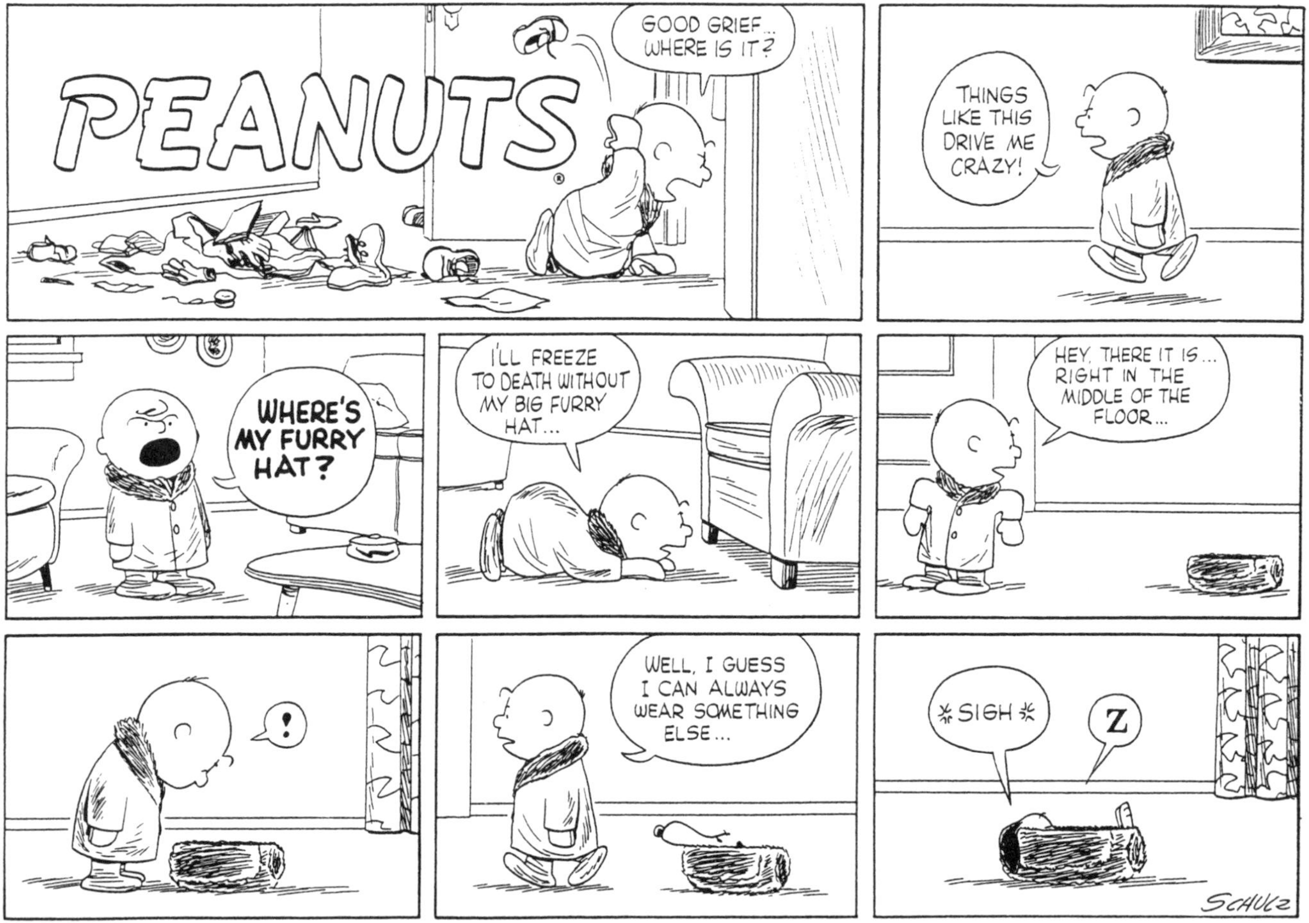
PEANUTS
GOOD GRIEF... WHERE IS IT?
THINGS LIKE THIS DRIVE ME CRAZY!
WHERE'S MY FURRY HAT?
I'LL FREEZE TO DEATH WITHOUT MY BIG FURRY HAT...
HEY, THERE IT IS... RIGHT IN THE MIDDLE OF THE FLOOR...
!
WELL, I GUESS I CAN ALWAYS WEAR SOMETHING ELSE...
SIGH
Z
SCHULZ

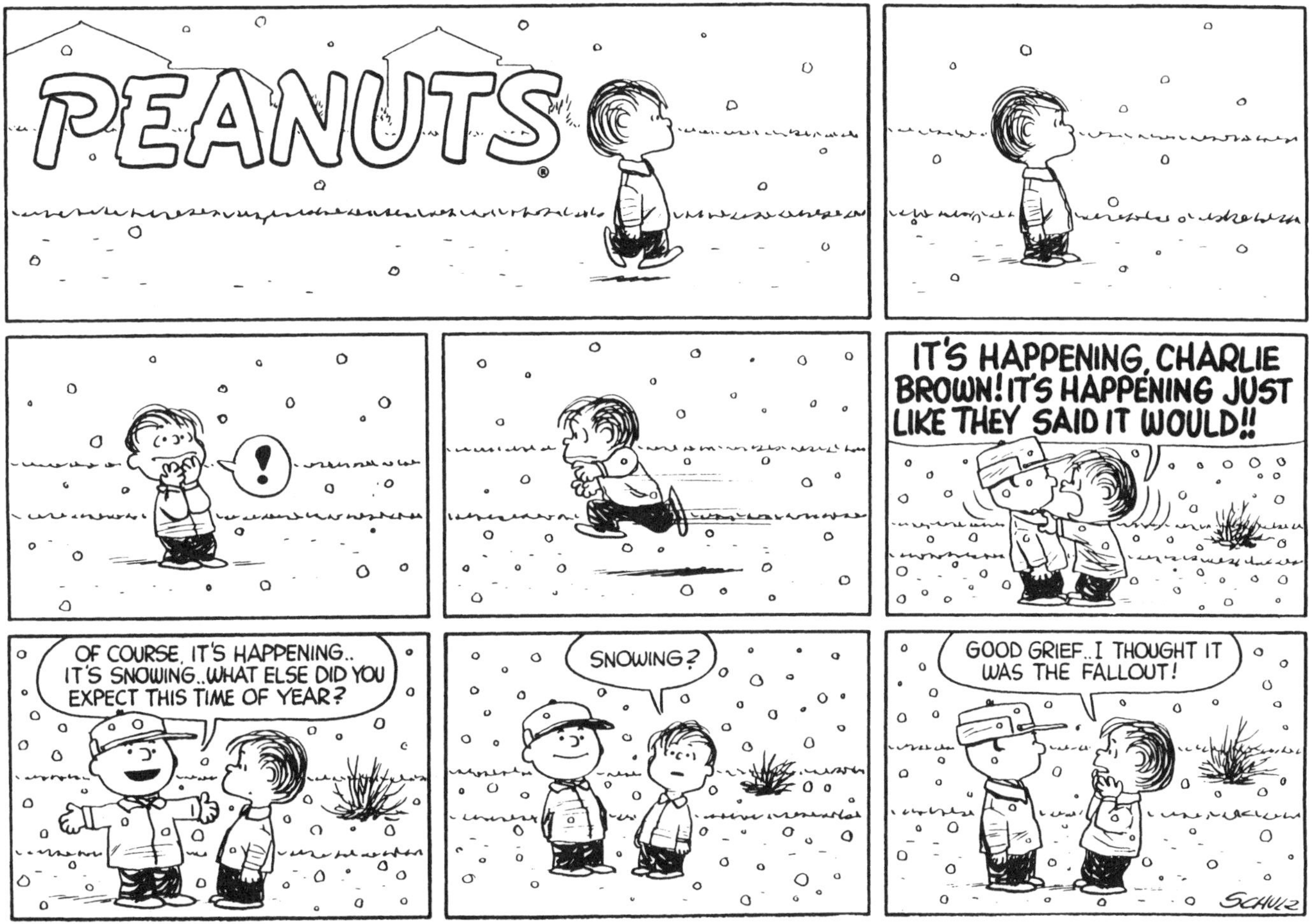
PEANUTS®
!
IT'S HAPPENING, CHARLIE BROWN! IT'S HAPPENING JUST LIKE THEY SAID IT WOULD!!
OF COURSE, IT'S HAPPENING.. IT'S SNOWING..WHAT ELSE DID YOU EXPECT THIS TIME OF YEAR?
SNOWING?
GOOD GRIEF..I THOUGHT IT WAS THE FALLOUT!
SCHULZ

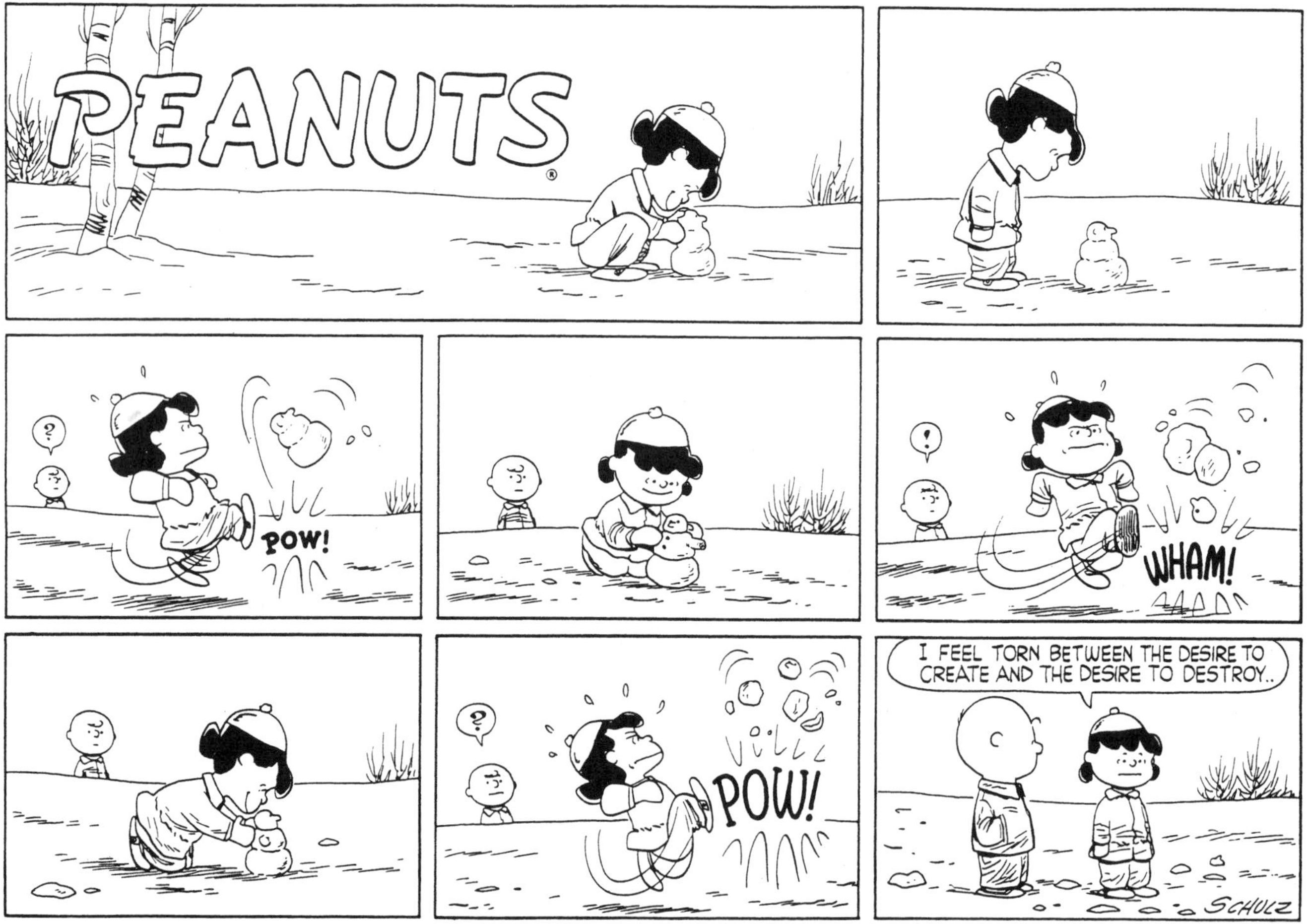
PEANUTS
?
POW!
!
WHAM!
?
POW!
I FEEL TORN BETWEEN THE DESIRE TO CREATE AND THE DESIRE TO DESTROY..
SCHULZ

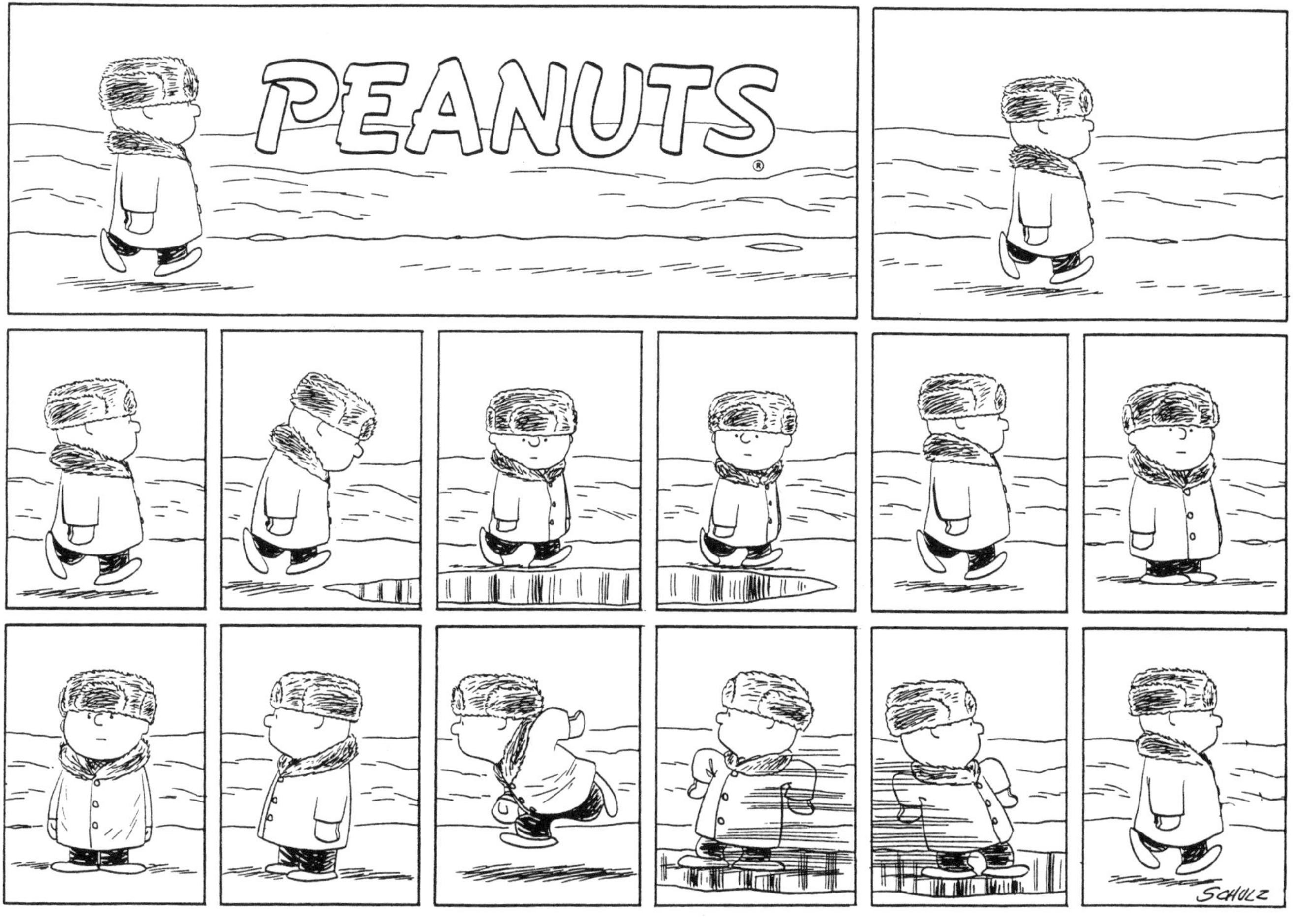
PEANUTS
SCHULZ

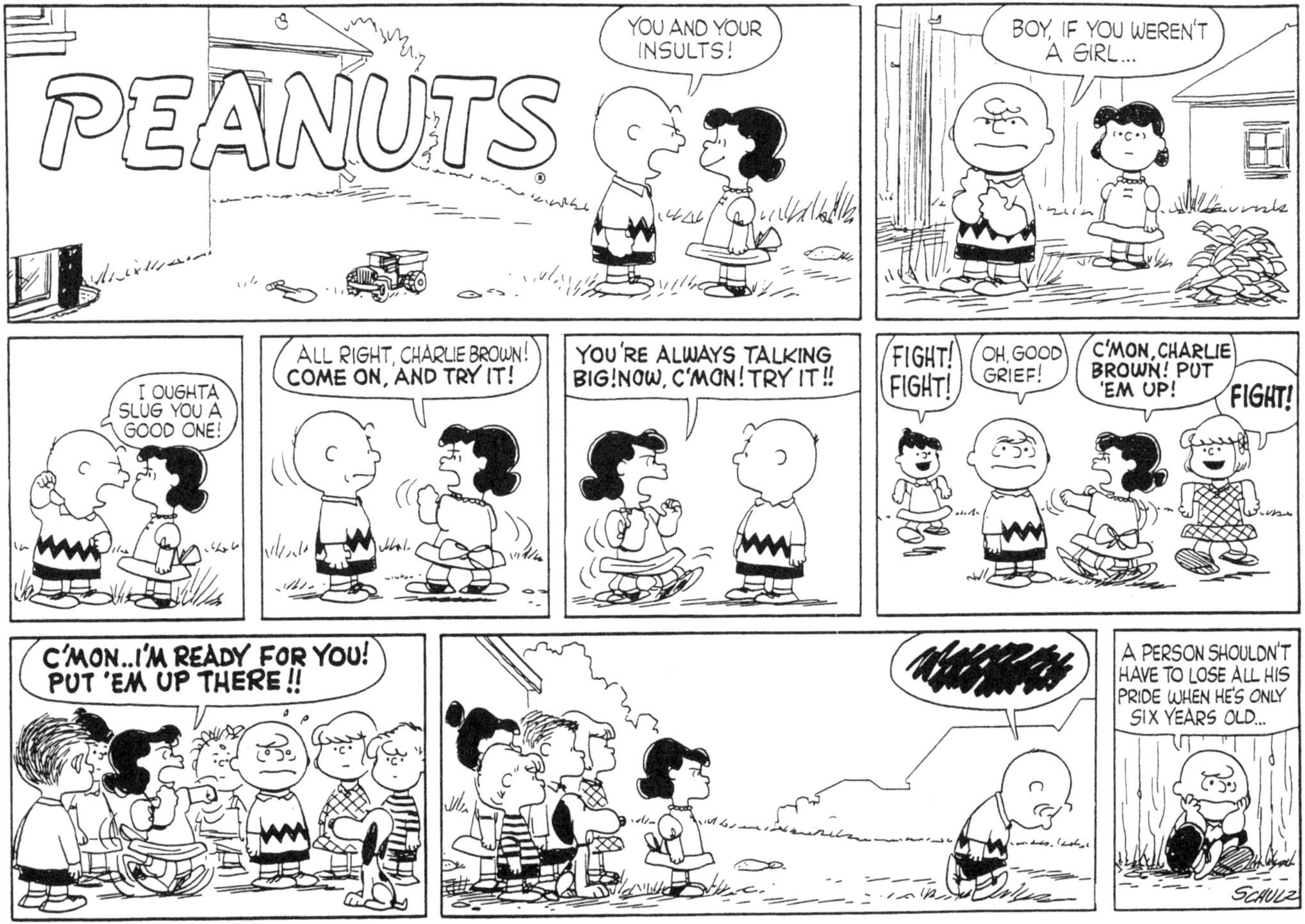
PEANUTS
YOU AND YOUR INSULTS!
BOY, IF YOU WEREN'T A GIRL...
I OUGHTA SLUG YOU A GOOD ONE!
ALL RIGHT, CHARLIE BROWN! COME ON, AND TRY IT!
YOU'RE ALWAYS TALKING BIG! NOW, C'MON! TRY IT!!
FIGHT! FIGHT!
OH, GOOD GRIEF!
C'MON, CHARLIE BROWN! PUT 'EM UP!
FIGHT!
C'MON..I'M READY FOR YOU! PUT 'EM UP THERE!!
A PERSON SHOULDN'T HAVE TO LOSE ALL HIS PRIDE WHEN HE'S ONLY SIX YEARS OLD...
SCHULZ

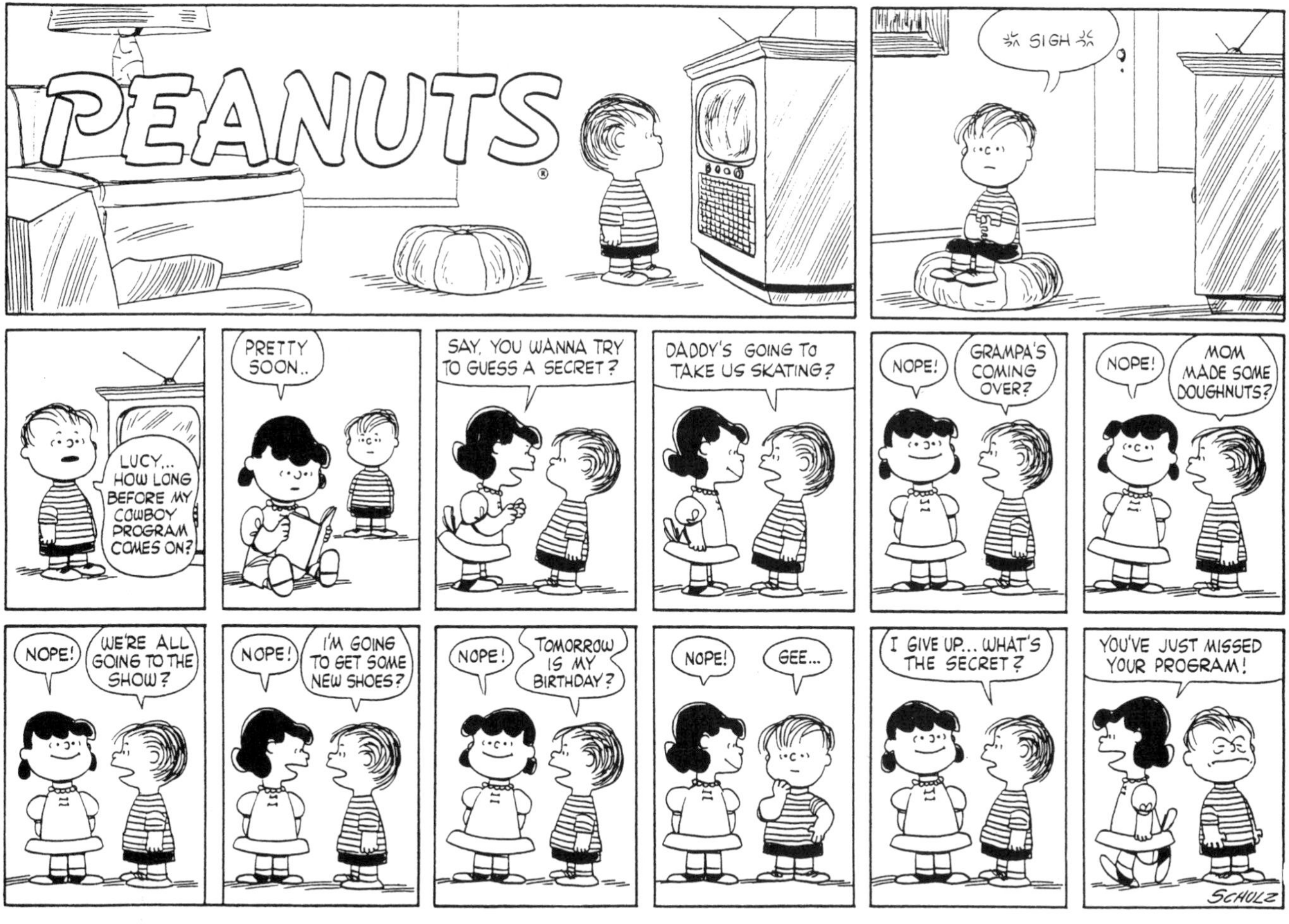
PEANUTS
SIGH
LUCY... HOW LONG BEFORE MY COWBOY PROGRAM COMES ON?
PRETTY SOON..
SAY, YOU WANNA TRY TO GUESS A SECRET?
DADDY'S GOING TO TAKE US SKATING?
NOPE!
GRAMPA'S COMING OVER?
NOPE!
MOM MADE SOME DOUGHNUTS?
NOPE!
WE'RE ALL GOING TO THE SHOW?
NOPE!
I'M GOING TO GET SOME NEW SHOES?
NOPE!
TOMORROW IS MY BIRTHDAY?
NOPE!
GEE...
I GIVE UP... WHAT'S THE SECRET?
YOU'VE JUST MISSED YOUR PROGRAM!
SCHULZ

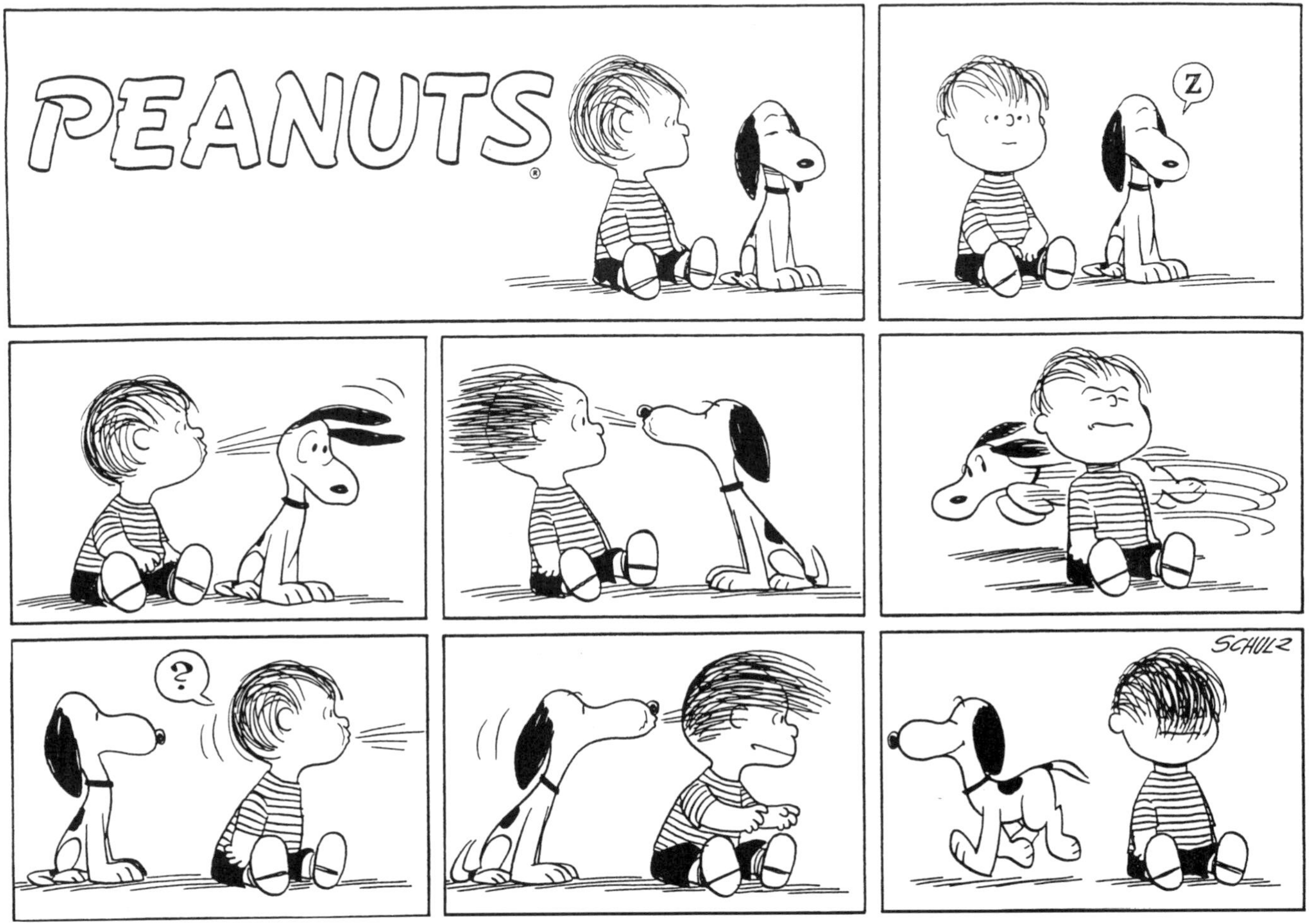
PEANUTS
Z
?
SCHULZ

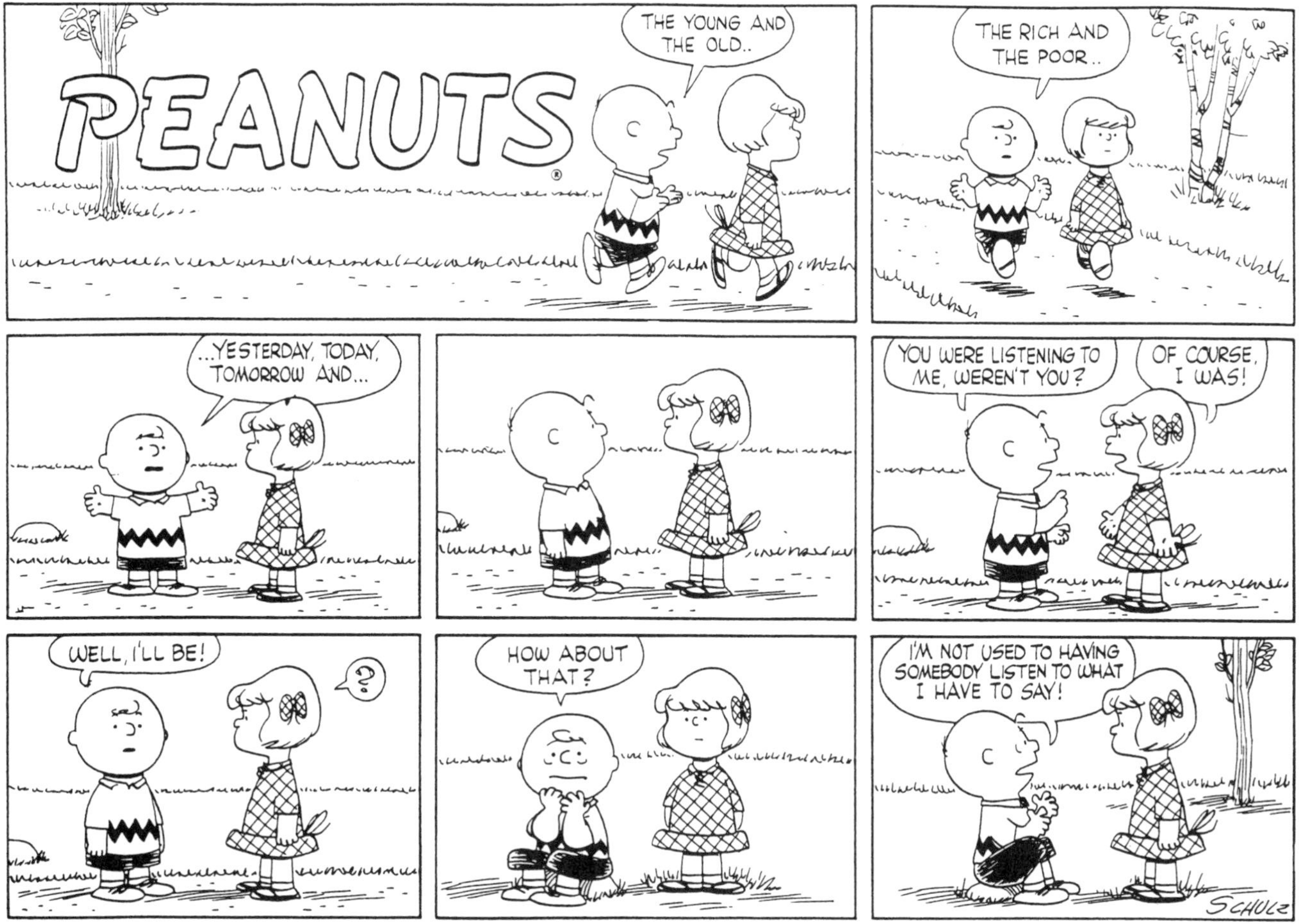
PEANUTS
THE YOUNG AND THE OLD..
THE RICH AND THE POOR..
...YESTERDAY, TODAY, TOMORROW AND...
YOU WERE LISTENING TO ME, WEREN'T YOU?
OF COURSE, I WAS!
WELL, I'LL BE!
?
HOW ABOUT THAT?
I'M NOT USED TO HAVING SOMEBODY LISTEN TO WHAT I HAVE TO SAY!
SCHULZ

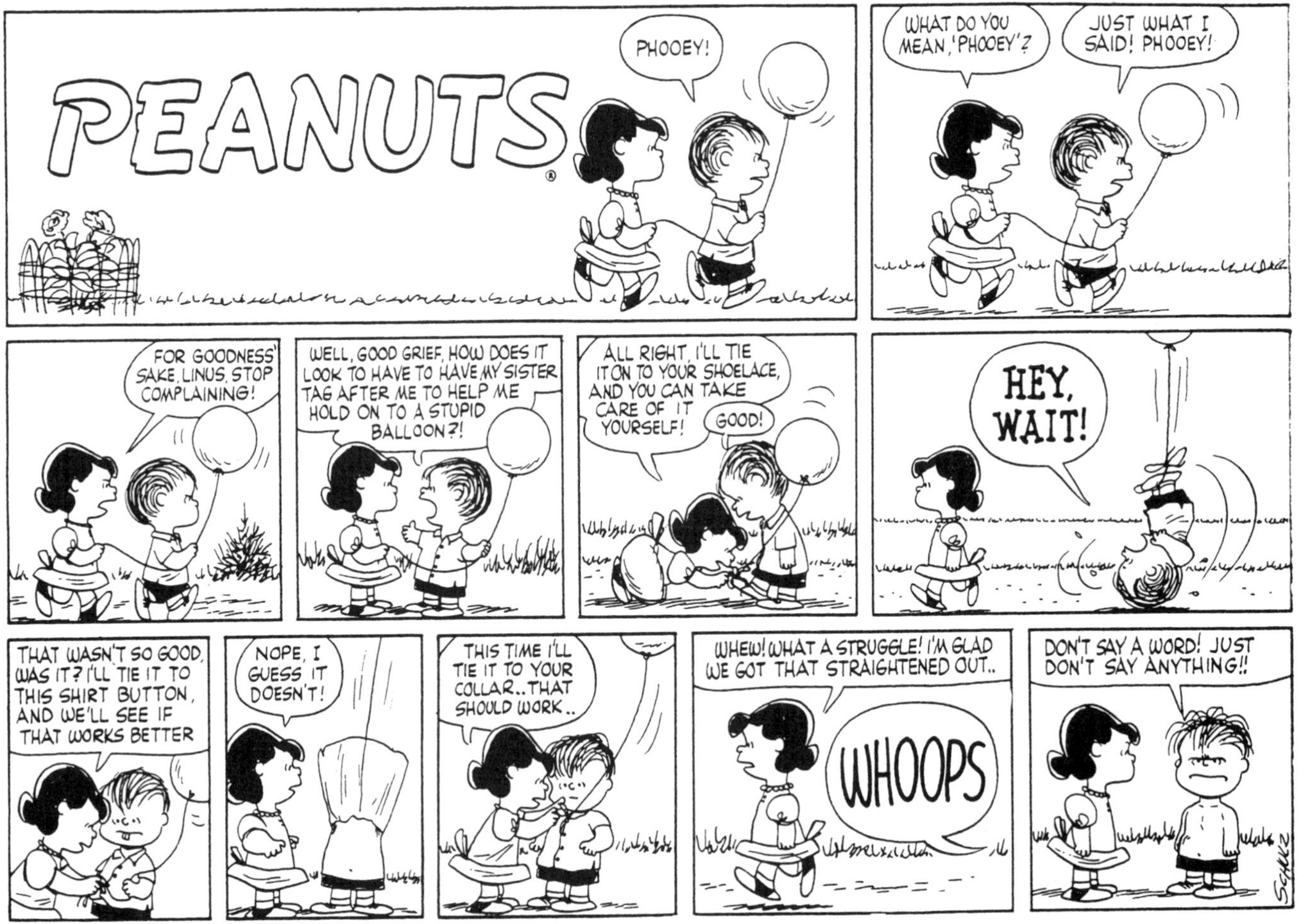
PEANUTS
PHOOEY!
WHAT DO YOU MEAN, 'PHOOEY'?
JUST WHAT I SAID! PHOOEY!
FOR GOODNESS' SAKE, LINUS, STOP COMPLAINING!
WELL, GOOD GRIEF, HOW DOES IT LOOK TO HAVE TO HAVE MY SISTER TAG AFTER ME TO HELP ME HOLD ON TO A STUPID BALLOON?!
ALL RIGHT, I'LL TIE IT ON TO YOUR SHOELACE, AND YOU CAN TAKE CARE OF IT YOURSELF!
GOOD!
HEY, WAIT!
THAT WASN'T SO GOOD, WAS IT? I'LL TIE IT TO THIS SHIRT BUTTON, AND WE'LL SEE IF THAT WORKS BETTER
NOPE, I GUESS IT DOESN'T!
THIS TIME I'LL TIE IT TO YOUR COLLAR..THAT SHOULD WORK..
WHEW! WHAT A STRUGGLE! I'M GLAD WE GOT THAT STRAIGHTENED OUT..
WHOOPS
DON'T SAY A WORD! JUST DON'T SAY ANYTHING!!
SCHULZ

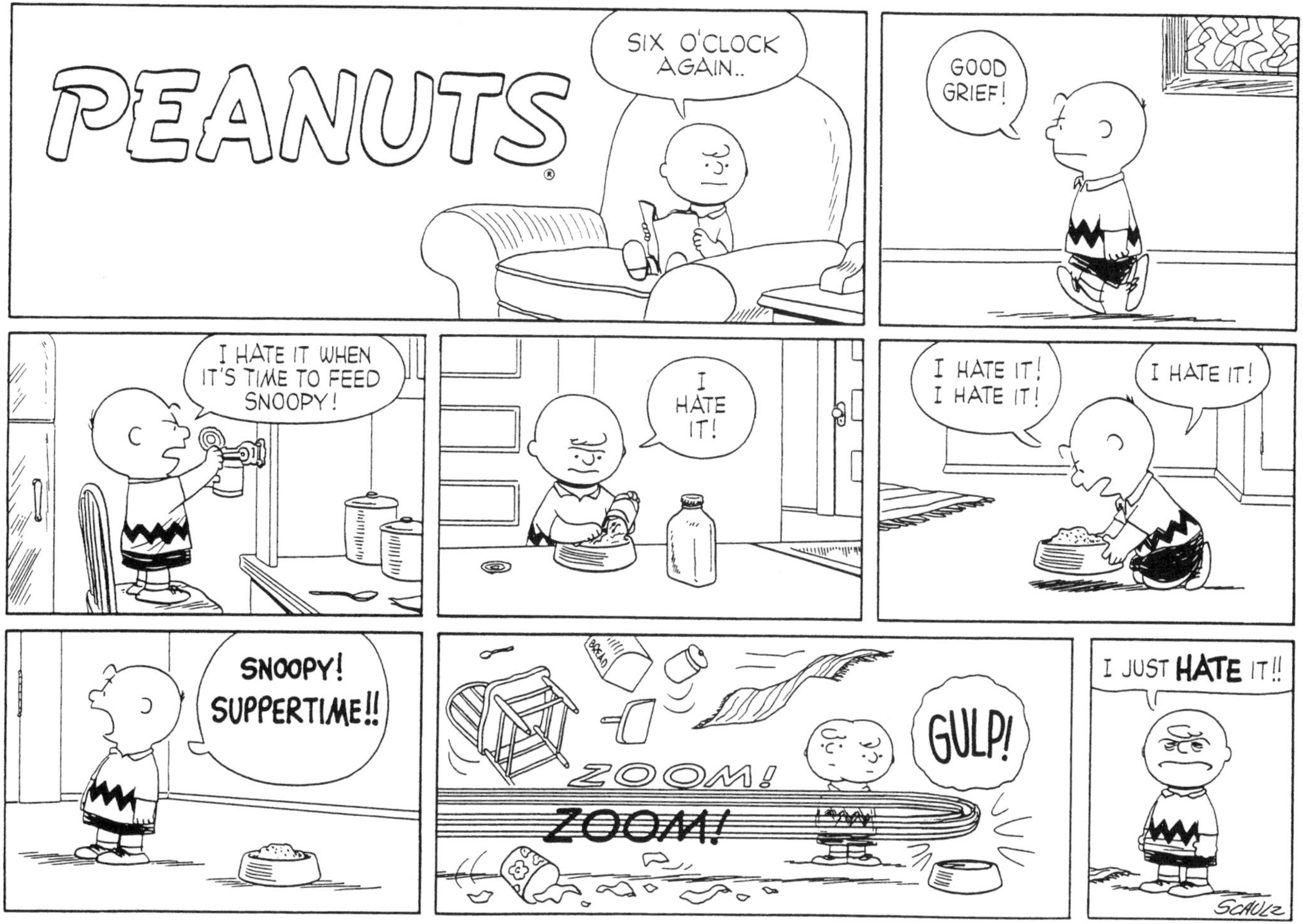
PEANUTS
SIX O'CLOCK AGAIN..
GOOD GRIEF!
I HATE IT WHEN IT'S TIME TO FEED SNOOPY!
I HATE IT!
I HATE IT! I HATE IT!
I HATE IT!
SNOOPY! SUPPERTIME!!
BREAD
ZOOM!
ZOOM!
GULP!
I JUST HATE IT!!
SCHULZ

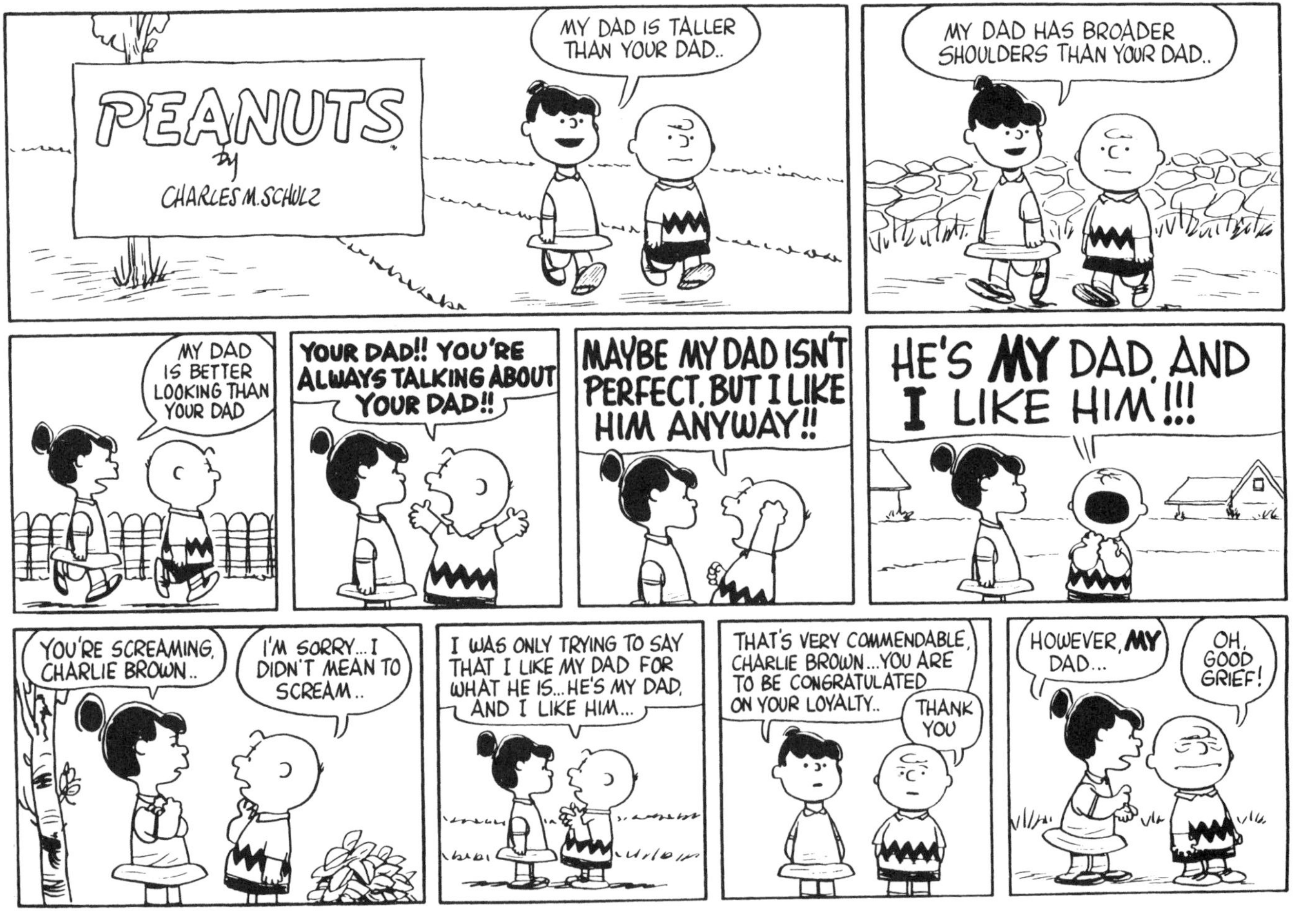
PEANUTS
by
CHARLES M. SCHULZ
MY DAD IS TALLER THAN YOUR DAD..
MY DAD HAS BROADER SHOULDERS THAN YOUR DAD..
MY DAD IS BETTER LOOKING THAN YOUR DAD
YOUR DAD!! YOU'RE ALWAYS TALKING ABOUT YOUR DAD!!
MAYBE MY DAD ISN'T PERFECT, BUT I LIKE HIM ANYWAY!!
HE'S MY DAD, AND I LIKE HIM!!!
YOU'RE SCREAMING, CHARLIE BROWN..
I'M SORRY...I DIDN'T MEAN TO SCREAM..
I WAS ONLY TRYING TO SAY THAT I LIKE MY DAD FOR WHAT HE IS...HE'S MY DAD, AND I LIKE HIM...
THAT'S VERY COMMENDABLE, CHARLIE BROWN...YOU ARE TO BE CONGRATULATED ON YOUR LOYALTY..
THANK YOU
HOWEVER, MY DAD...
OH, GOOD GRIEF!

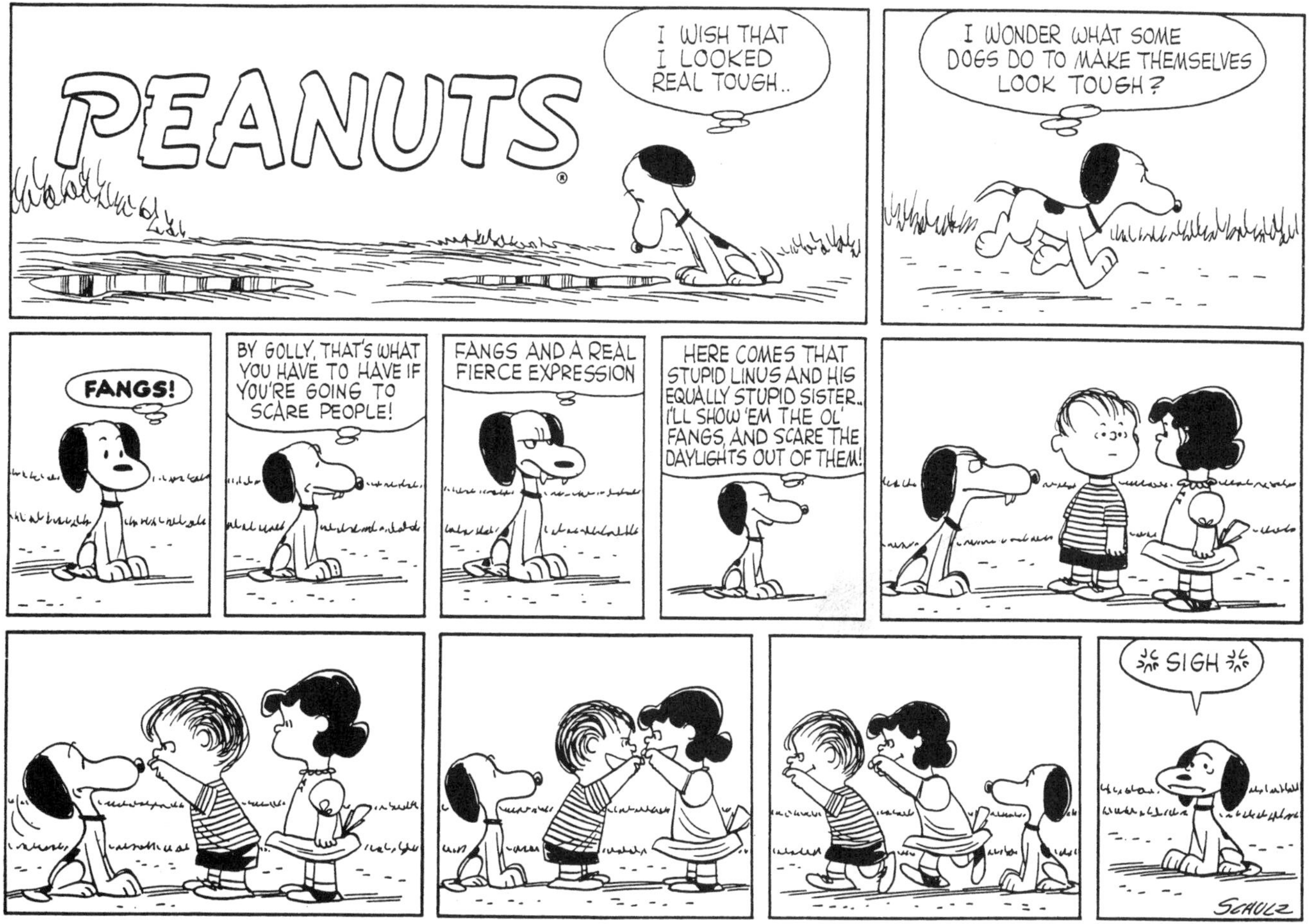
PEANUTS®
I WISH THAT I LOOKED REAL TOUGH..
I WONDER WHAT SOME DOGS DO TO MAKE THEMSELVES LOOK TOUGH?
FANGS!
BY GOLLY, THAT'S WHAT YOU HAVE TO HAVE IF YOU'RE GOING TO SCARE PEOPLE!
FANGS AND A REAL FIERCE EXPRESSION
HERE COMES THAT STUPID LINUS AND HIS EQUALLY STUPID SISTER.. I'LL SHOW 'EM THE OL' FANGS, AND SCARE THE DAYLIGHTS OUT OF THEM!
SIGH
SCHULZ

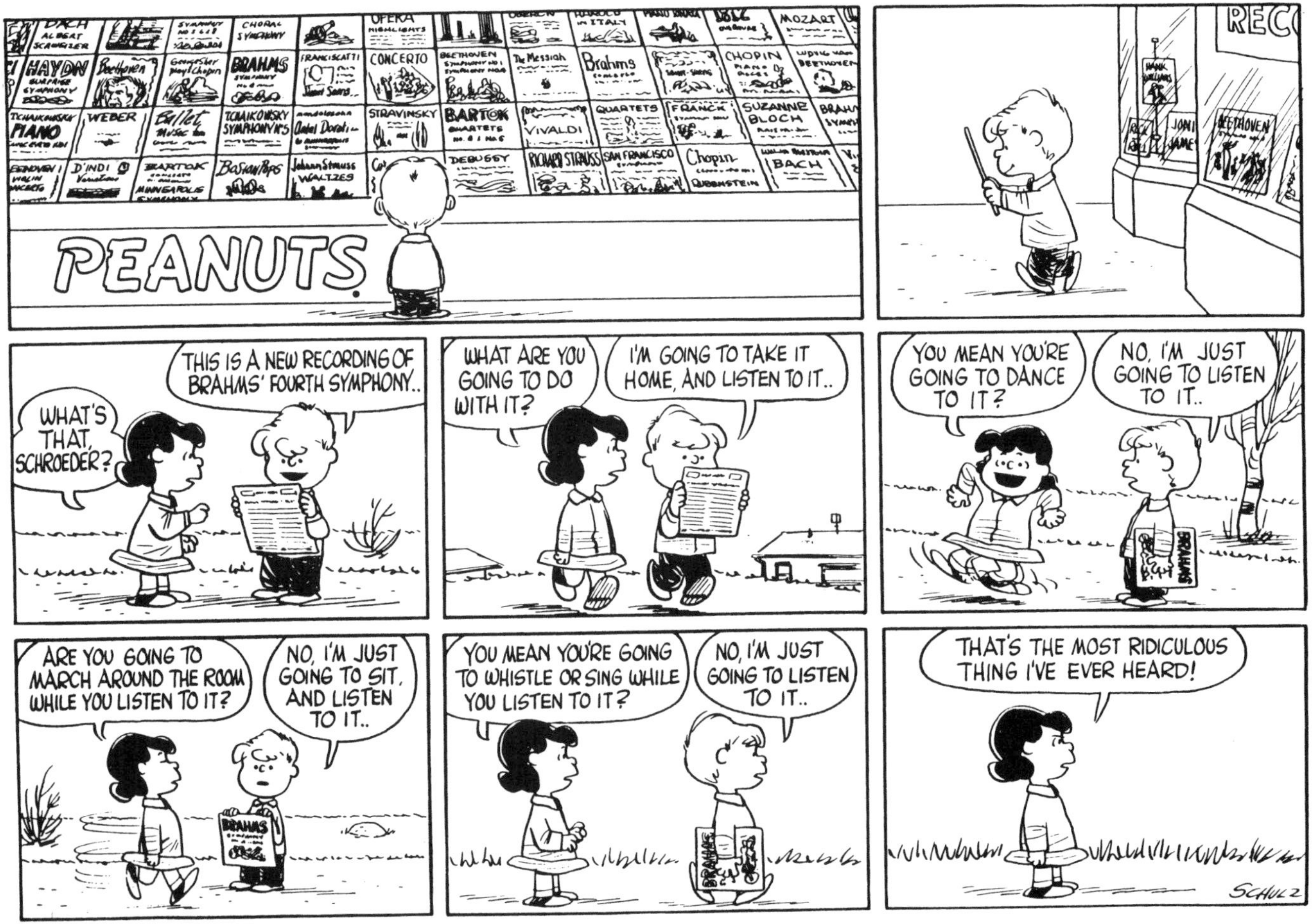
PEANUTS
WHAT'S THAT, SCHROEDER?
THIS IS A NEW RECORDING OF BRAHMS' FOURTH SYMPHONY..
WHAT ARE YOU GOING TO DO WITH IT?
I'M GOING TO TAKE IT HOME, AND LISTEN TO IT..
YOU MEAN YOU'RE GOING TO DANCE TO IT?
NO, I'M JUST GOING TO LISTEN TO IT..
ARE YOU GOING TO MARCH AROUND THE ROOM WHILE YOU LISTEN TO IT?
NO, I'M JUST GOING TO SIT, AND LISTEN TO IT..
YOU MEAN YOU'RE GOING TO WHISTLE OR SING WHILE YOU LISTEN TO IT?
NO, I'M JUST GOING TO LISTEN TO IT..
THAT'S THE MOST RIDICULOUS THING I'VE EVER HEARD!
SCHULZ

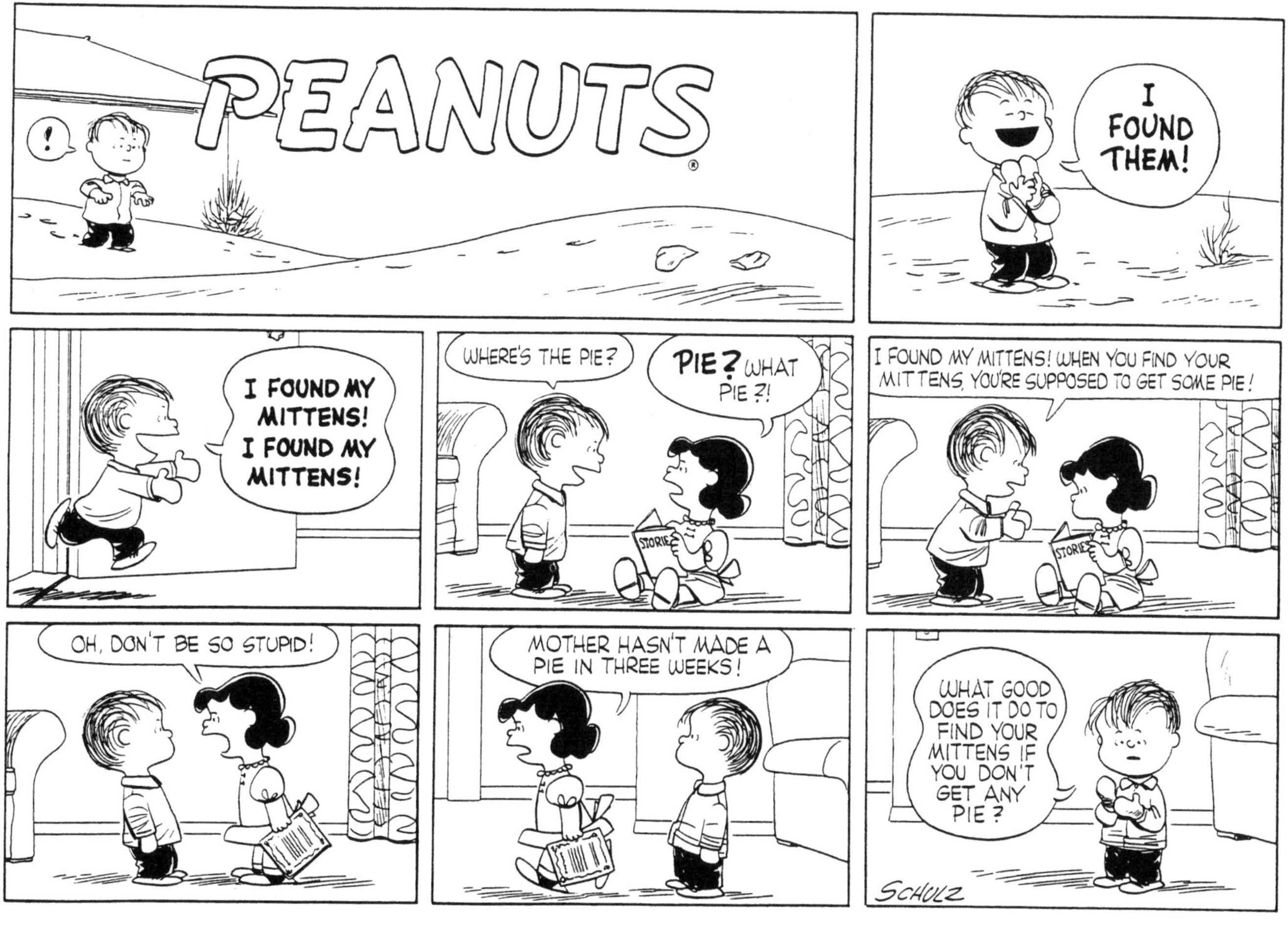
PEANUTS®
!
I FOUND THEM!
I FOUND MY MITTENS! I FOUND MY MITTENS!
WHERE'S THE PIE?
PIE? WHAT PIE?!
STORIES
I FOUND MY MITTENS! WHEN YOU FIND YOUR MITTENS, YOU'RE SUPPOSED TO GET SOME PIE!
STORIES
OH, DON'T BE SO STUPID!
MOTHER HASN'T MADE A PIE IN THREE WEEKS!
WHAT GOOD DOES IT DO TO FIND YOUR MITTENS IF YOU DON'T GET ANY PIE?
SCHULZ

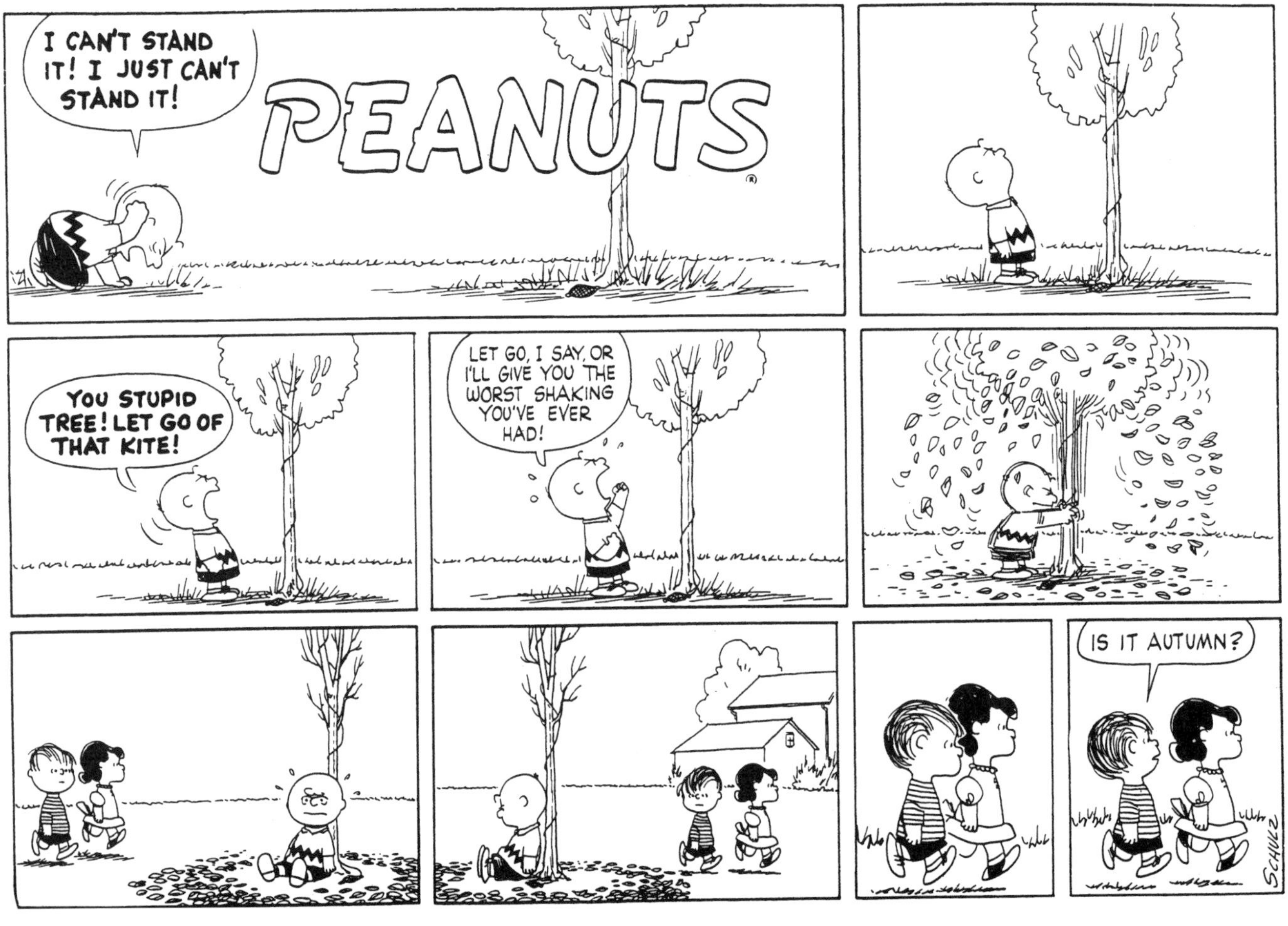
I CAN'T STAND IT! I JUST CAN'T STAND IT!
PEANUTS
YOU STUPID TREE! LET GO OF THAT KITE!
LET GO, I SAY, OR I'LL GIVE YOU THE WORST SHAKING YOU'VE EVER HAD!
IS IT AUTUMN?
SCHULZ

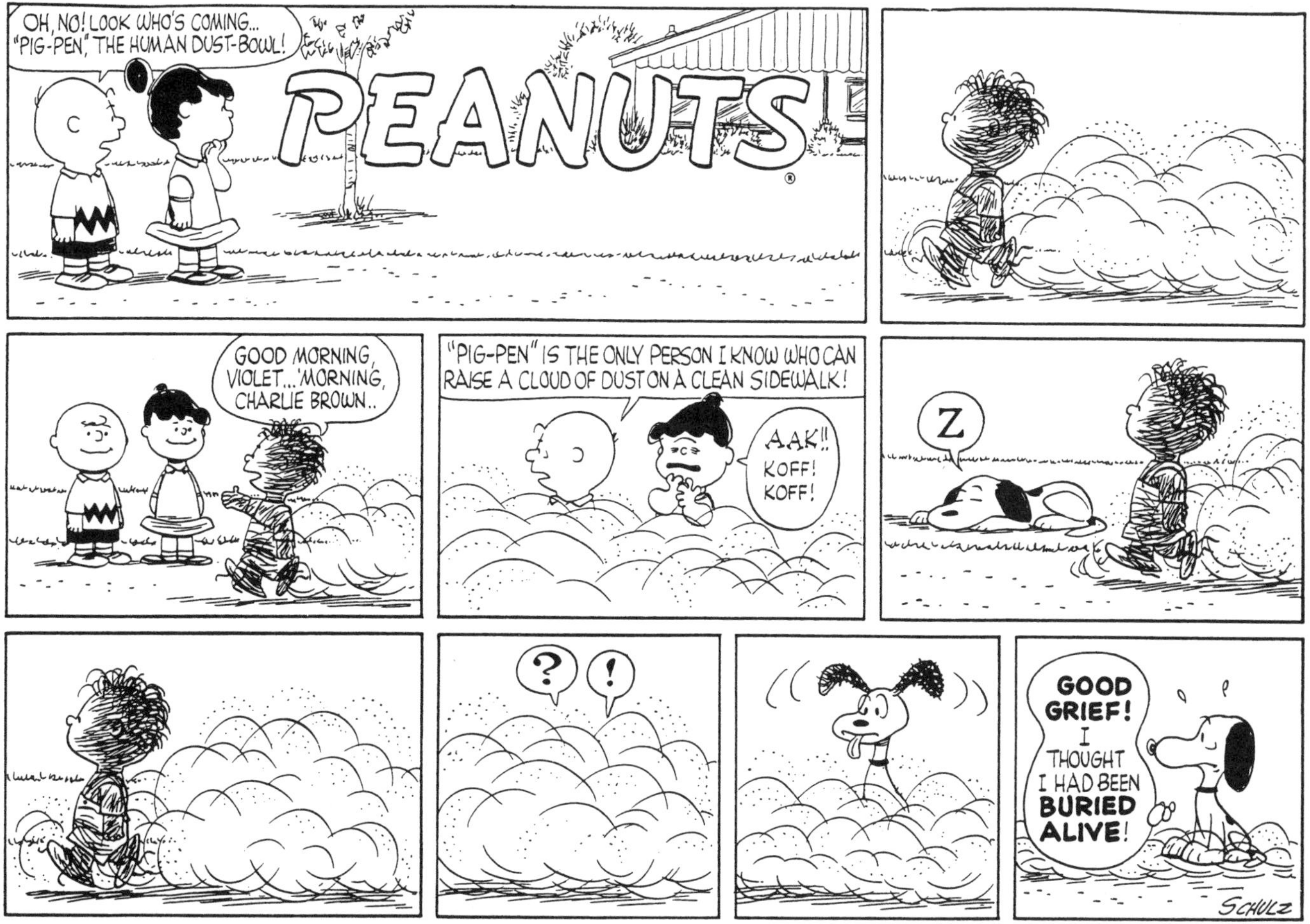
OH, NO! LOOK WHO'S COMING... "PIG-PEN," THE HUMAN DUST-BOWL!
PEANUTS
GOOD MORNING, VIOLET...'MORNING, CHARLIE BROWN..
"PIG-PEN" IS THE ONLY PERSON I KNOW WHO CAN RAISE A CLOUD OF DUST ON A CLEAN SIDEWALK!
AAK!! KOFF! KOFF!
Z
?
!
GOOD GRIEF! I THOUGHT I HAD BEEN BURIED ALIVE!
SCHULZ

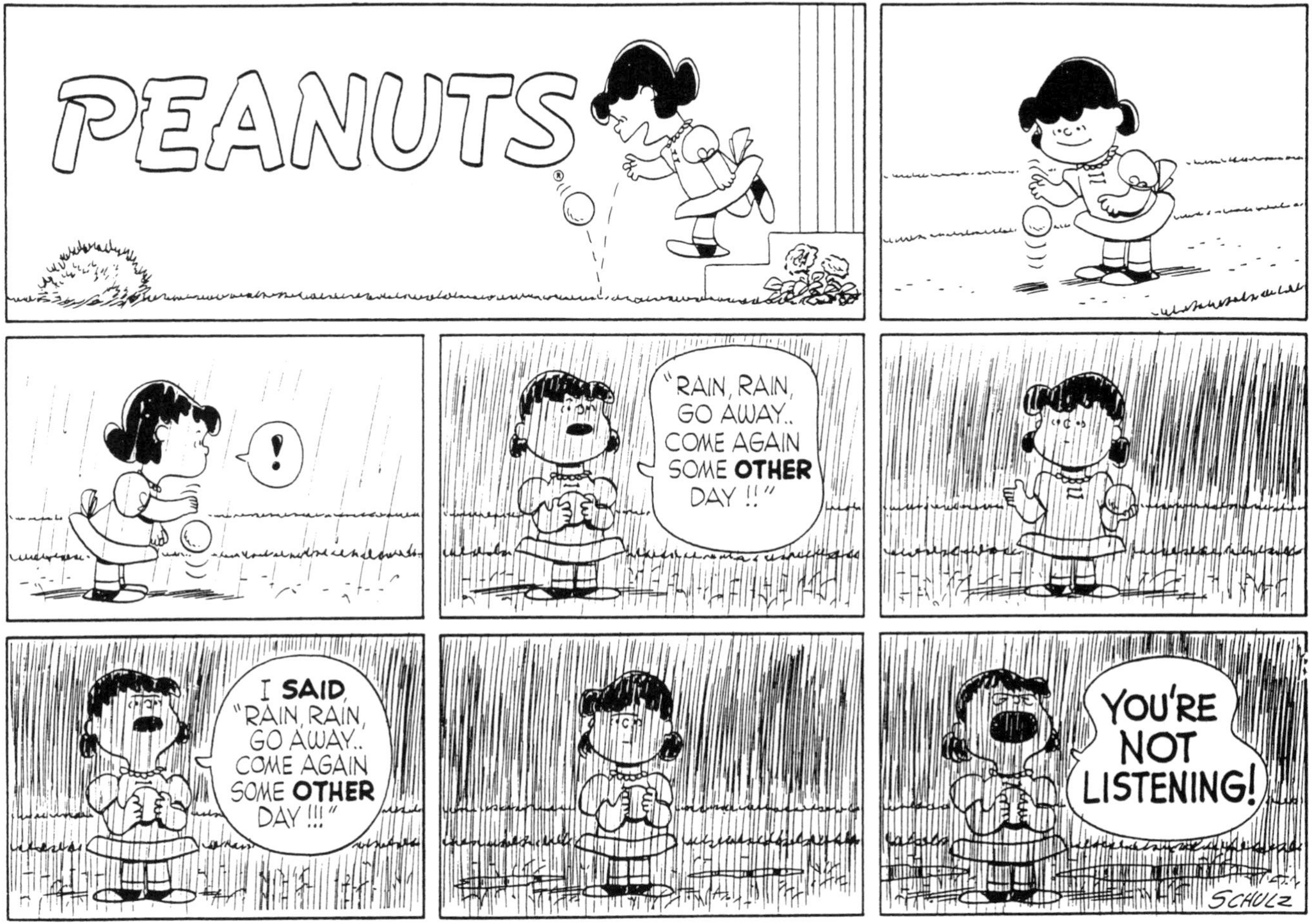
PEANUTS
!
"RAIN, RAIN, GO AWAY.. COME AGAIN SOME OTHER DAY !!"
I SAID, "RAIN, RAIN, GO AWAY.. COME AGAIN SOME OTHER DAY !!!"
YOU'RE NOT LISTENING!
SCHULZ

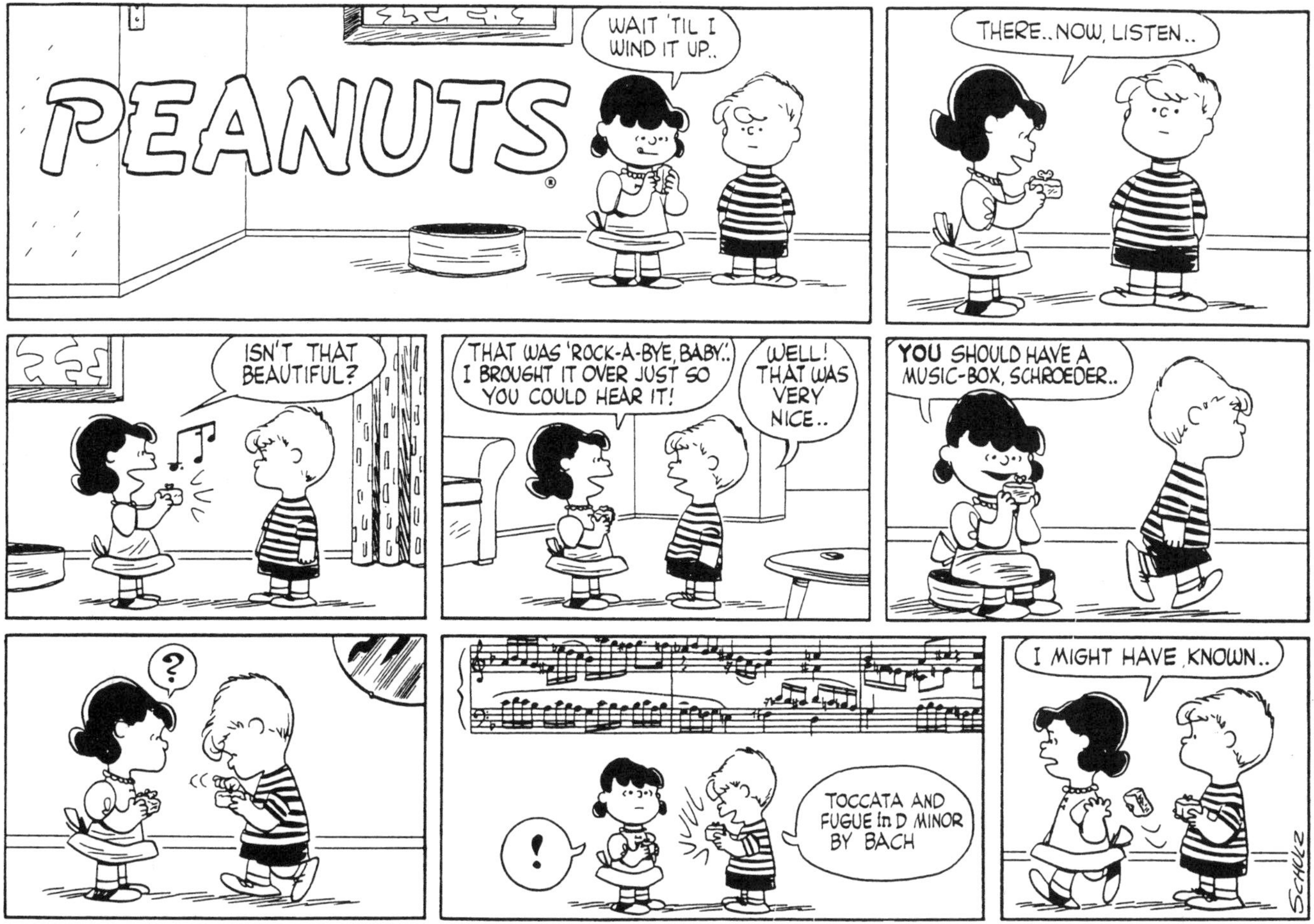
PEANUTS
WAIT 'TIL I WIND IT UP..
THERE..NOW, LISTEN..
ISN'T THAT BEAUTIFUL?
THAT WAS 'ROCK-A-BYE, BABY.'.. I BROUGHT IT OVER JUST SO YOU COULD HEAR IT!
WELL! THAT WAS VERY NICE..
YOU SHOULD HAVE A MUSIC-BOX, SCHROEDER..
?
!
TOCCATA AND FUGUE in D MINOR BY BACH
I MIGHT HAVE KNOWN..
SCHULZ

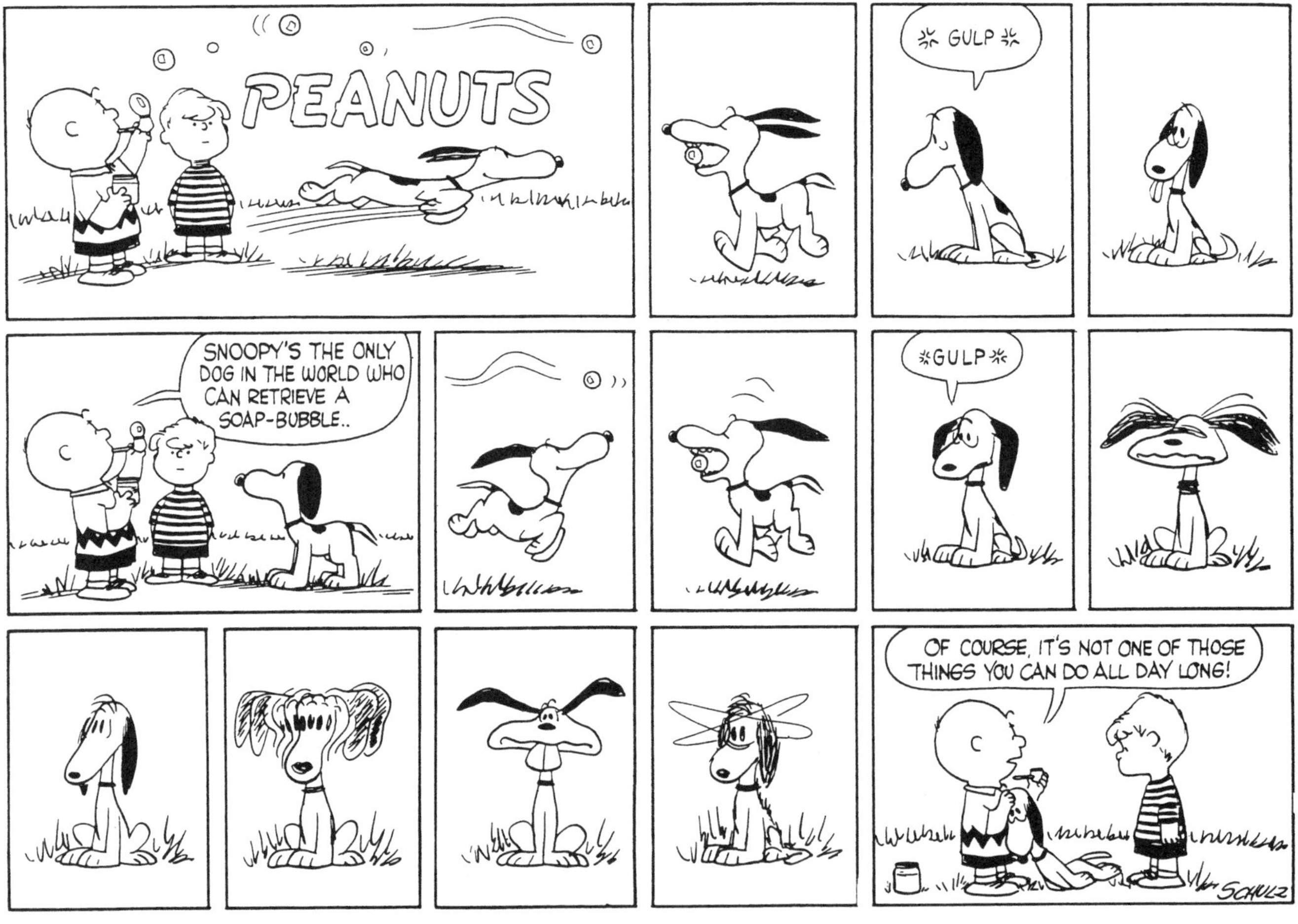
PEANUTS
GULP
SNOOPY'S THE ONLY DOG IN THE WORLD WHO CAN RETRIEVE A SOAP-BUBBLE..
GULP
OF COURSE, IT'S NOT ONE OF THOSE THINGS YOU CAN DO ALL DAY LONG!
SCHULZ

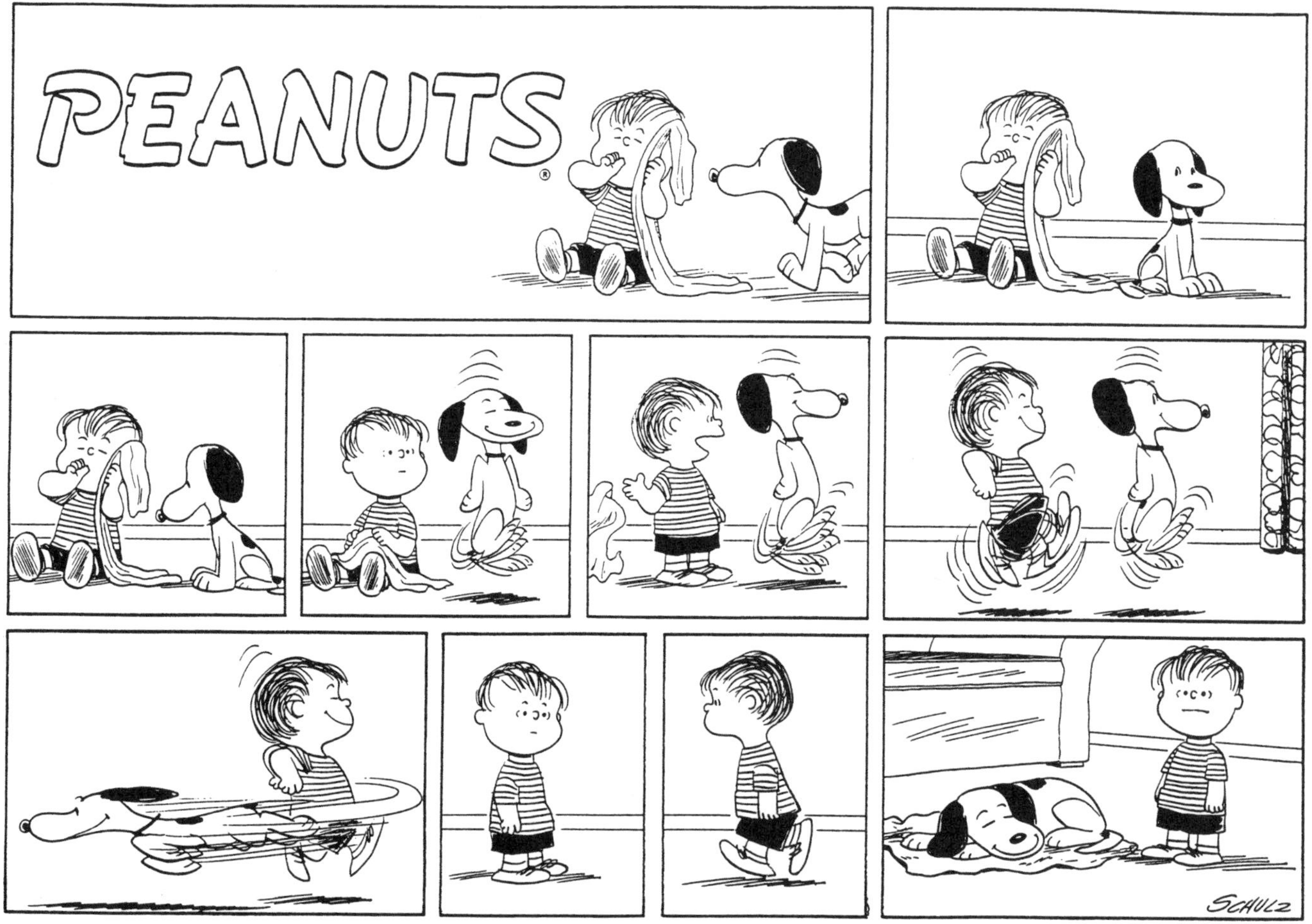
PEANUTS
SCHULZ

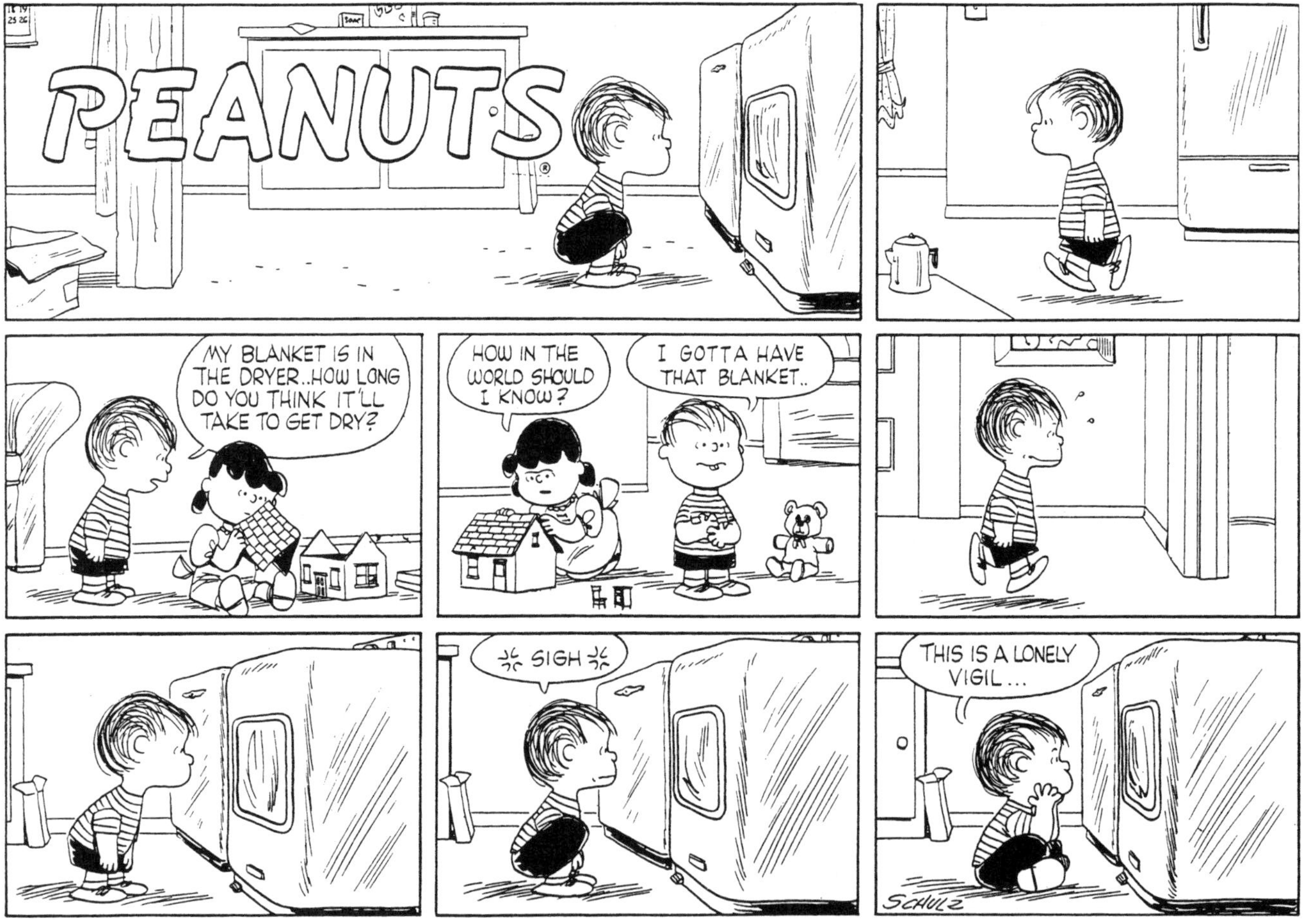
PEANUTS
MY BLANKET IS IN THE DRYER..HOW LONG DO YOU THINK IT'LL TAKE TO GET DRY?
HOW IN THE WORLD SHOULD I KNOW?
I GOTTA HAVE THAT BLANKET..
SIGH
THIS IS A LONELY VIGIL...
SCHULZ

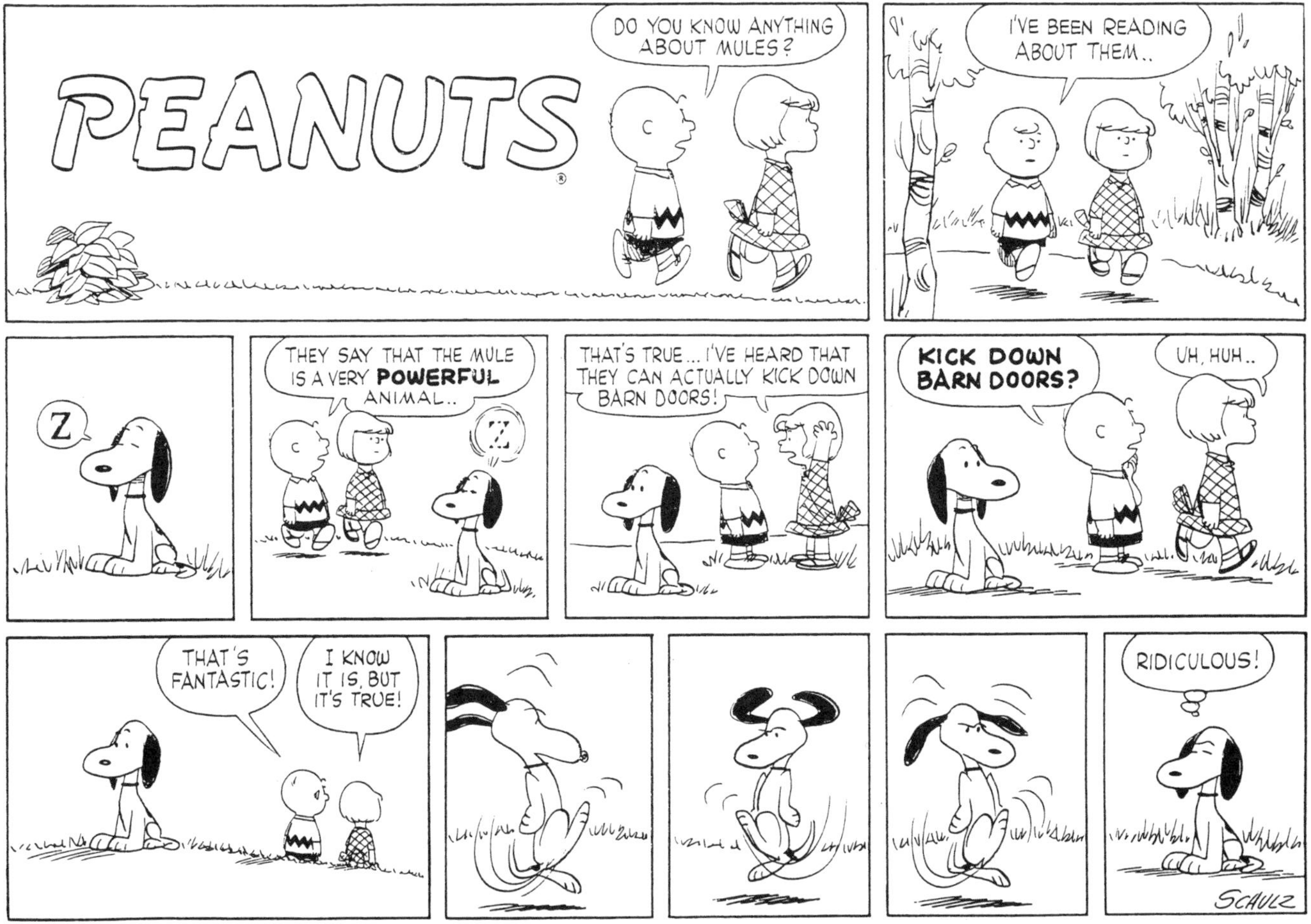
PEANUTS
DO YOU KNOW ANYTHING ABOUT MULES?
I'VE BEEN READING ABOUT THEM..
Z
THEY SAY THAT THE MULE IS A VERY POWERFUL ANIMAL..
Z
THAT'S TRUE... I'VE HEARD THAT THEY CAN ACTUALLY KICK DOWN BARN DOORS!
KICK DOWN BARN DOORS?
UH, HUH..
THAT'S FANTASTIC!
I KNOW IT IS, BUT IT'S TRUE!
RIDICULOUS!
SCHULZ

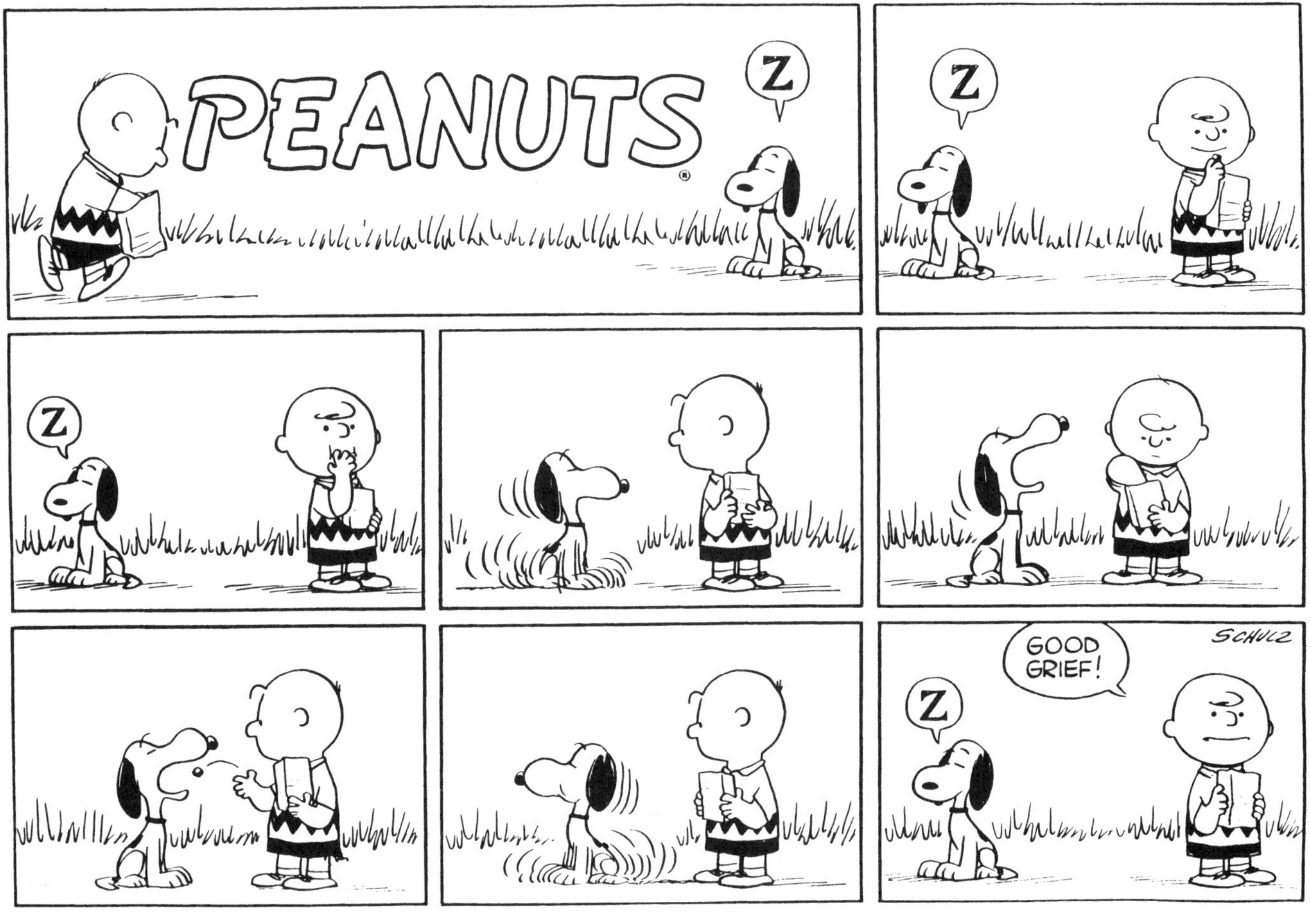
PEANUTS
Z
Z
Z
GOOD GRIEF!
Z
SCHULZ

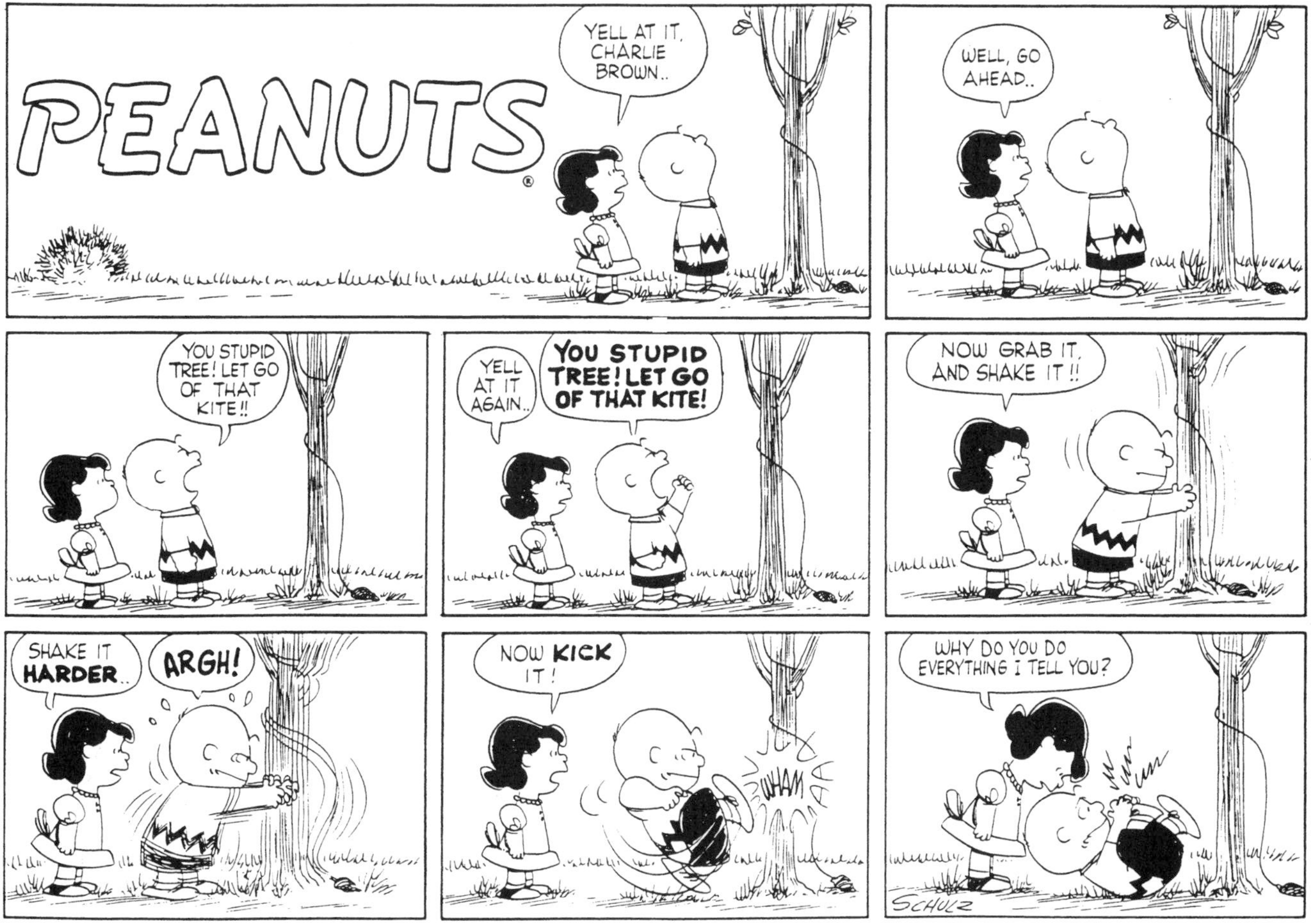
PEANUTS
YELL AT IT, CHARLIE BROWN..
WELL, GO AHEAD..
YOU STUPID TREE! LET GO OF THAT KITE!!
YELL AT IT AGAIN..
YOU STUPID TREE! LET GO OF THAT KITE!
NOW GRAB IT, AND SHAKE IT!!
SHAKE IT HARDER..
ARGH!
NOW KICK IT!
WHAM
WHY DO YOU DO EVERYTHING I TELL YOU?
SCHULZ

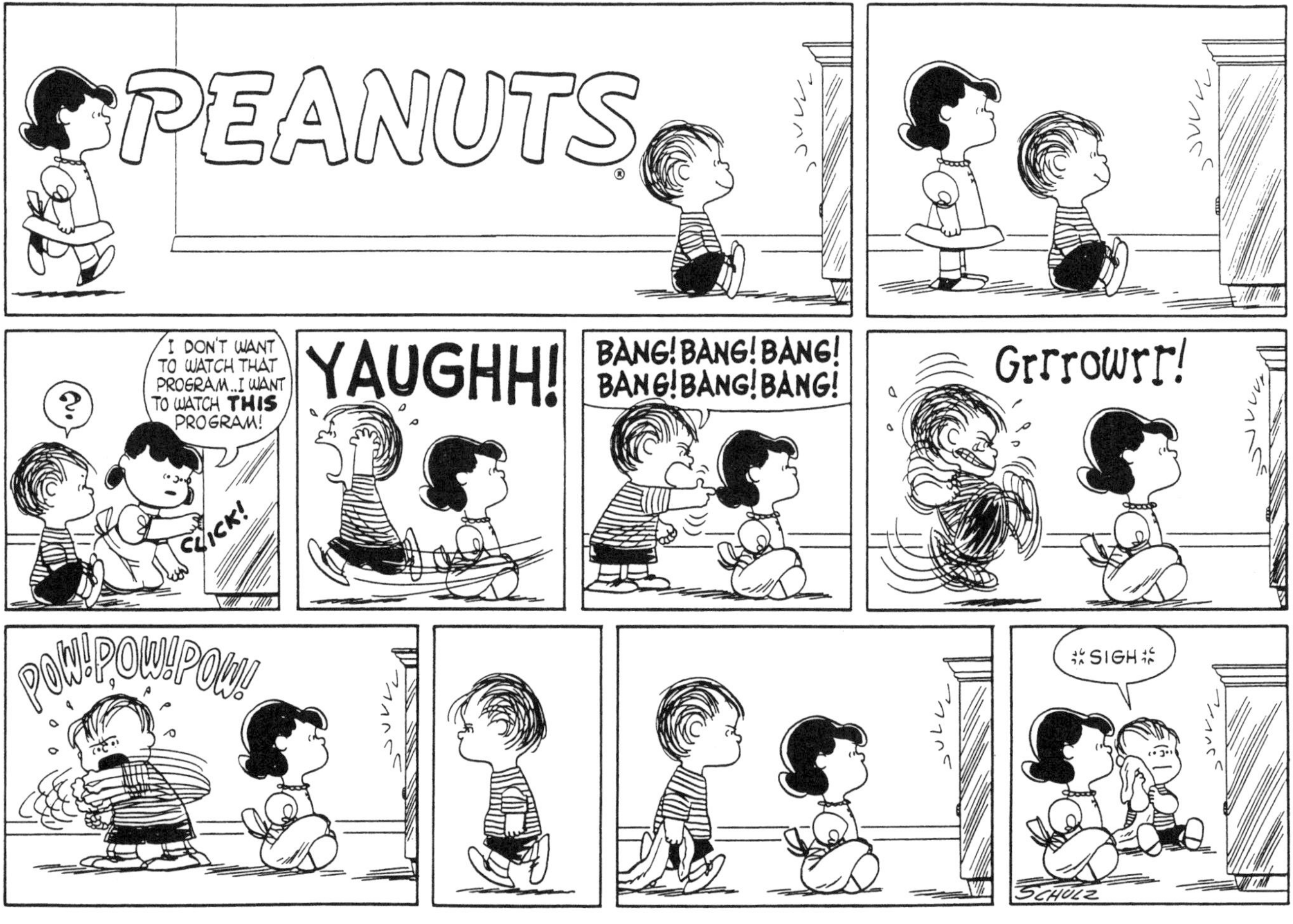
PEANUTS®
?
I DON'T WANT TO WATCH THAT PROGRAM..I WANT TO WATCH THIS PROGRAM!
CLICK!
YAUGHH!
BANG! BANG! BANG! BANG! BANG! BANG!
Grrrowrr!
POW! POW! POW!
SIGH
SCHULZ

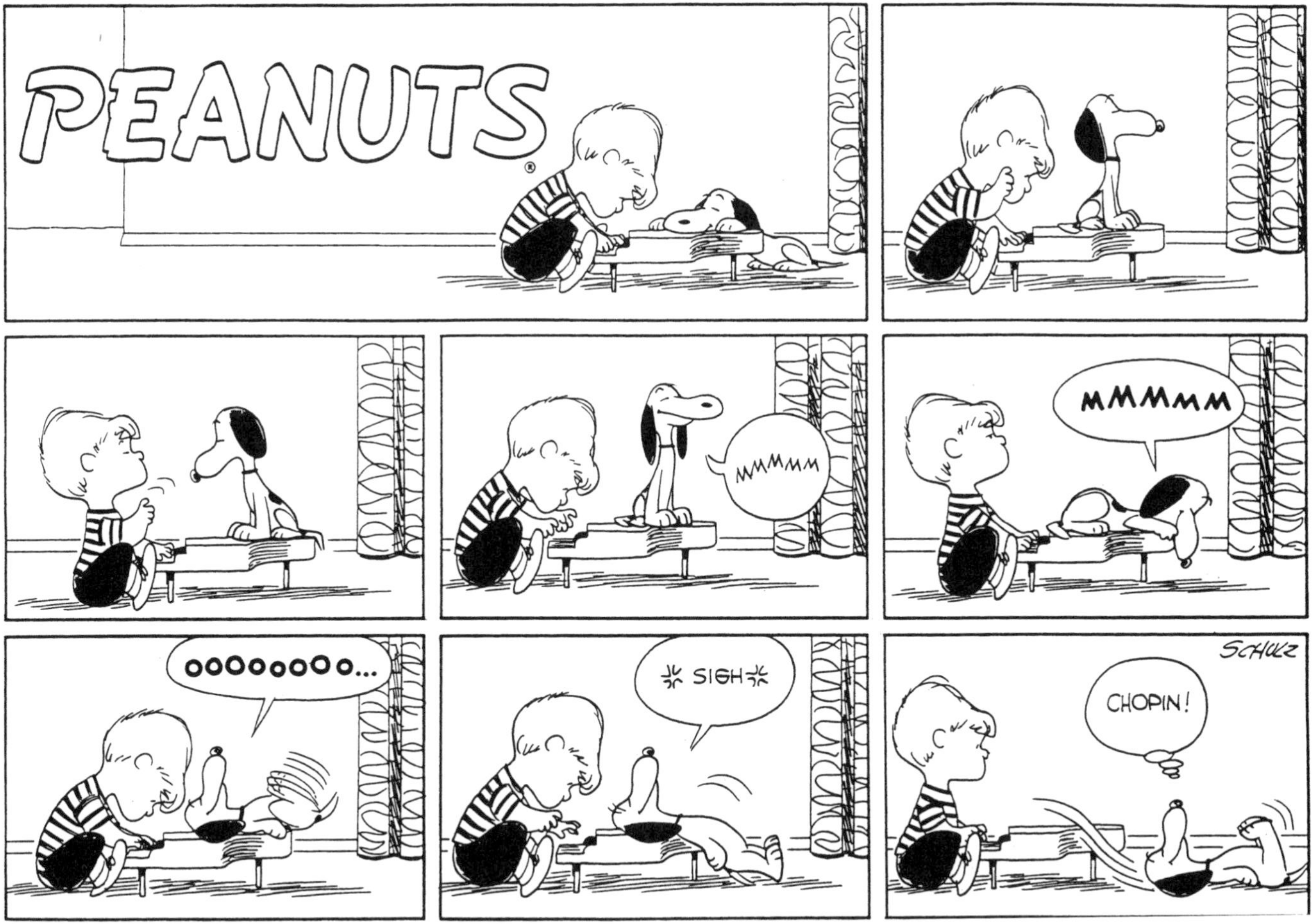
PEANUTS
MMMMM
MMMMM
OOOOOOOOO...
SIGH
CHOPIN!
SCHULZ

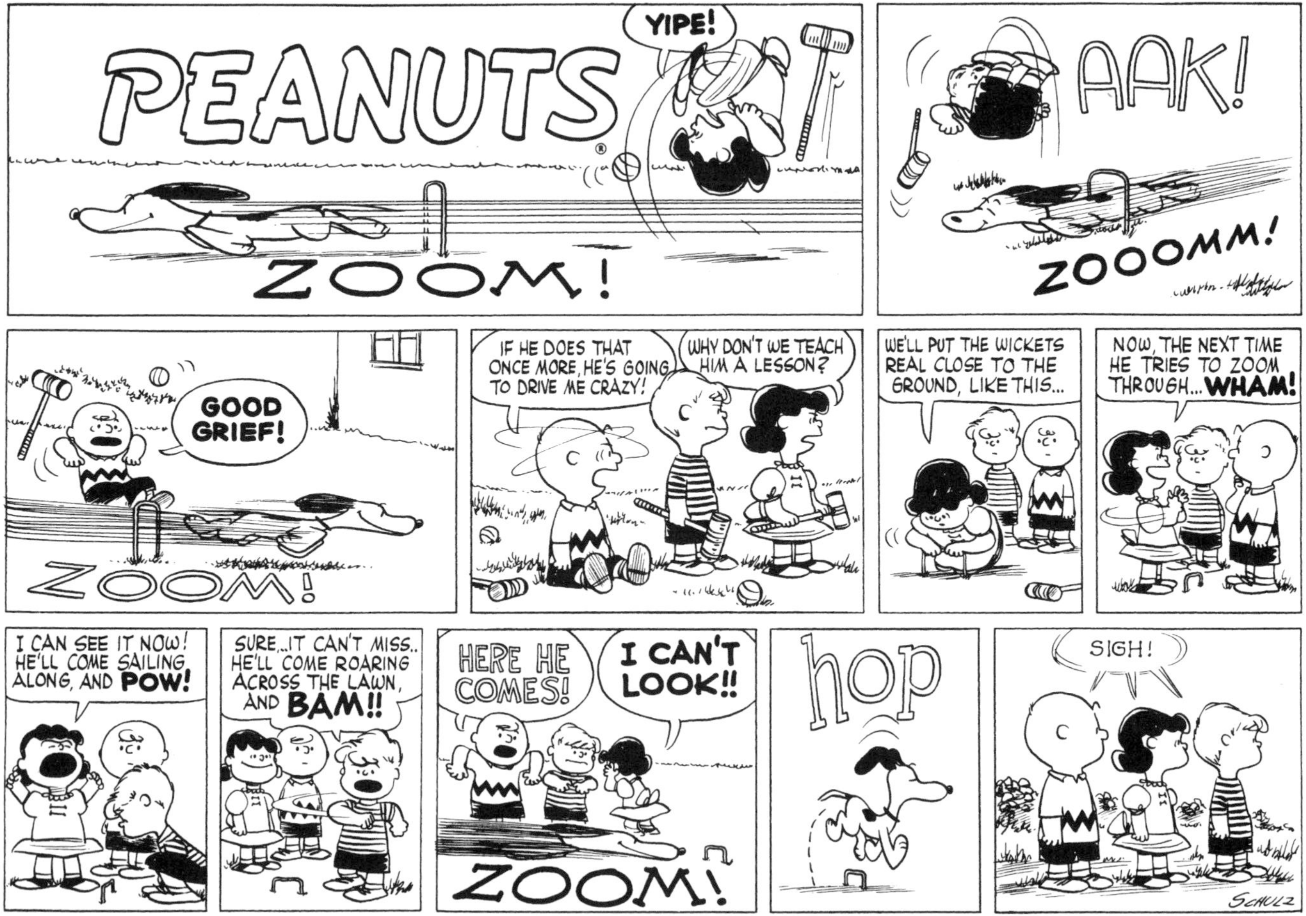
PEANUTS
YIPE!
ZOOM!
AAK!
ZOOOMM!
GOOD GRIEF!
ZOOM!
IF HE DOES THAT ONCE MORE, HE'S GOING TO DRIVE ME CRAZY!
WHY DON'T WE TEACH HIM A LESSON?
WE'LL PUT THE WICKETS REAL CLOSE TO THE GROUND, LIKE THIS...
NOW, THE NEXT TIME HE TRIES TO ZOOM THROUGH... WHAM!
I CAN SEE IT NOW! HE'LL COME SAILING ALONG, AND POW!
SURE...IT CAN'T MISS.. HE'LL COME ROARING ACROSS THE LAWN, AND BAM!!
HERE HE COMES!
I CAN'T LOOK!!
ZOOM!
hop
SIGH!
SCHULZ

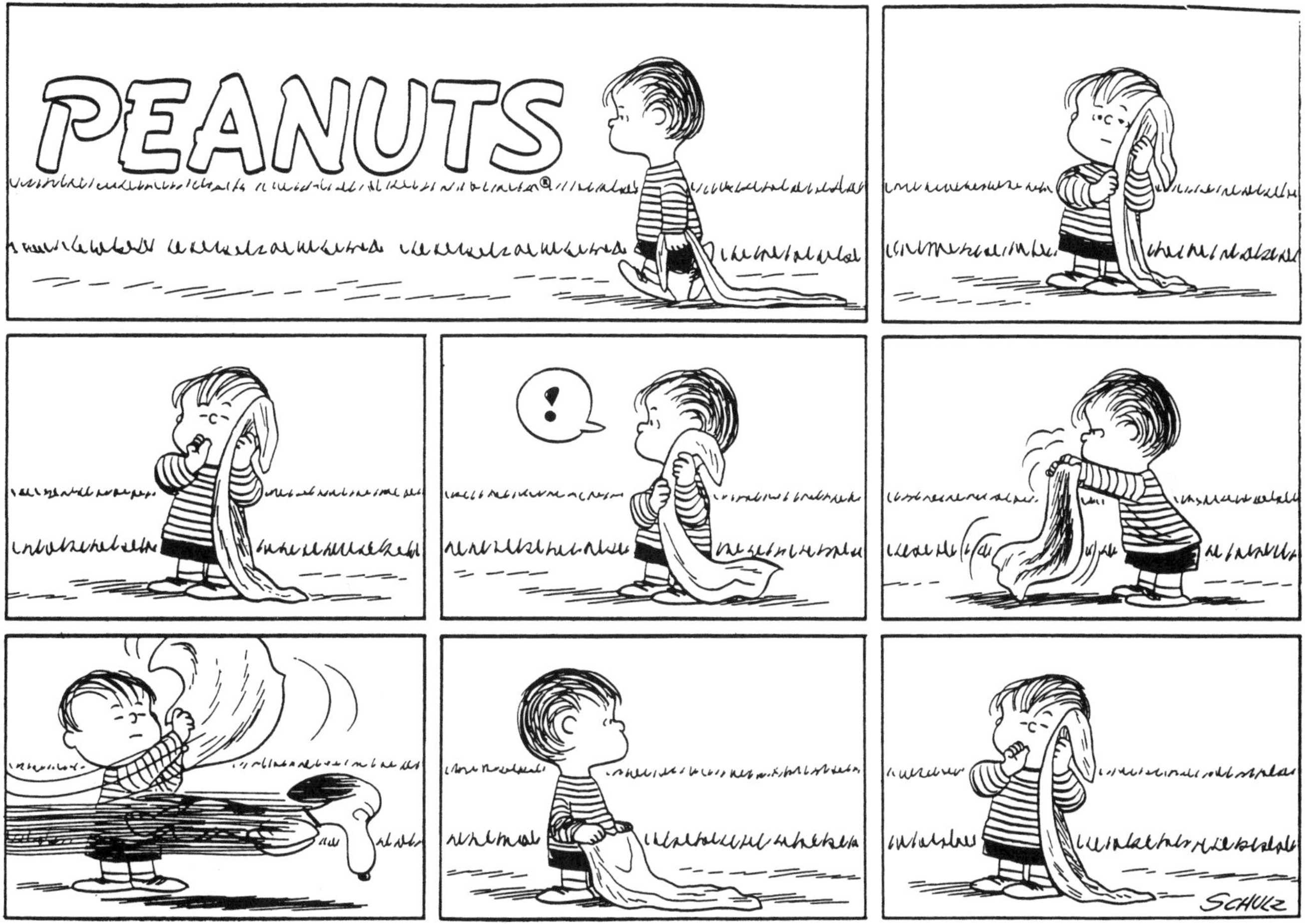
PEANUTS
!
SCHULZ

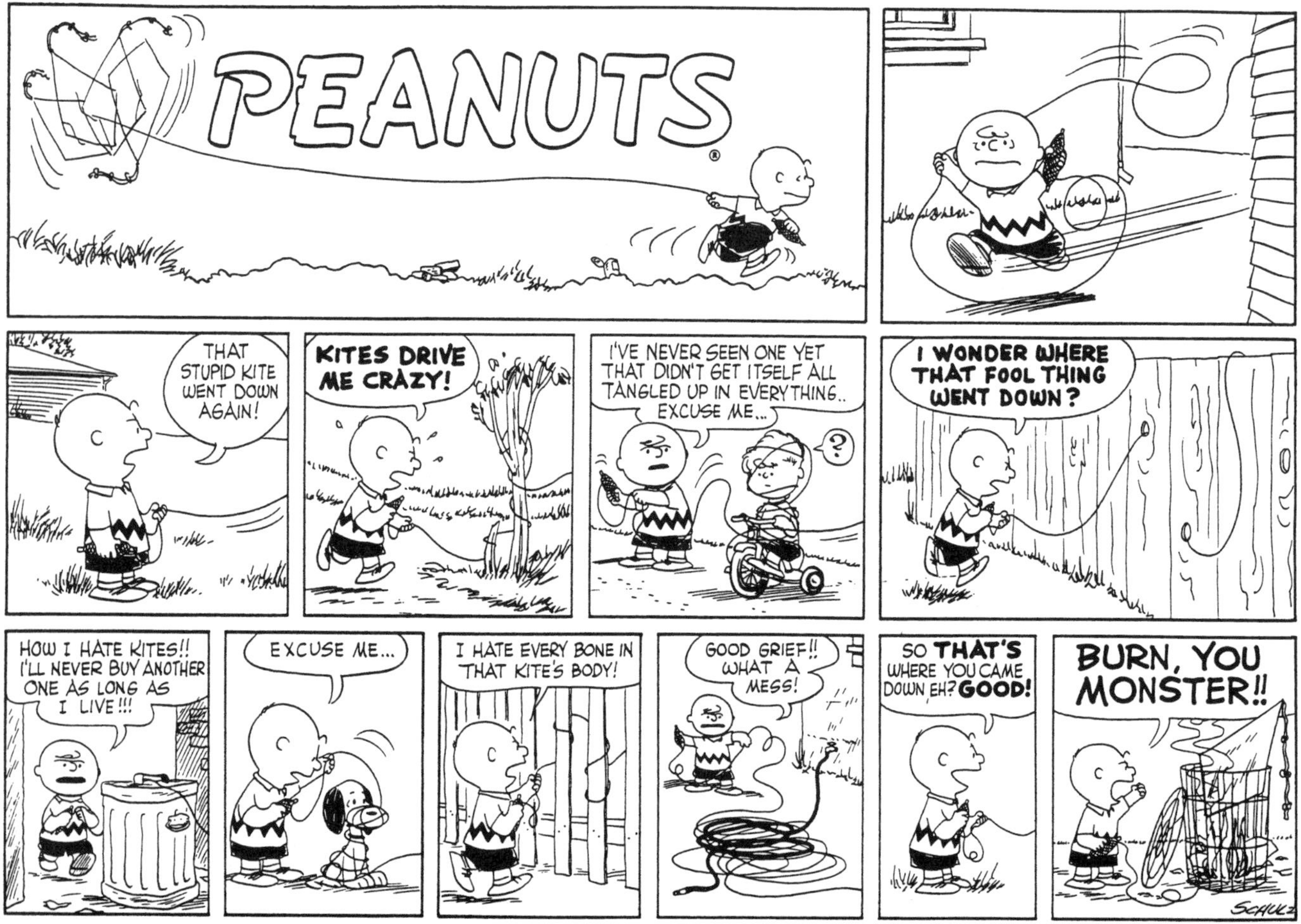
PEANUTS
THAT STUPID KITE WENT DOWN AGAIN!
KITES DRIVE ME CRAZY!
I'VE NEVER SEEN ONE YET THAT DIDN'T GET ITSELF ALL TANGLED UP IN EVERYTHING.. EXCUSE ME...
?
I WONDER WHERE THAT FOOL THING WENT DOWN?
HOW I HATE KITES!! I'LL NEVER BUY ANOTHER ONE AS LONG AS I LIVE!!!
EXCUSE ME...
I HATE EVERY BONE IN THAT KITE'S BODY!
GOOD GRIEF!! WHAT A MESS!
SO THAT'S WHERE YOU CAME DOWN, EH? GOOD!
BURN, YOU MONSTER!!
SCHULZ

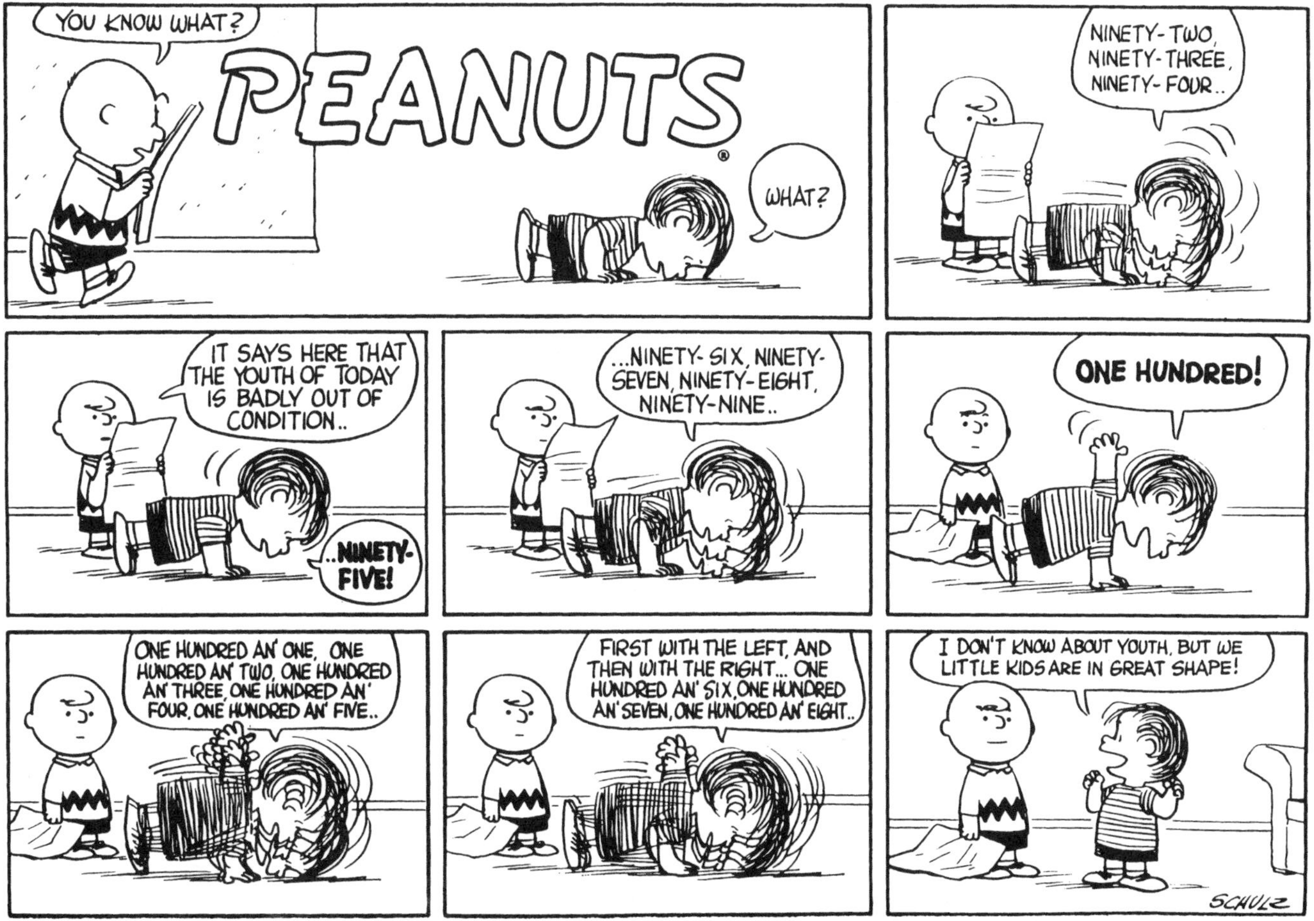
YOU KNOW WHAT?
PEANUTS
WHAT?
NINETY-TWO, NINETY-THREE, NINETY-FOUR..
IT SAYS HERE THAT THE YOUTH OF TODAY IS BADLY OUT OF CONDITION..
..NINETY-FIVE!
...NINETY-SIX, NINETY-SEVEN, NINETY-EIGHT, NINETY-NINE..
ONE HUNDRED!
ONE HUNDRED AN' ONE, ONE HUNDRED AN' TWO, ONE HUNDRED AN' THREE, ONE HUNDRED AN' FOUR, ONE HUNDRED AN' FIVE..
FIRST WITH THE LEFT, AND THEN WITH THE RIGHT... ONE HUNDRED AN' SIX, ONE HUNDRED AN' SEVEN, ONE HUNDRED AN' EIGHT..
I DON'T KNOW ABOUT YOUTH, BUT WE LITTLE KIDS ARE IN GREAT SHAPE!
SCHULZ

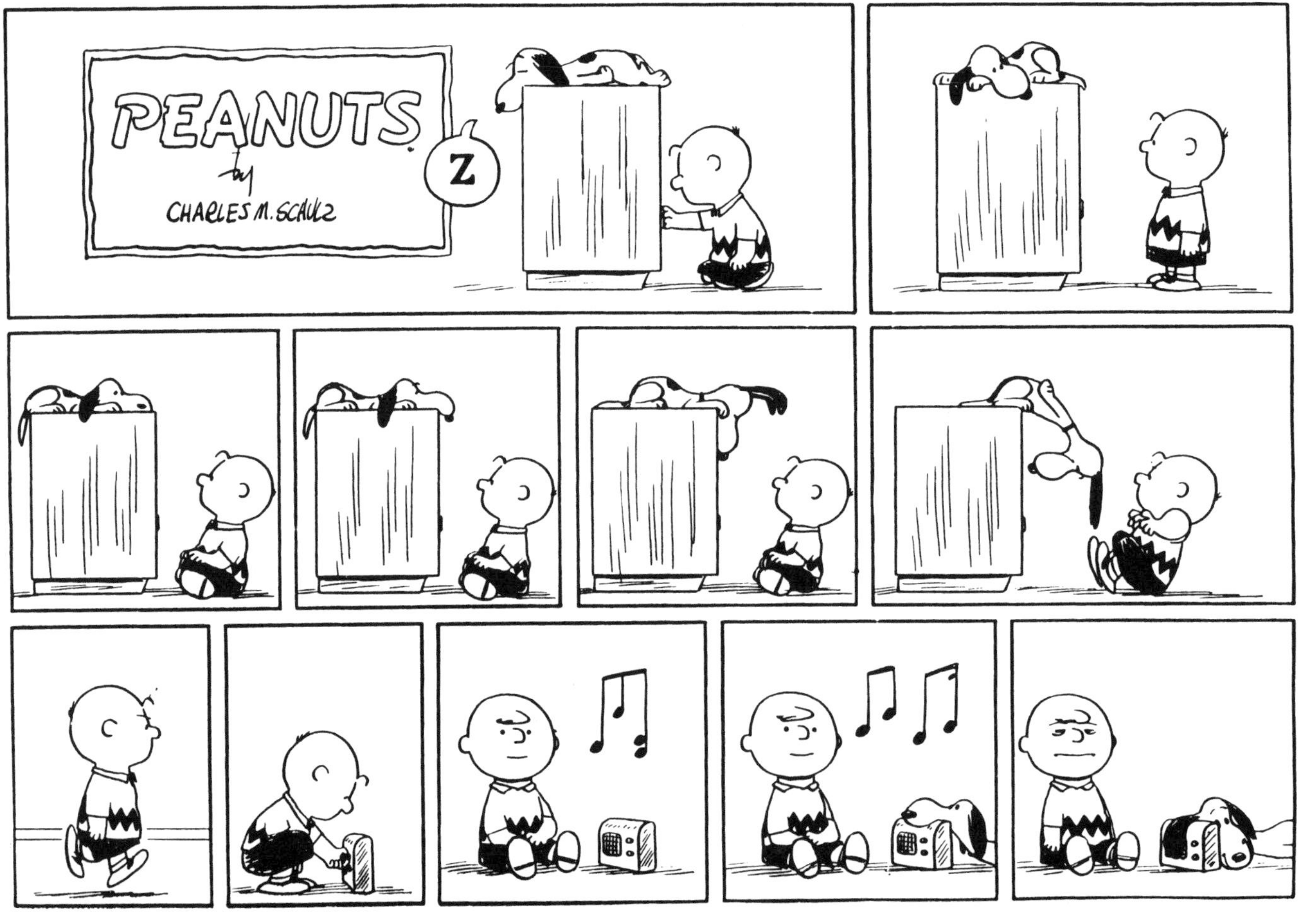
PEANUTS
by
CHARLES M. SCHULZ
Z

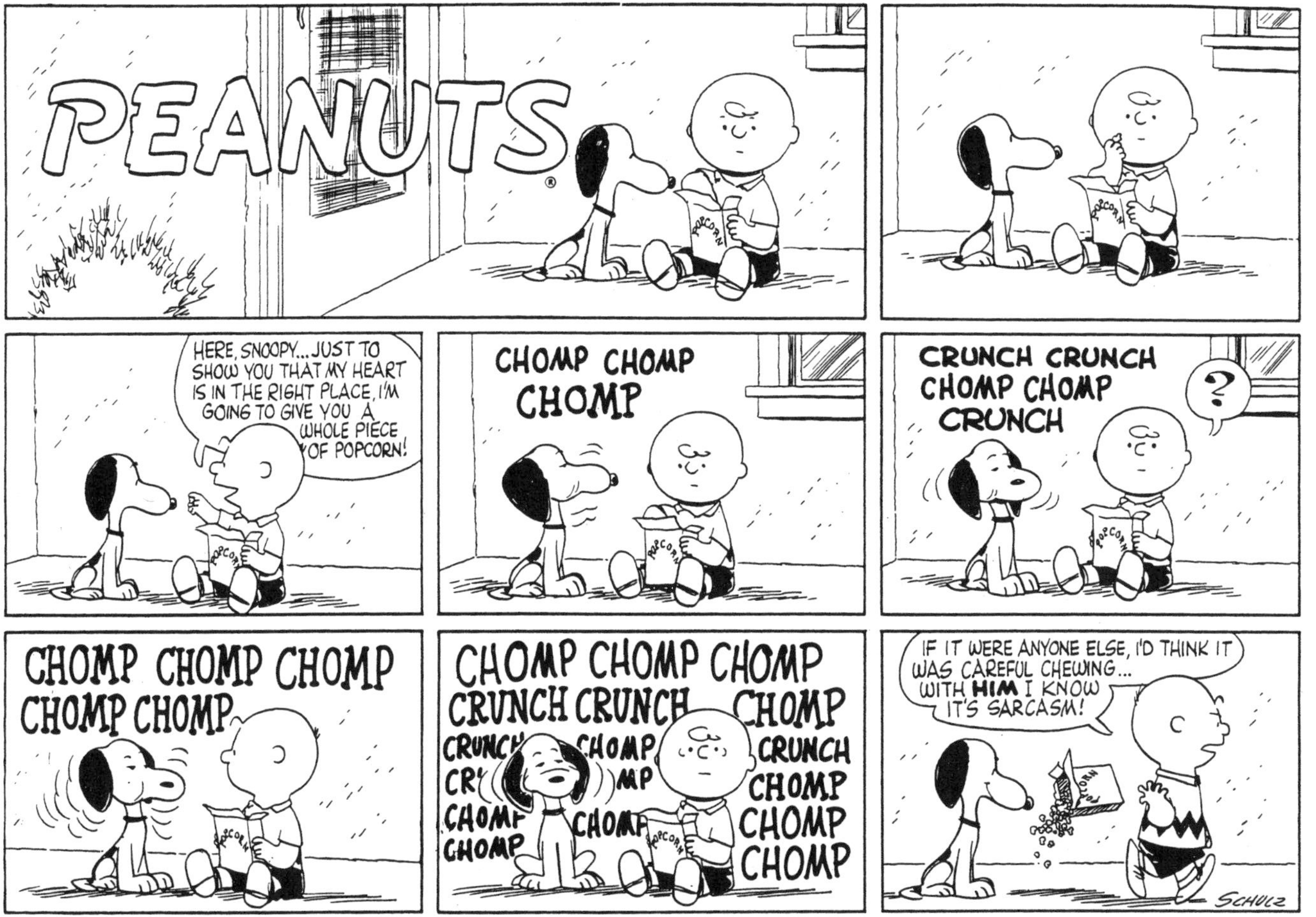
PEANUTS®
POPCORN
HERE, SNOOPY...JUST TO SHOW YOU THAT MY HEART IS IN THE RIGHT PLACE, I'M GOING TO GIVE YOU A WHOLE PIECE OF POPCORN!
CHOMP CHOMP CHOMP
CRUNCH CRUNCH CHOMP CHOMP CRUNCH
?
CHOMP CHOMP CHOMP CHOMP CHOMP
CHOMP CHOMP CHOMP CRUNCH CRUNCH CHOMP CRUNCH CHOMP CRUNCH CHOMP CHOMP CHOMP CHOMP
IF IT WERE ANYONE ELSE, I'D THINK IT WAS CAREFUL CHEWING... WITH **HIM** I KNOW IT'S SARCASM!
SCHULZ

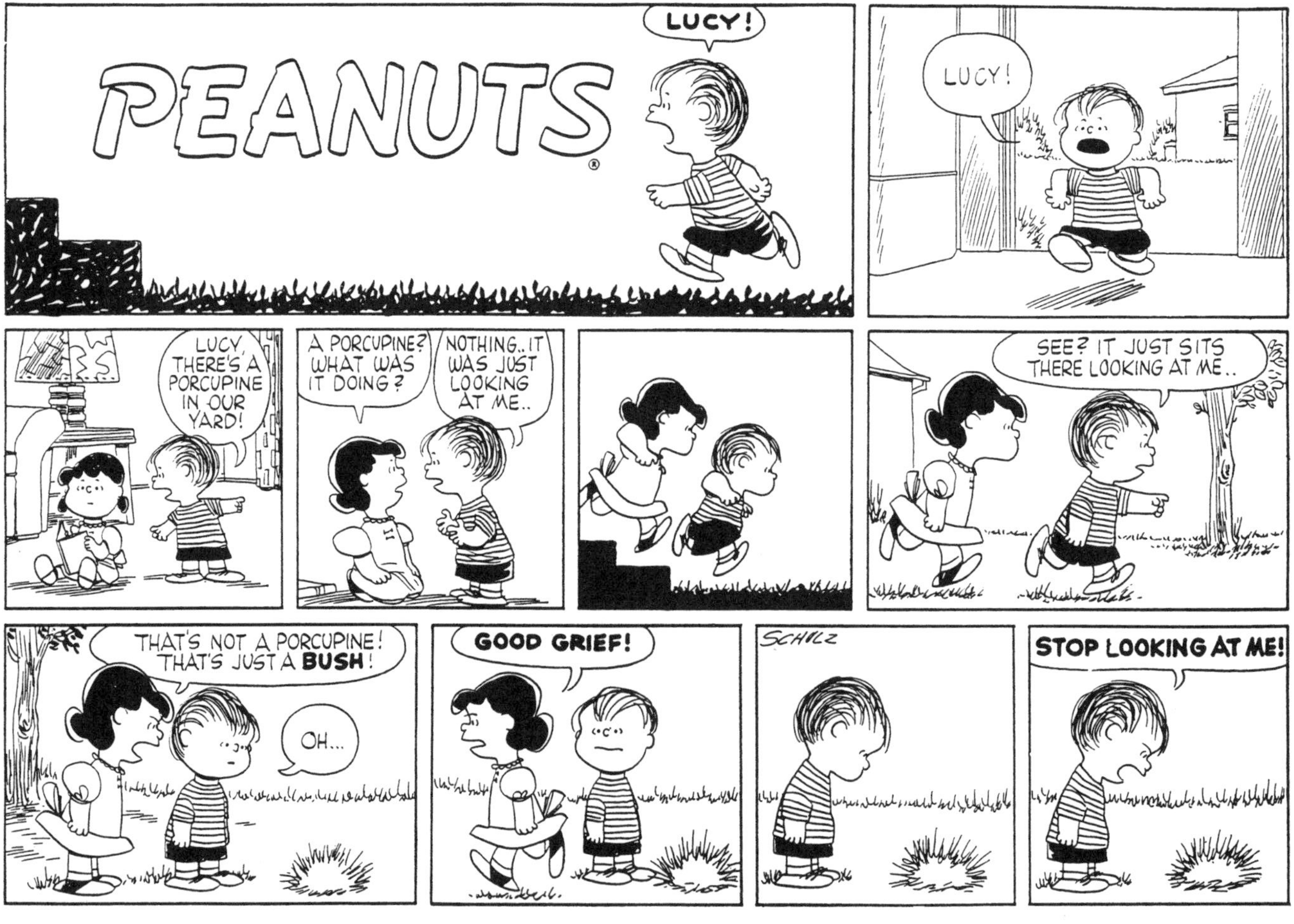
PEANUTS
LUCY!
LUCY!
LUCY, THERE'S A PORCUPINE IN OUR YARD!
A PORCUPINE? WHAT WAS IT DOING?
NOTHING.. IT WAS JUST LOOKING AT ME..
SEE? IT JUST SITS THERE LOOKING AT ME..
THAT'S NOT A PORCUPINE! THAT'S JUST A **BUSH**!
OH...
GOOD GRIEF!
SCHULZ
STOP LOOKING AT ME!

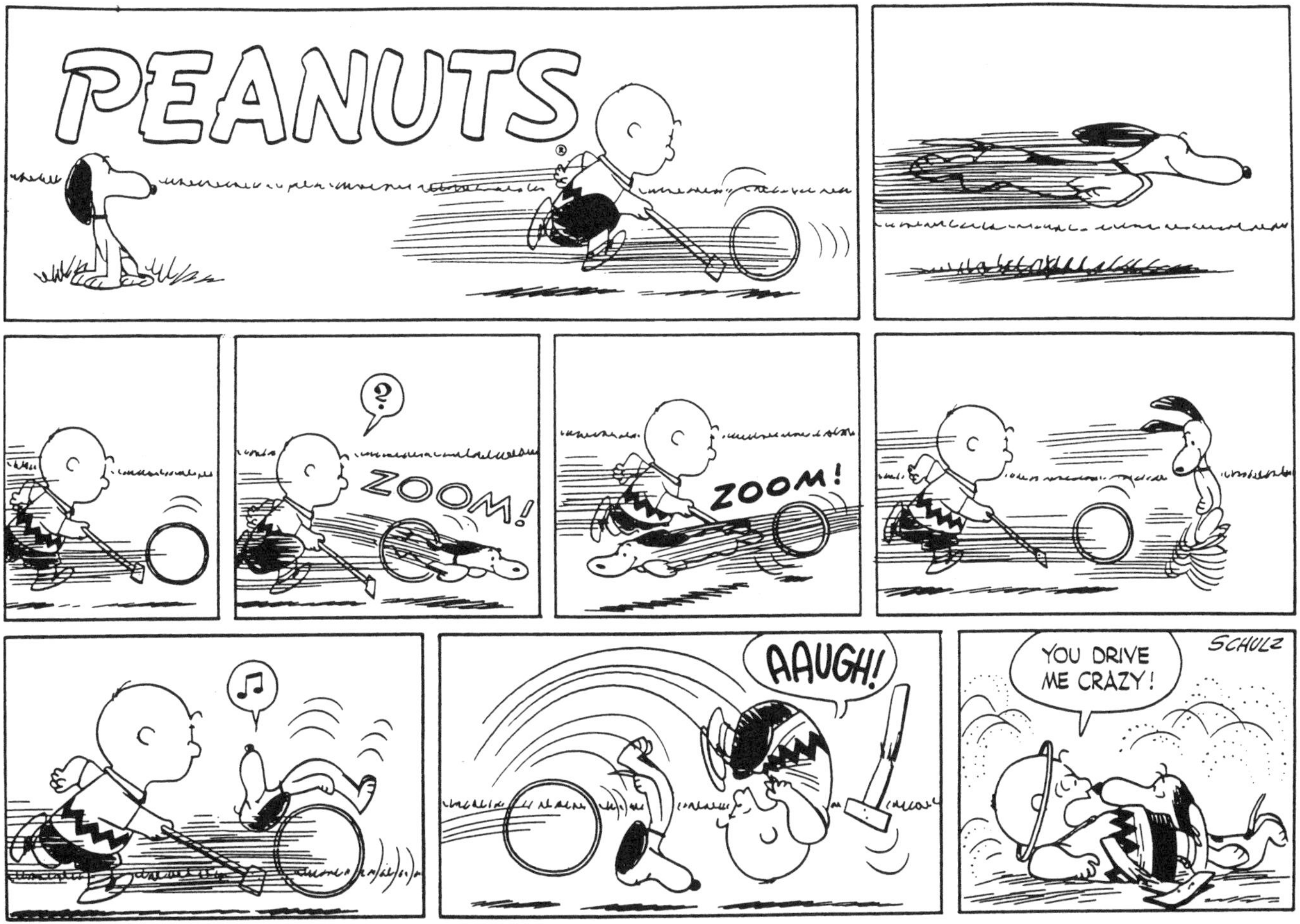

PEANUTS
?
ZOOM!
ZOOM!
♫
AAUGH!
YOU DRIVE ME CRAZY!
SCHULZ

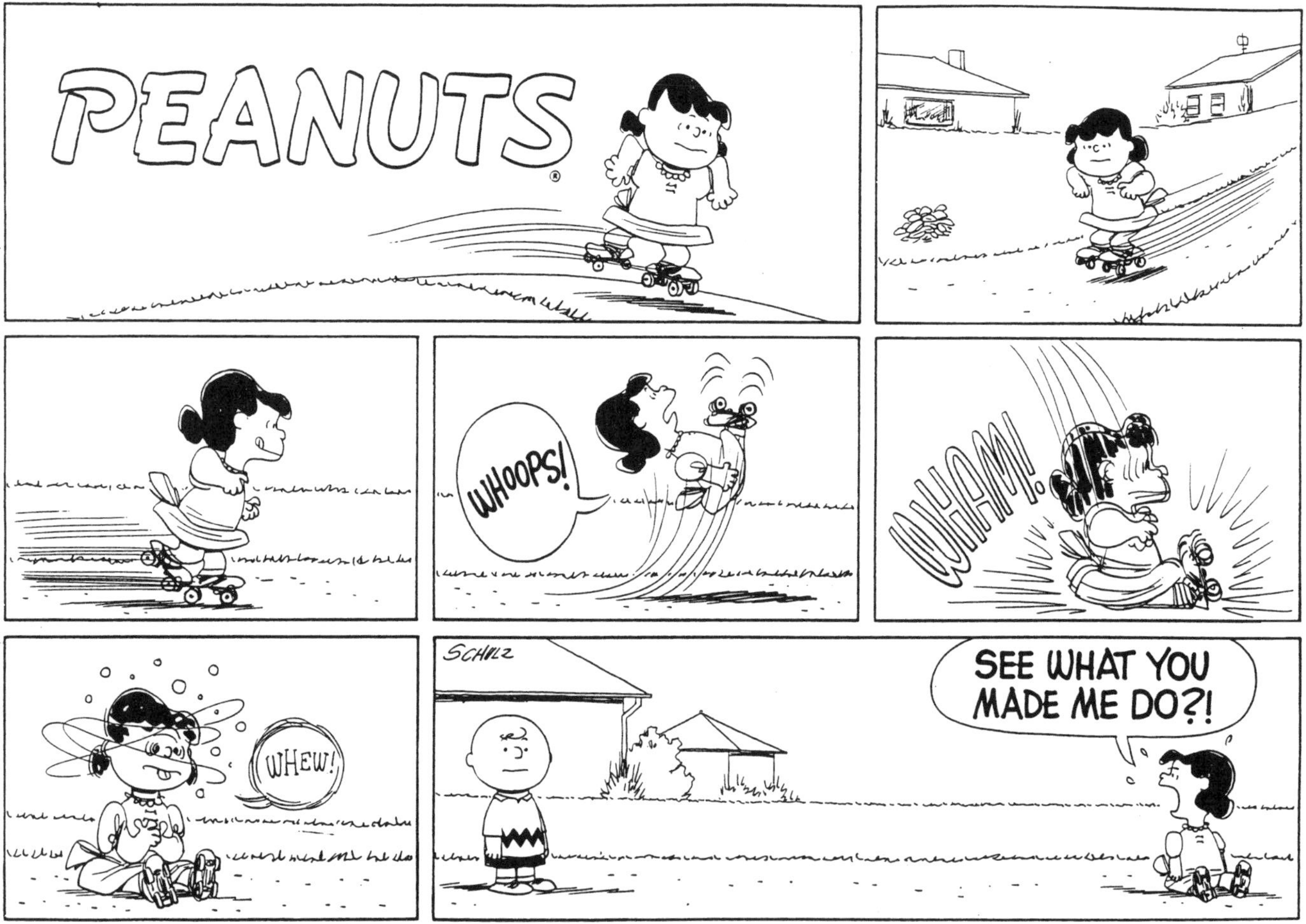
PEANUTS
WHOOPS!
WHAM!
WHEW!
SCHULZ
SEE WHAT YOU MADE ME DO?!

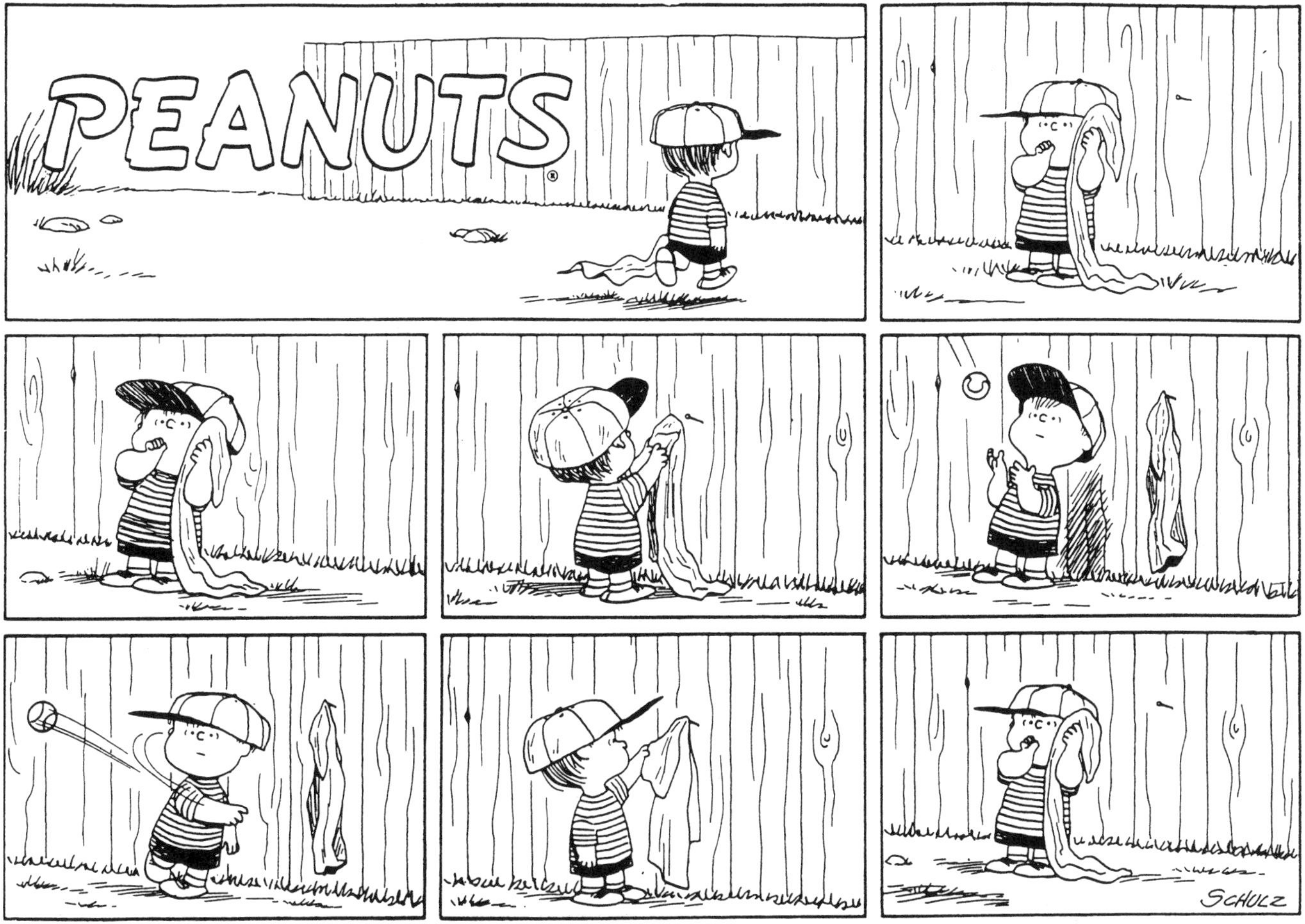
PEANUTS
SCHULZ

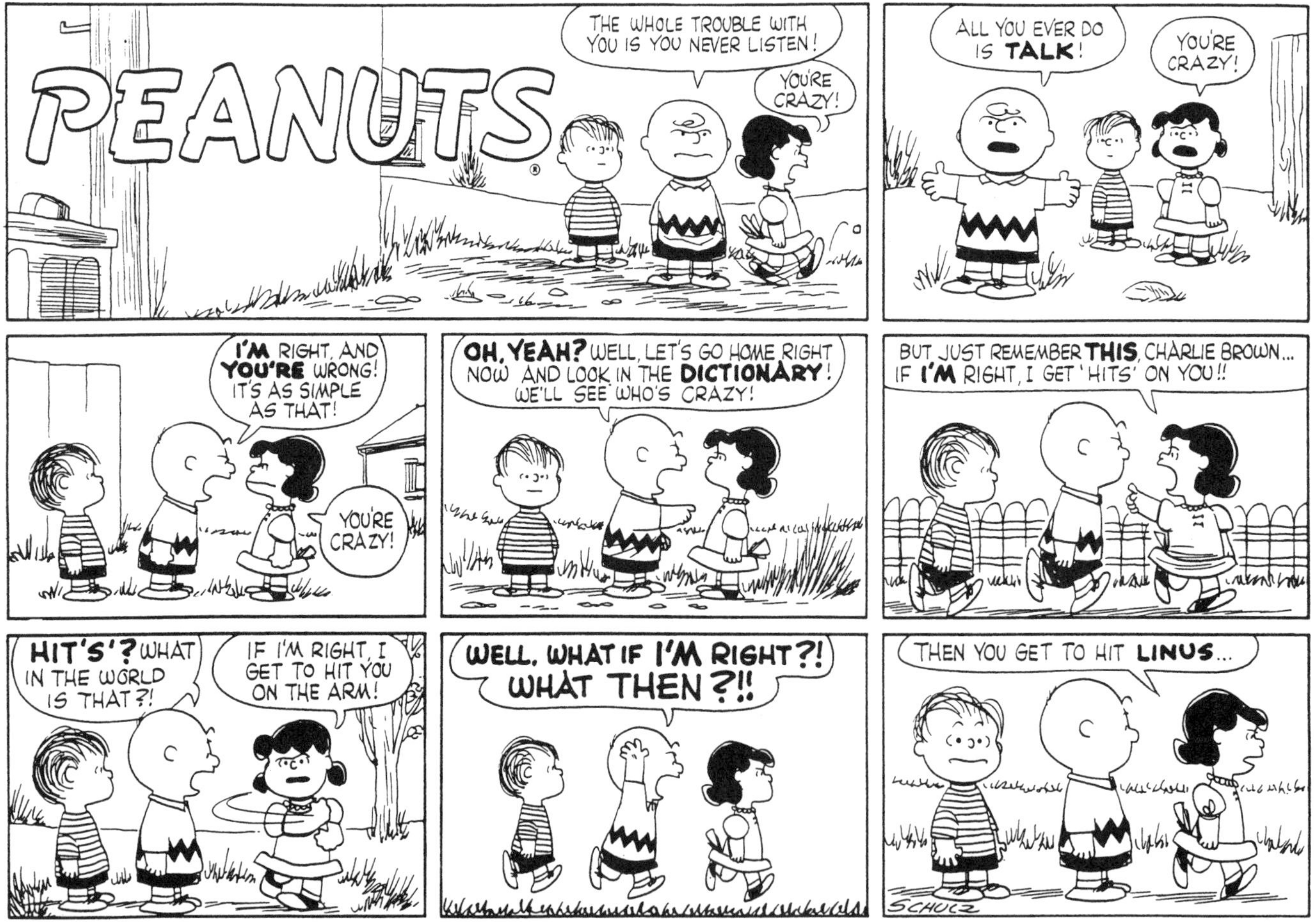
PEANUTS®
THE WHOLE TROUBLE WITH YOU IS YOU NEVER LISTEN!
YOU'RE CRAZY!
ALL YOU EVER DO IS TALK!
YOU'RE CRAZY!
I'M RIGHT, AND YOU'RE WRONG! IT'S AS SIMPLE AS THAT!
YOU'RE CRAZY!
OH, YEAH? WELL, LET'S GO HOME RIGHT NOW AND LOOK IN THE DICTIONARY! WE'LL SEE WHO'S CRAZY!
BUT JUST REMEMBER THIS, CHARLIE BROWN... IF I'M RIGHT, I GET 'HITS' ON YOU!!
HIT'S'? WHAT IN THE WORLD IS THAT?!
IF I'M RIGHT, I GET TO HIT YOU ON THE ARM!
WELL, WHAT IF I'M RIGHT?! WHAT THEN?!!
THEN YOU GET TO HIT LINUS...
SCHULZ

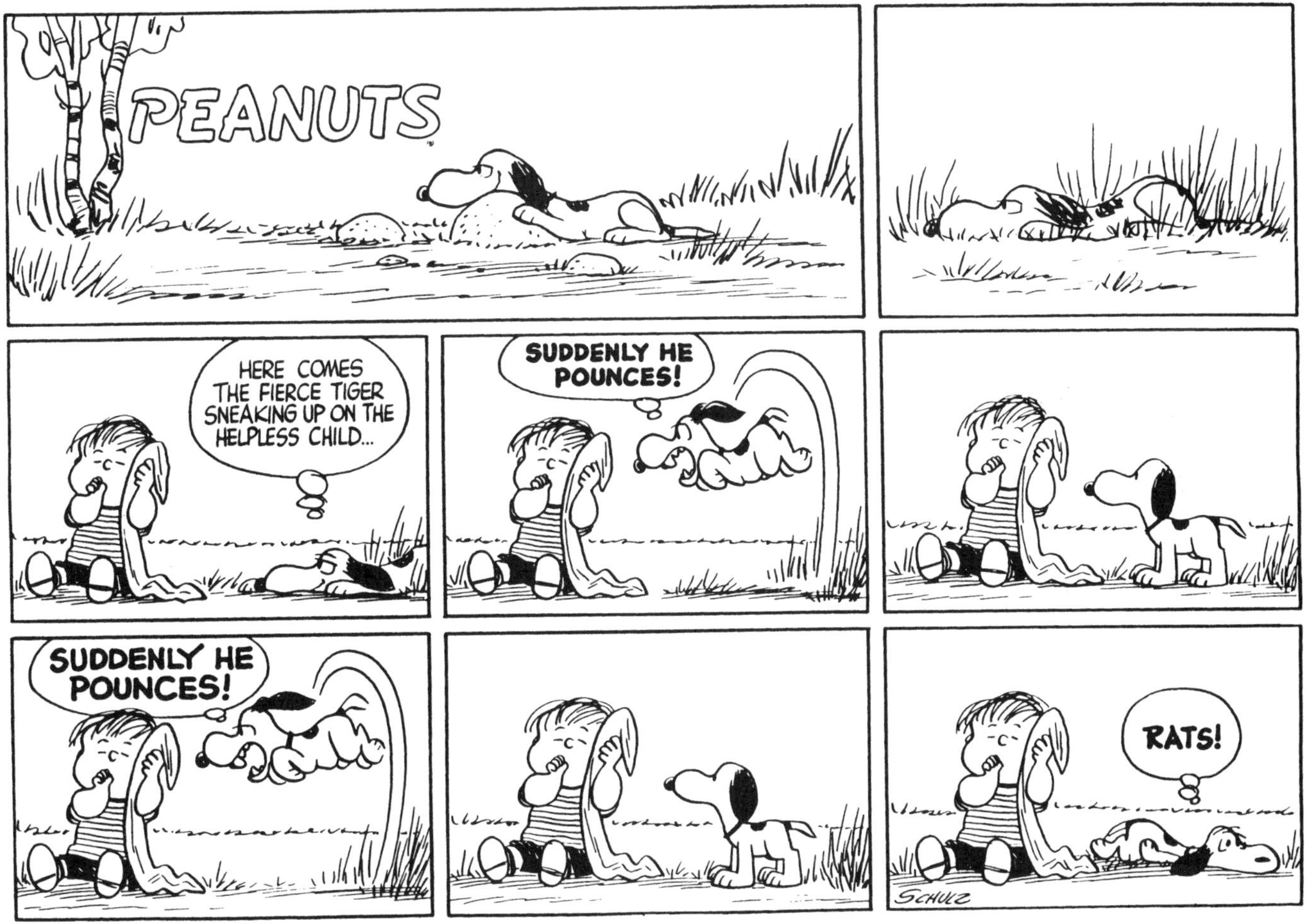
PEANUTS
HERE COMES THE FIERCE TIGER SNEAKING UP ON THE HELPLESS CHILD...
SUDDENLY HE POUNCES!
SUDDENLY HE POUNCES!
RATS!
SCHULZ

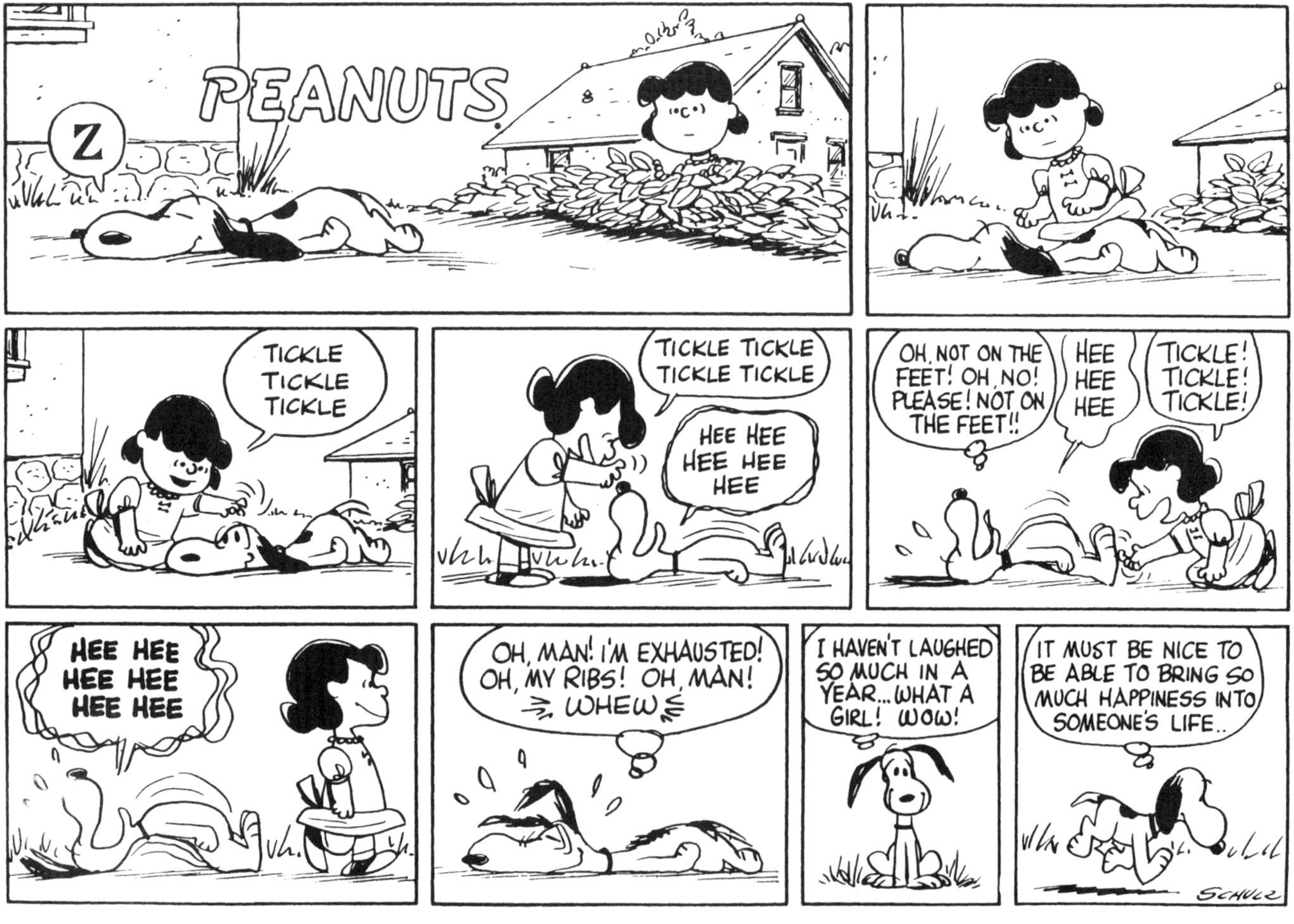
PEANUTS
Z
TICKLE TICKLE TICKLE
TICKLE TICKLE TICKLE TICKLE
HEE HEE HEE HEE HEE
OH, NOT ON THE FEET! OH, NO! PLEASE! NOT ON THE FEET!!
HEE HEE HEE
TICKLE! TICKLE! TICKLE!
HEE HEE HEE HEE HEE HEE
OH, MAN! I'M EXHAUSTED! OH, MY RIBS! OH, MAN! WHEW
I HAVEN'T LAUGHED SO MUCH IN A YEAR... WHAT A GIRL! WOW!
IT MUST BE NICE TO BE ABLE TO BRING SO MUCH HAPPINESS INTO SOMEONE'S LIFE..
SCHULZ

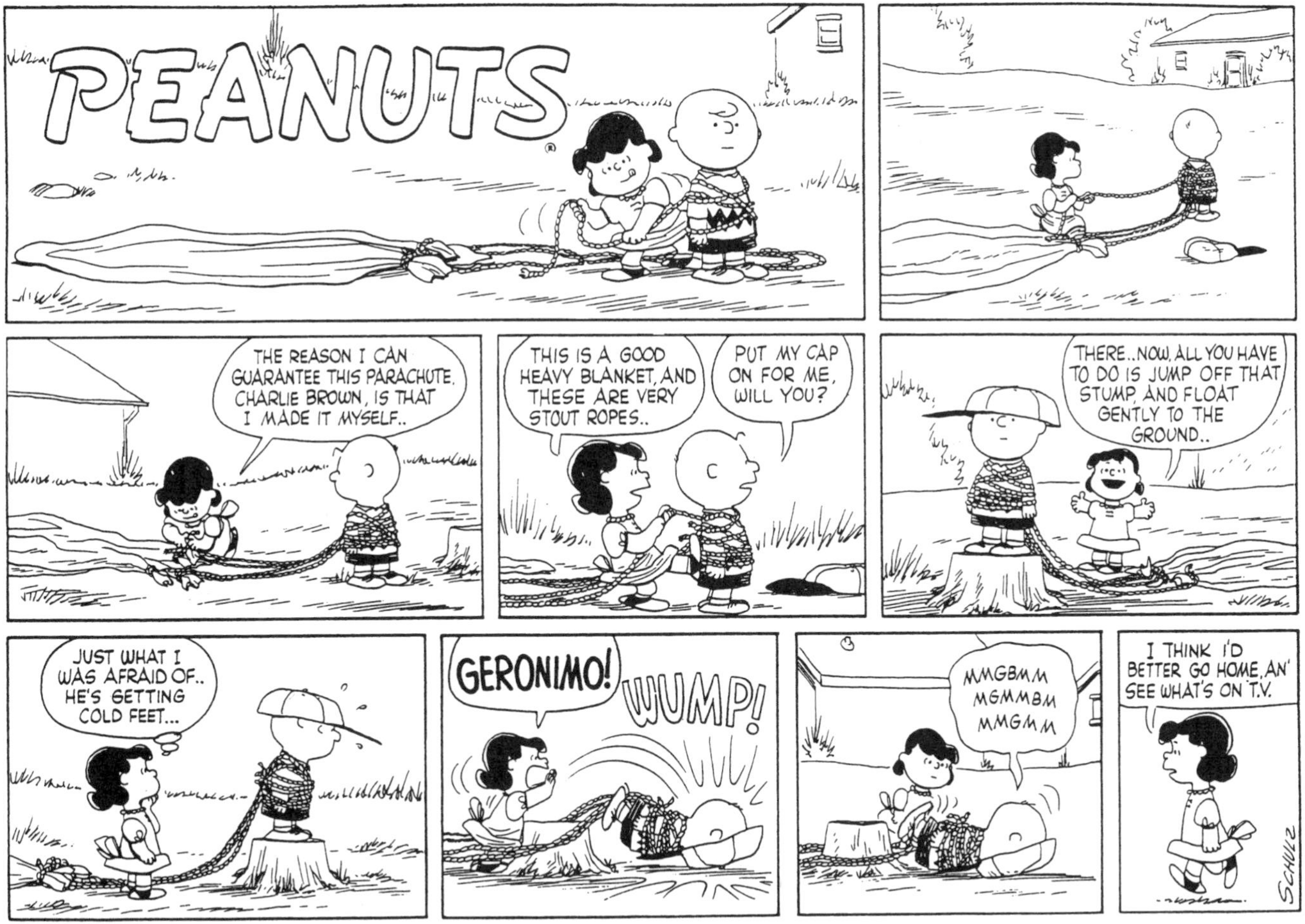
PEANUTS
THE REASON I CAN GUARANTEE THIS PARACHUTE, CHARLIE BROWN, IS THAT I MADE IT MYSELF..
THIS IS A GOOD HEAVY BLANKET, AND THESE ARE VERY STOUT ROPES..
PUT MY CAP ON FOR ME, WILL YOU?
THERE..NOW, ALL YOU HAVE TO DO IS JUMP OFF THAT STUMP, AND FLOAT GENTLY TO THE GROUND..
JUST WHAT I WAS AFRAID OF.. HE'S GETTING COLD FEET...
GERONIMO!
WUMP!
MMGBMM MGMMBM MMGMM
I THINK I'D BETTER GO HOME, AN' SEE WHAT'S ON T.V.
SCHULZ

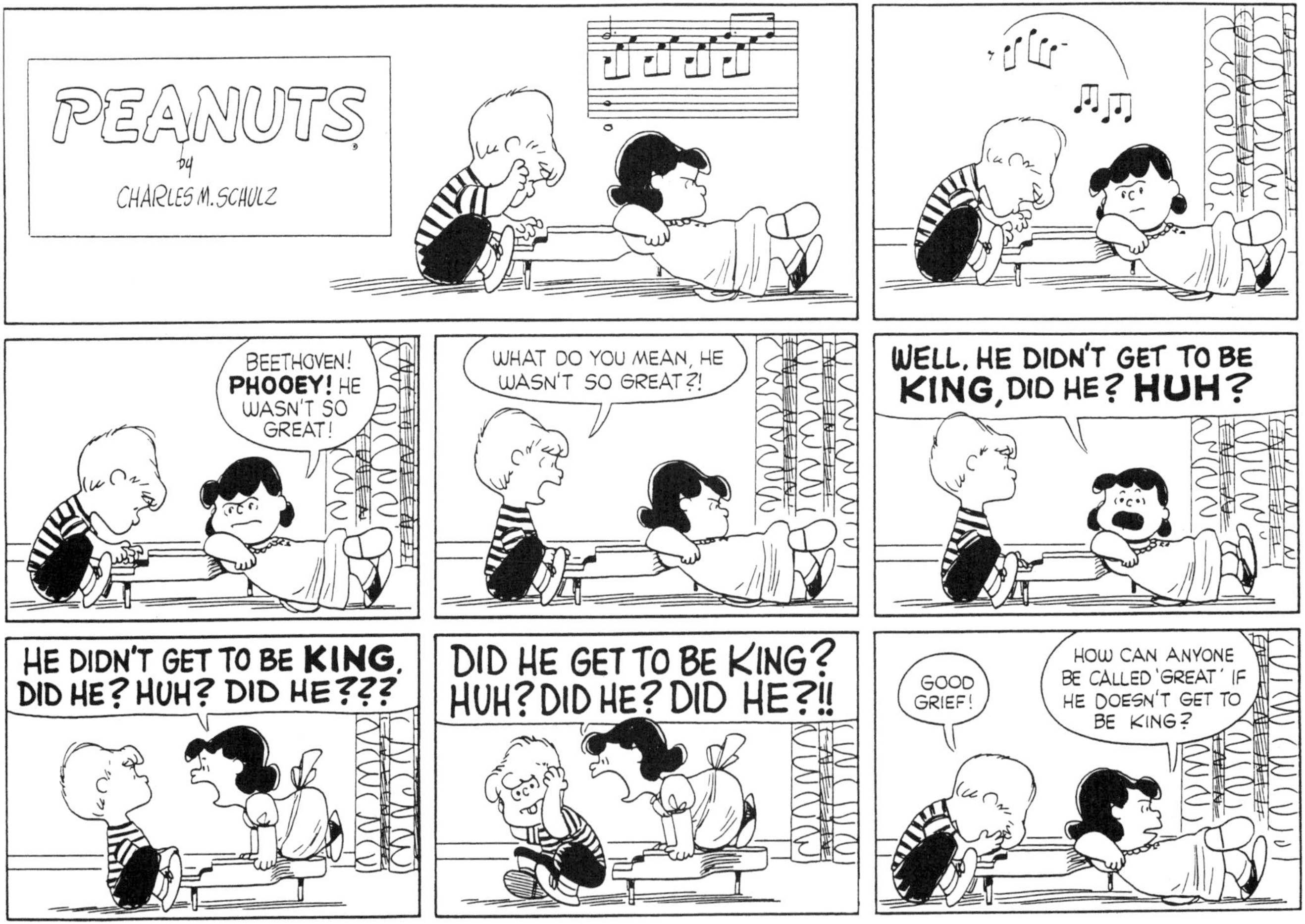
PEANUTS
by CHARLES M. SCHULZ
BEETHOVEN! PHOOEY! HE WASN'T SO GREAT!
WHAT DO YOU MEAN, HE WASN'T SO GREAT?!
WELL, HE DIDN'T GET TO BE KING, DID HE? HUH?
HE DIDN'T GET TO BE KING, DID HE? HUH? DID HE???
DID HE GET TO BE KING? HUH? DID HE? DID HE?!!
GOOD GRIEF!
HOW CAN ANYONE BE CALLED 'GREAT' IF HE DOESN'T GET TO BE KING?

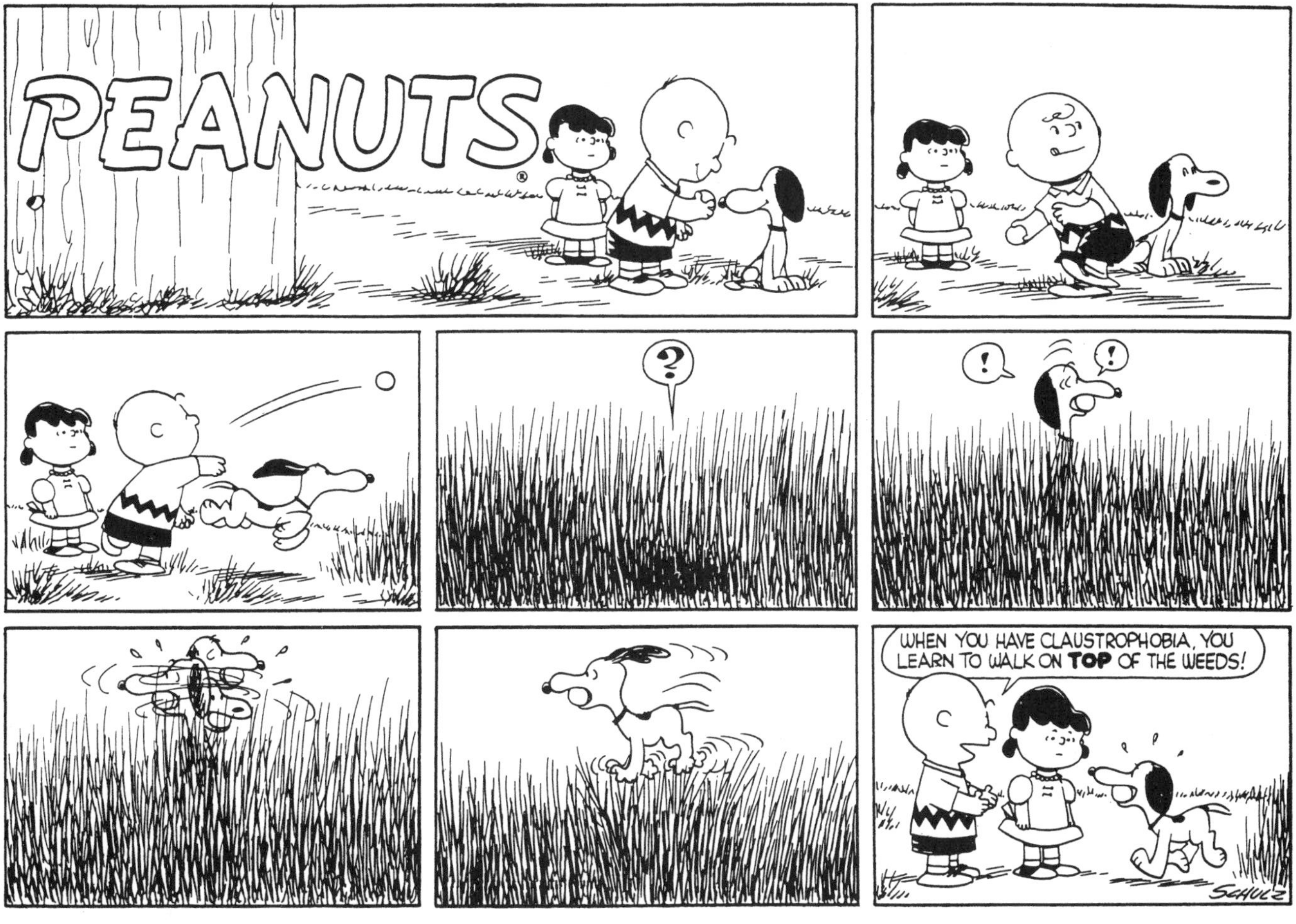
PEANUTS
?
!
!
WHEN YOU HAVE CLAUSTROPHOBIA, YOU LEARN TO WALK ON **TOP** OF THE WEEDS!
SCHULZ

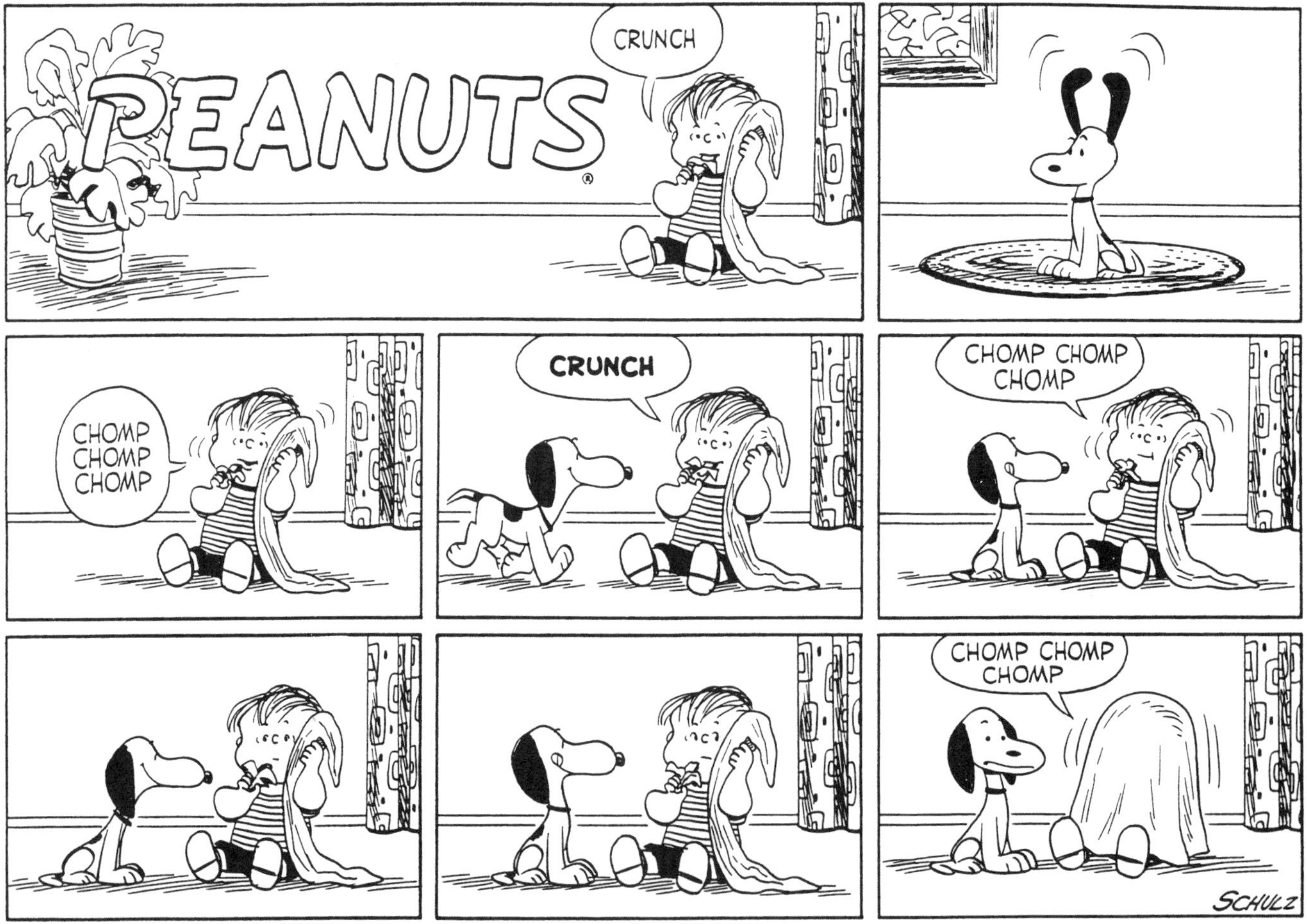
PEANUTS
CRUNCH
CHOMP CHOMP CHOMP
CRUNCH
CHOMP CHOMP CHOMP
CHOMP CHOMP CHOMP
SCHULZ

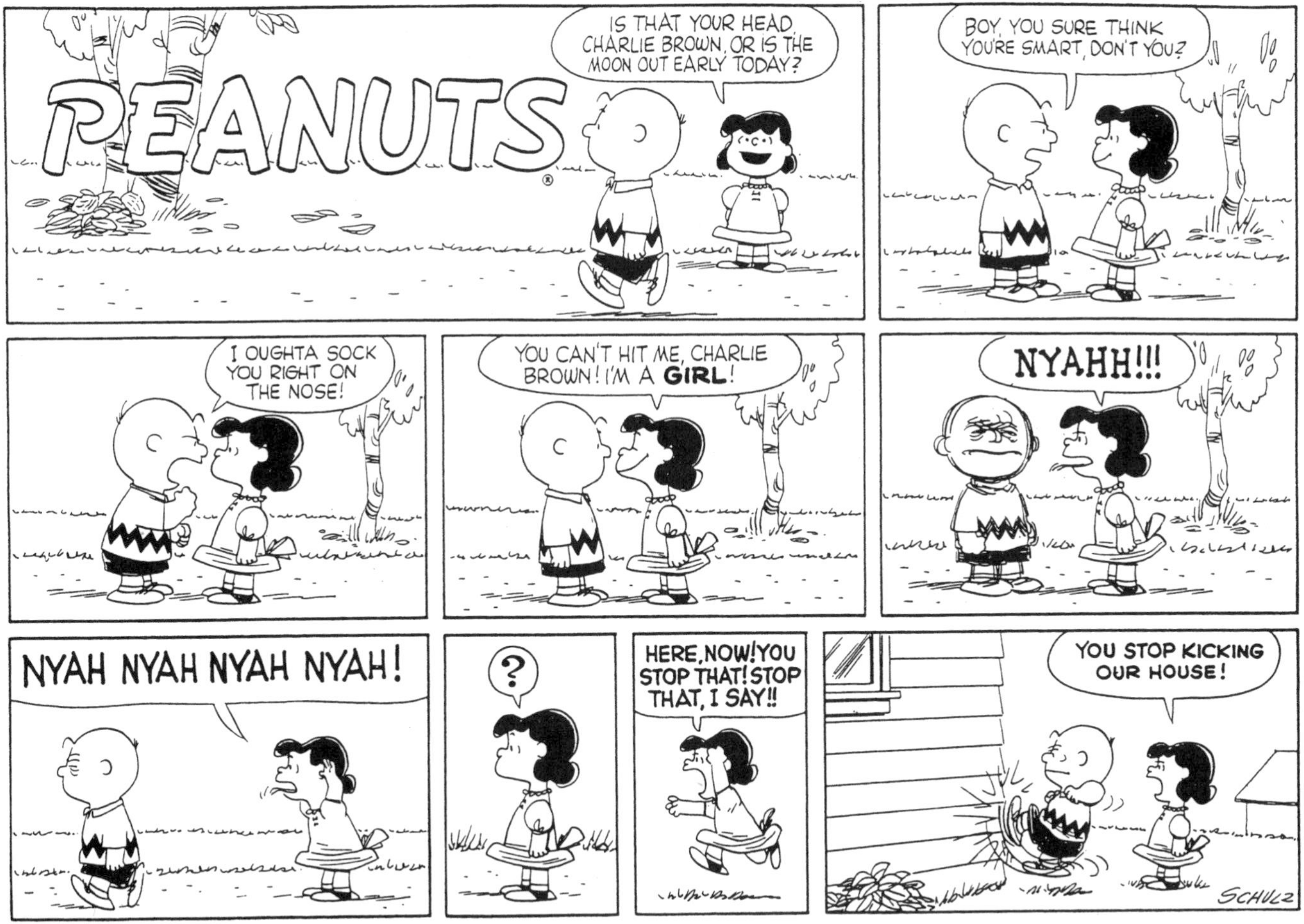
PEANUTS
IS THAT YOUR HEAD, CHARLIE BROWN, OR IS THE MOON OUT EARLY TODAY?
BOY, YOU SURE THINK YOU'RE SMART, DON'T YOU?
I OUGHTA SOCK YOU RIGHT ON THE NOSE!
YOU CAN'T HIT ME, CHARLIE BROWN! I'M A GIRL!
NYAHH!!!
NYAH NYAH NYAH NYAH!
?
HERE, NOW! YOU STOP THAT! STOP THAT, I SAY!!
YOU STOP KICKING OUR HOUSE!
SCHULZ

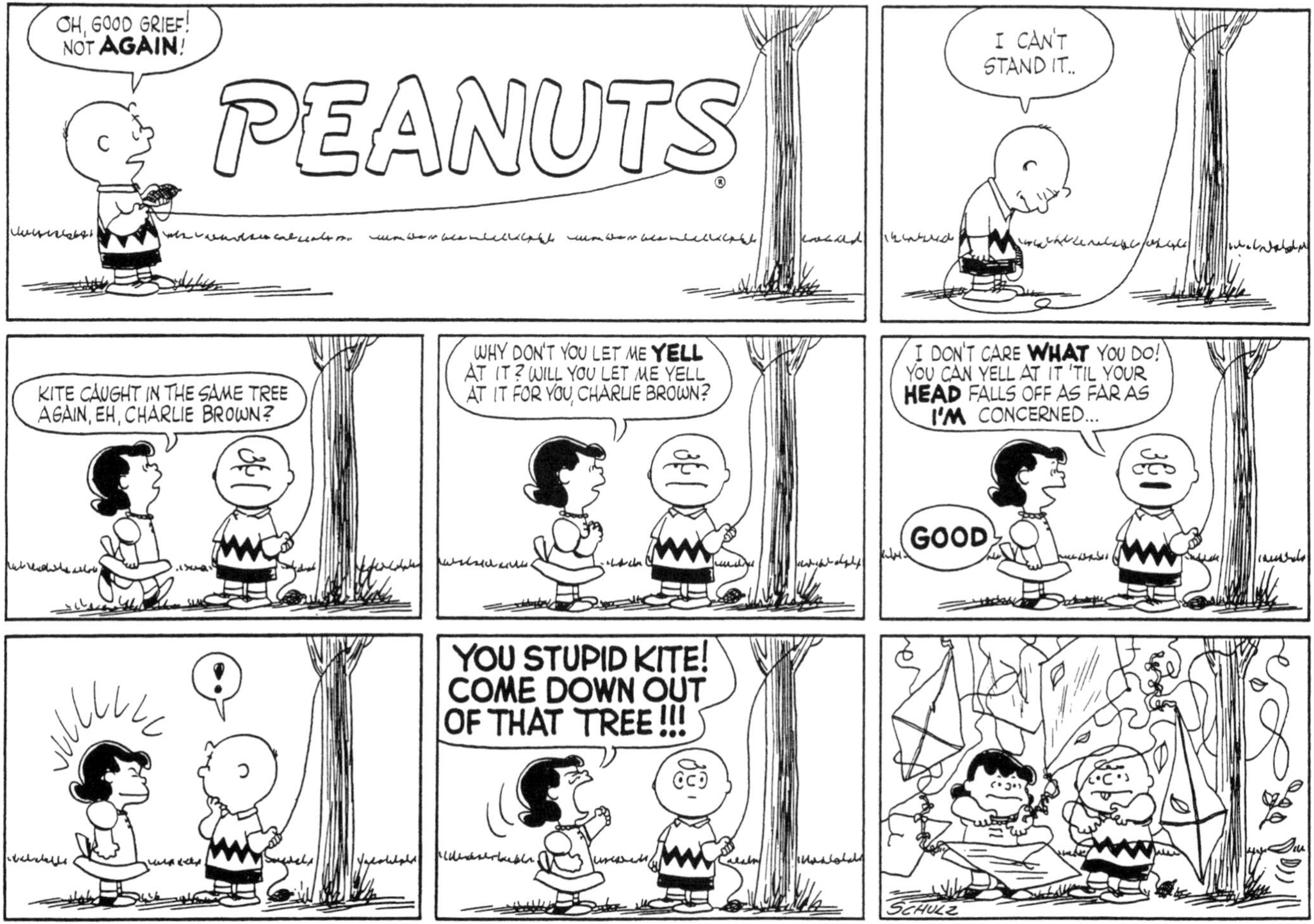

OH, GOOD GRIEF! NOT AGAIN!
PEANUTS®
I CAN'T STAND IT..
KITE CAUGHT IN THE SAME TREE AGAIN, EH, CHARLIE BROWN?
WHY DON'T YOU LET ME YELL AT IT? WILL YOU LET ME YELL AT IT FOR YOU, CHARLIE BROWN?
I DON'T CARE WHAT YOU DO! YOU CAN YELL AT IT 'TIL YOUR HEAD FALLS OFF AS FAR AS I'M CONCERNED...
GOOD
!
YOU STUPID KITE! COME DOWN OUT OF THAT TREE!!!
SCHULZ

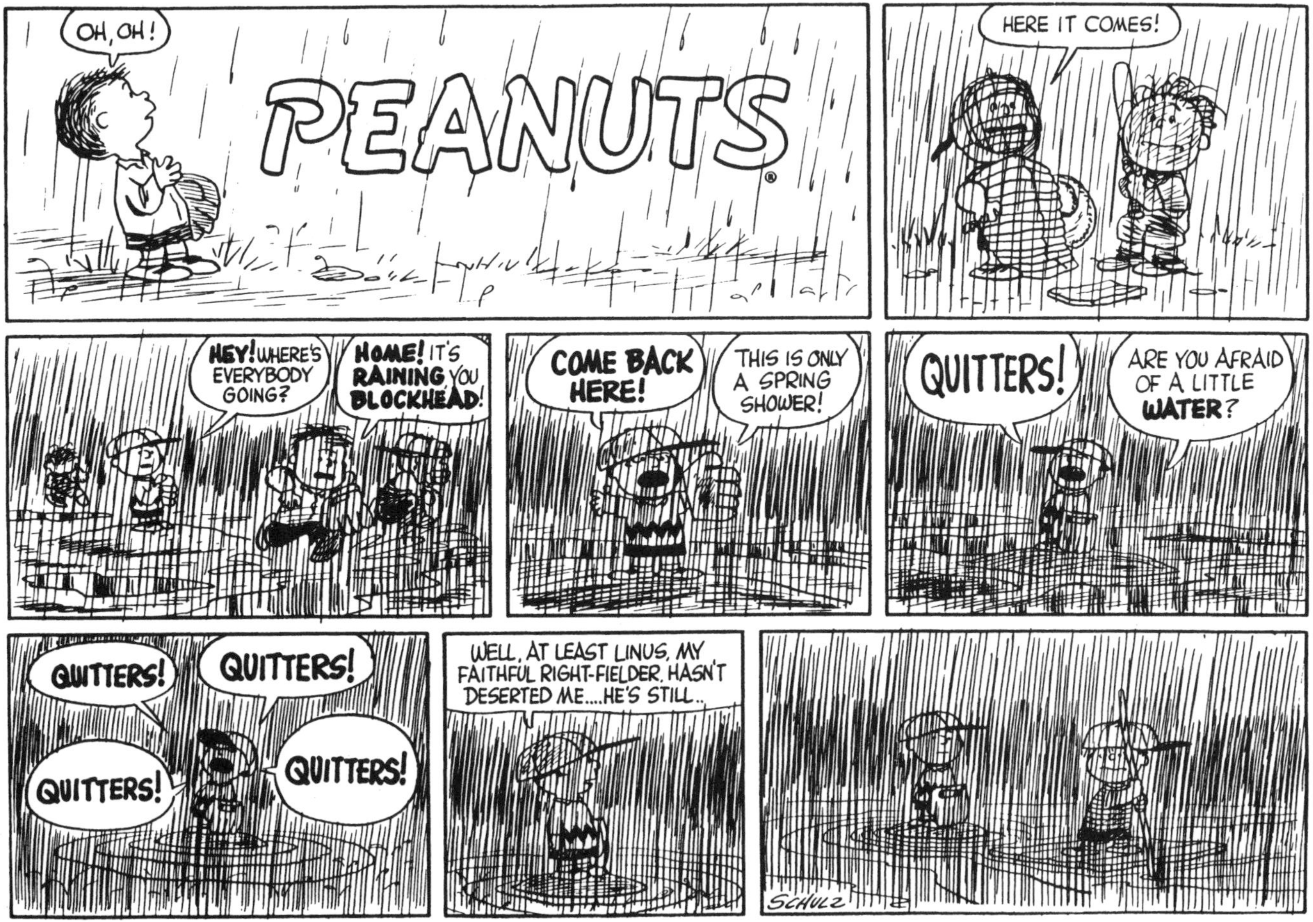
OH, OH!
PEANUTS®
HERE IT COMES!
HEY! WHERE'S EVERYBODY GOING?
HOME! IT'S RAINING YOU BLOCKHEAD!
COME BACK HERE!
THIS IS ONLY A SPRING SHOWER!
QUITTERS!
ARE YOU AFRAID OF A LITTLE WATER?
QUITTERS!
QUITTERS!
QUITTERS!
QUITTERS!
WELL, AT LEAST LINUS, MY FAITHFUL RIGHT-FIELDER, HASN'T DESERTED ME....HE'S STILL..
SCHULZ

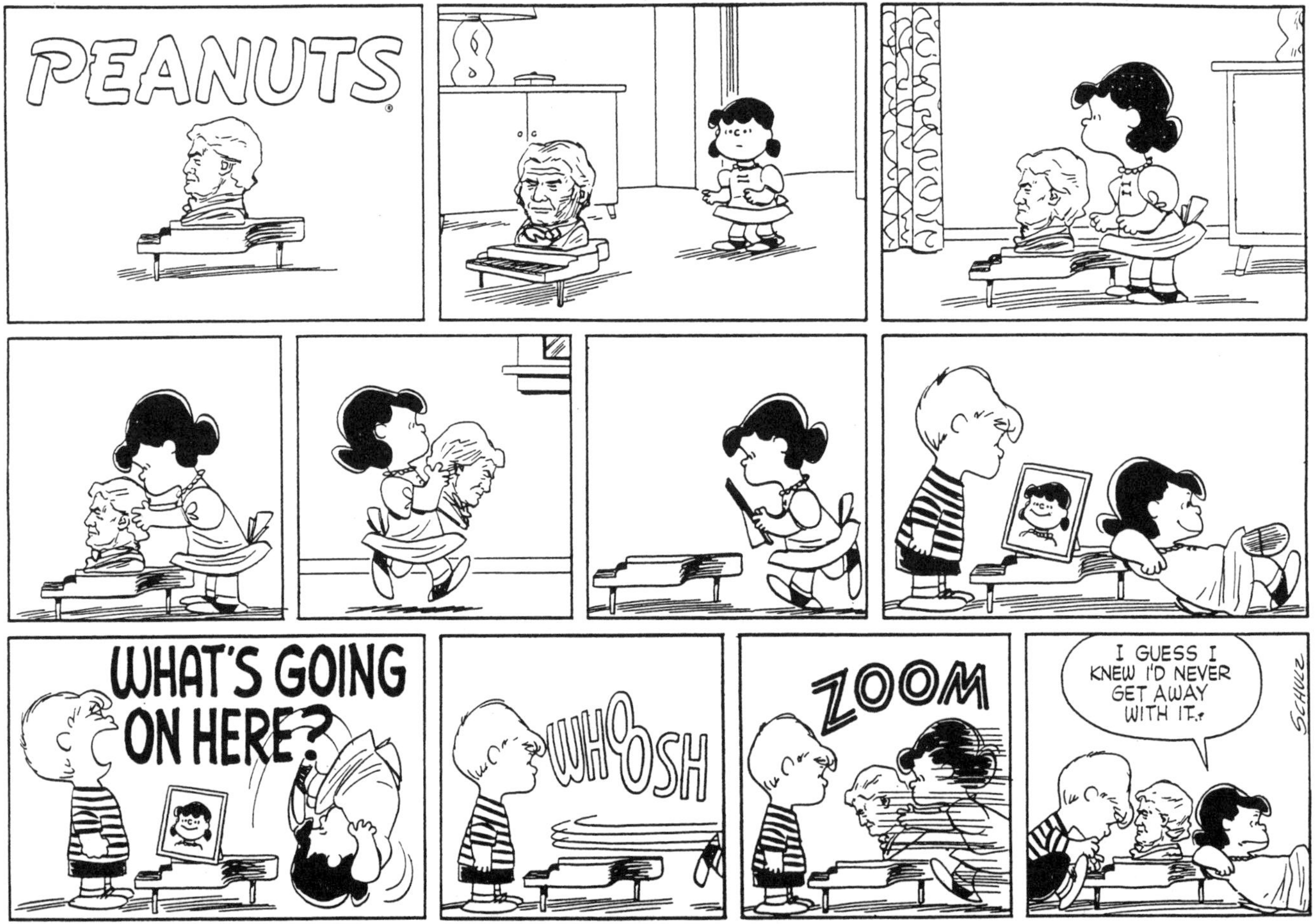
PEANUTS
WHAT'S GOING ON HERE?
WHOOSH
ZOOM
I GUESS I KNEW I'D NEVER GET AWAY WITH IT..
SCHULZ

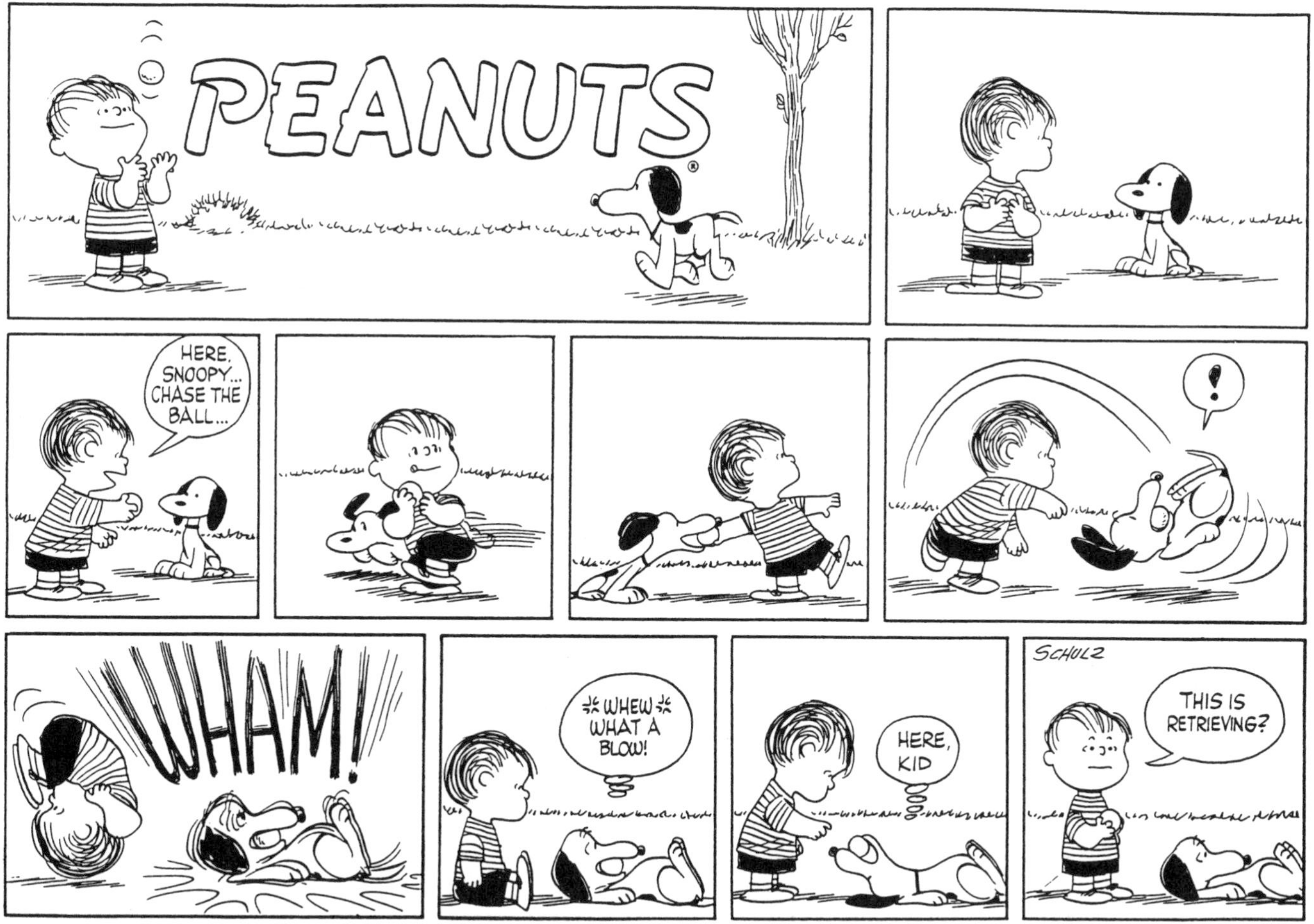
PEANUTS®
HERE, SNOOPY... CHASE THE BALL...
!
WHAM!
WHEW WHAT A BLOW!
HERE, KID
SCHULZ
THIS IS RETRIEVING?

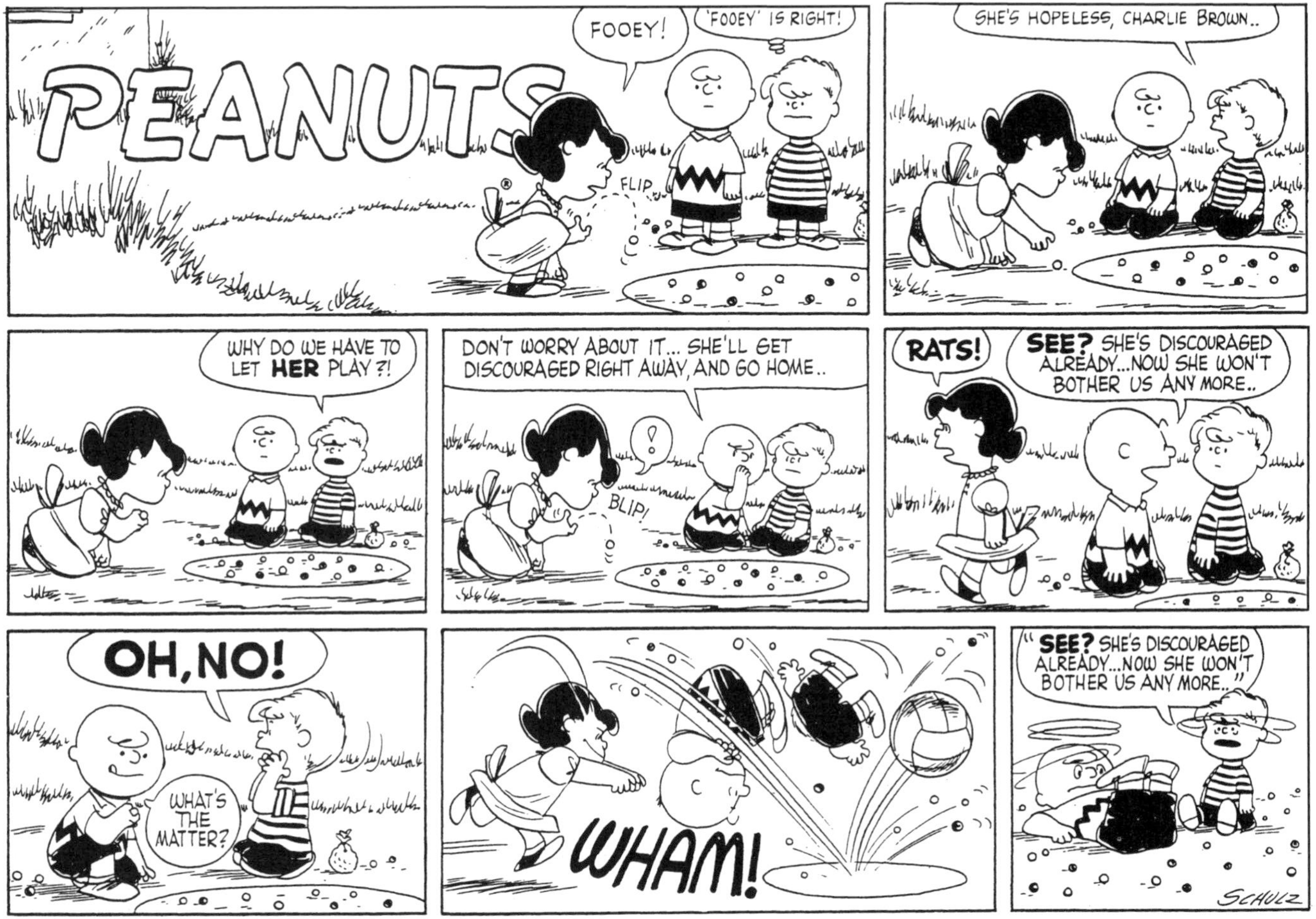
PEANUTS
FOOEY!
'FOOEY' IS RIGHT!
FLIP
SHE'S HOPELESS, CHARLIE BROWN..
WHY DO WE HAVE TO LET **HER** PLAY ?!
DON'T WORRY ABOUT IT... SHE'LL GET DISCOURAGED RIGHT AWAY, AND GO HOME..
!
BLIP!
RATS!
SEE? SHE'S DISCOURAGED ALREADY...NOW SHE WON'T BOTHER US ANY MORE..
OH, NO!
WHAT'S THE MATTER?
WHAM!
"**SEE?** SHE'S DISCOURAGED ALREADY...NOW SHE WON'T BOTHER US ANY MORE.."
SCHULZ

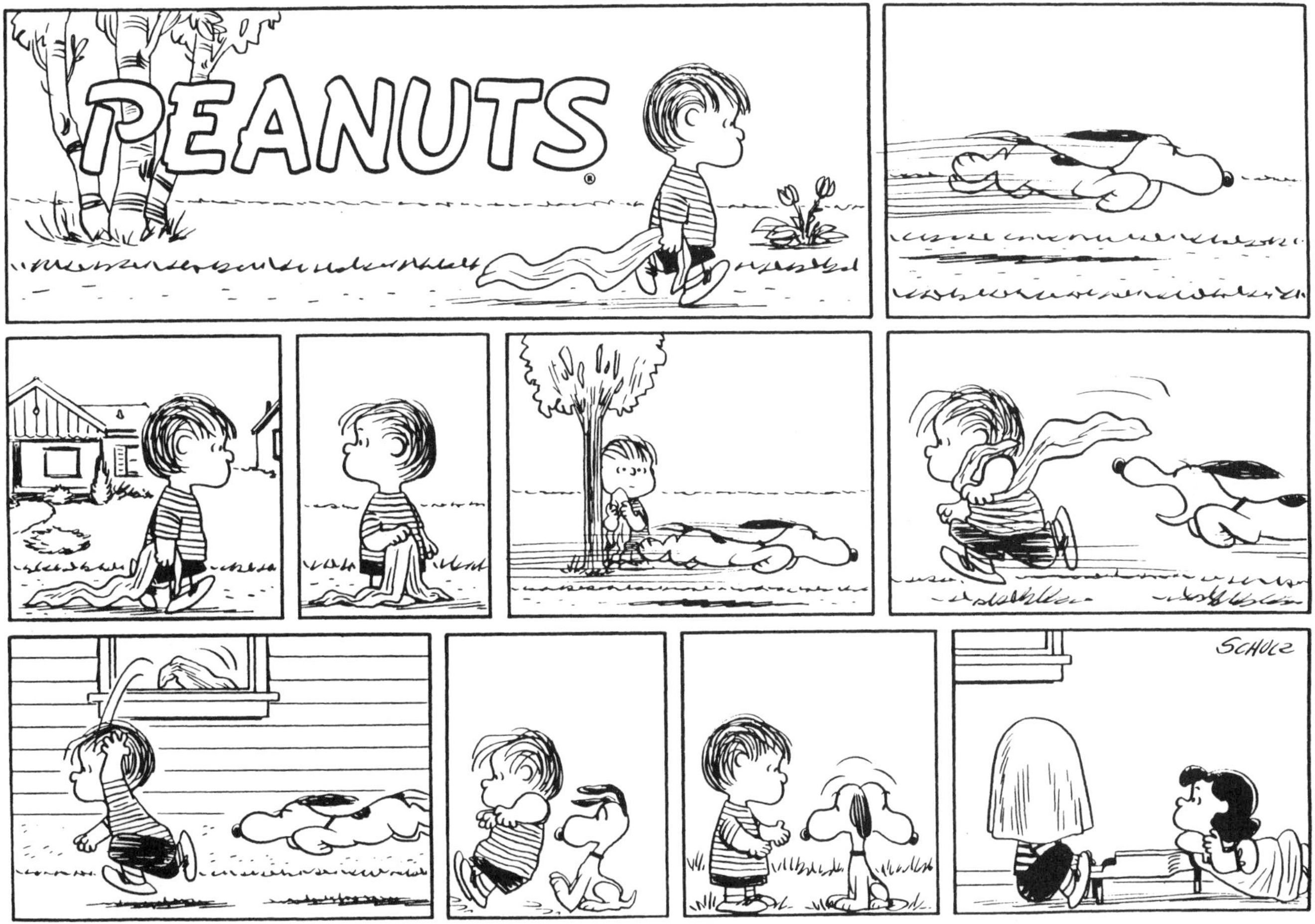
PEANUTS
SCHULZ

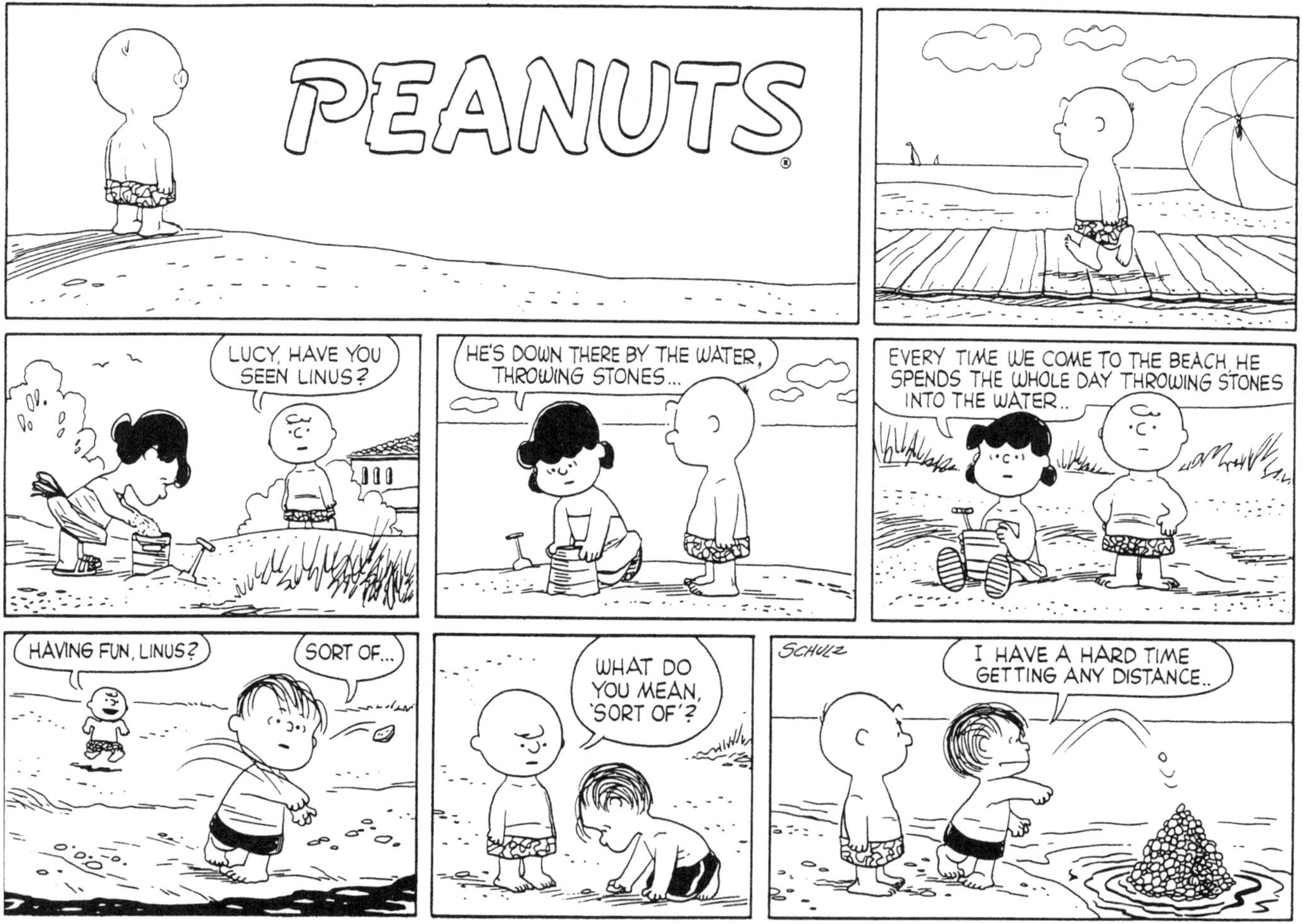
PEANUTS
LUCY, HAVE YOU SEEN LINUS?
HE'S DOWN THERE BY THE WATER, THROWING STONES...
EVERY TIME WE COME TO THE BEACH, HE SPENDS THE WHOLE DAY THROWING STONES INTO THE WATER..
HAVING FUN, LINUS?
SORT OF...
WHAT DO YOU MEAN, 'SORT OF'?
SCHULZ
I HAVE A HARD TIME GETTING ANY DISTANCE..

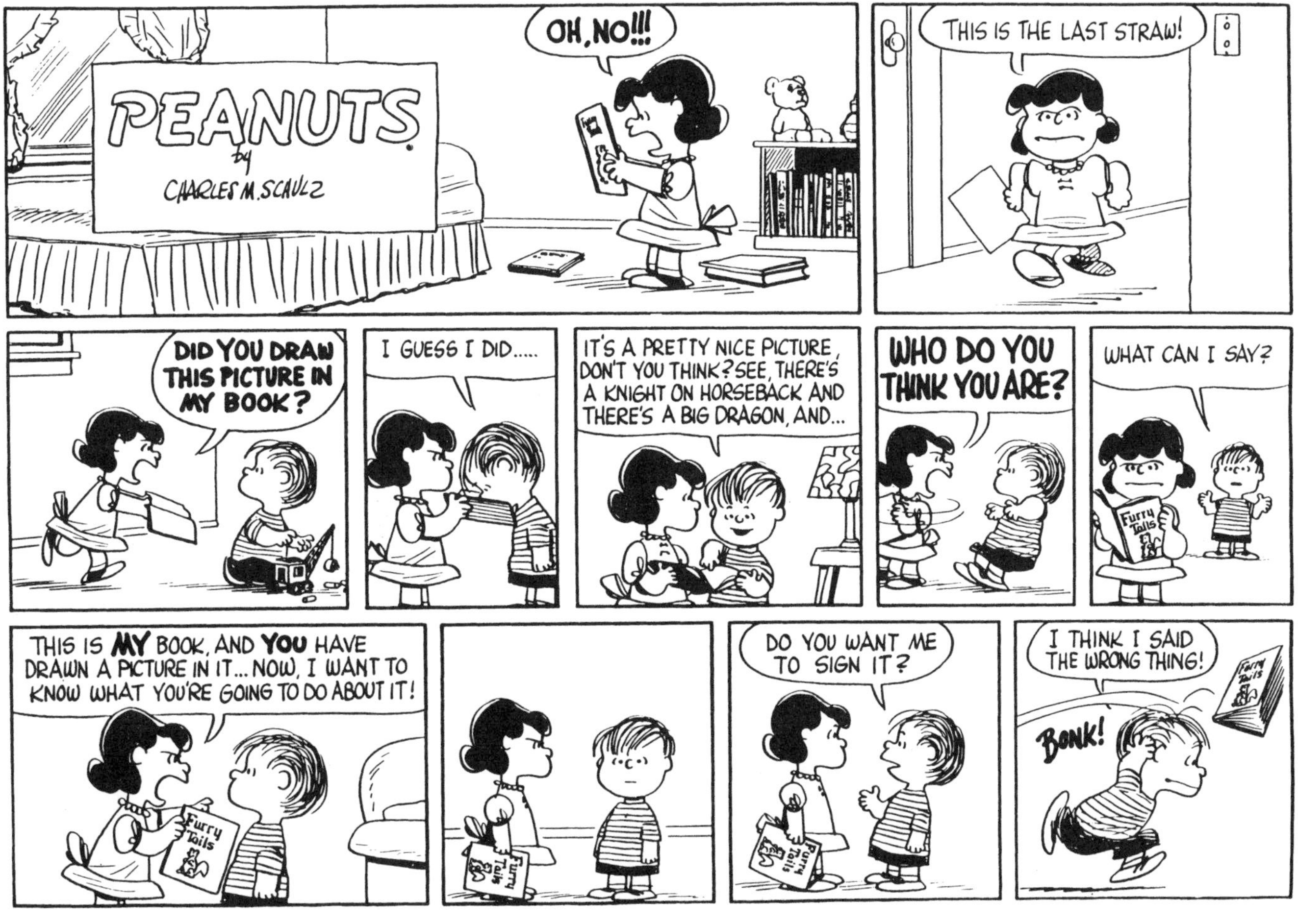
PEANUTS
by
CHARLES M. SCHULZ
OH, NO!!!
THIS IS THE LAST STRAW!
DID YOU DRAW THIS PICTURE IN MY BOOK?
I GUESS I DID.....
IT'S A PRETTY NICE PICTURE, DON'T YOU THINK? SEE, THERE'S A KNIGHT ON HORSEBACK AND THERE'S A BIG DRAGON, AND...
WHO DO YOU THINK YOU ARE?
WHAT CAN I SAY?
Furry Tails
THIS IS MY BOOK, AND YOU HAVE DRAWN A PICTURE IN IT... NOW, I WANT TO KNOW WHAT YOU'RE GOING TO DO ABOUT IT!
DO YOU WANT ME TO SIGN IT?
I THINK I SAID THE WRONG THING!
BONK!

PEANUTS

SAY! I THOUGHT WE WERE GONNA TAKE TURNS USING THAT UMBRELLA?

WELL, WE WERE, BUT I'VE DECIDED THAT AS LONG AS YOU'RE ALL WET ALREADY, THERE'S REALLY NO SENSE IN MY GIVING YOU THE UMBRELLA, AND THEN GETTING WET, TOO...

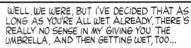

THAT WOULDN'T MAKE SENSE, WOULD IT? NO, IT WOULDN'T...

SO MUCH IN THIS WORLD DEPENDS UPON WHO GETS BORN FIRST!

SCHULZ

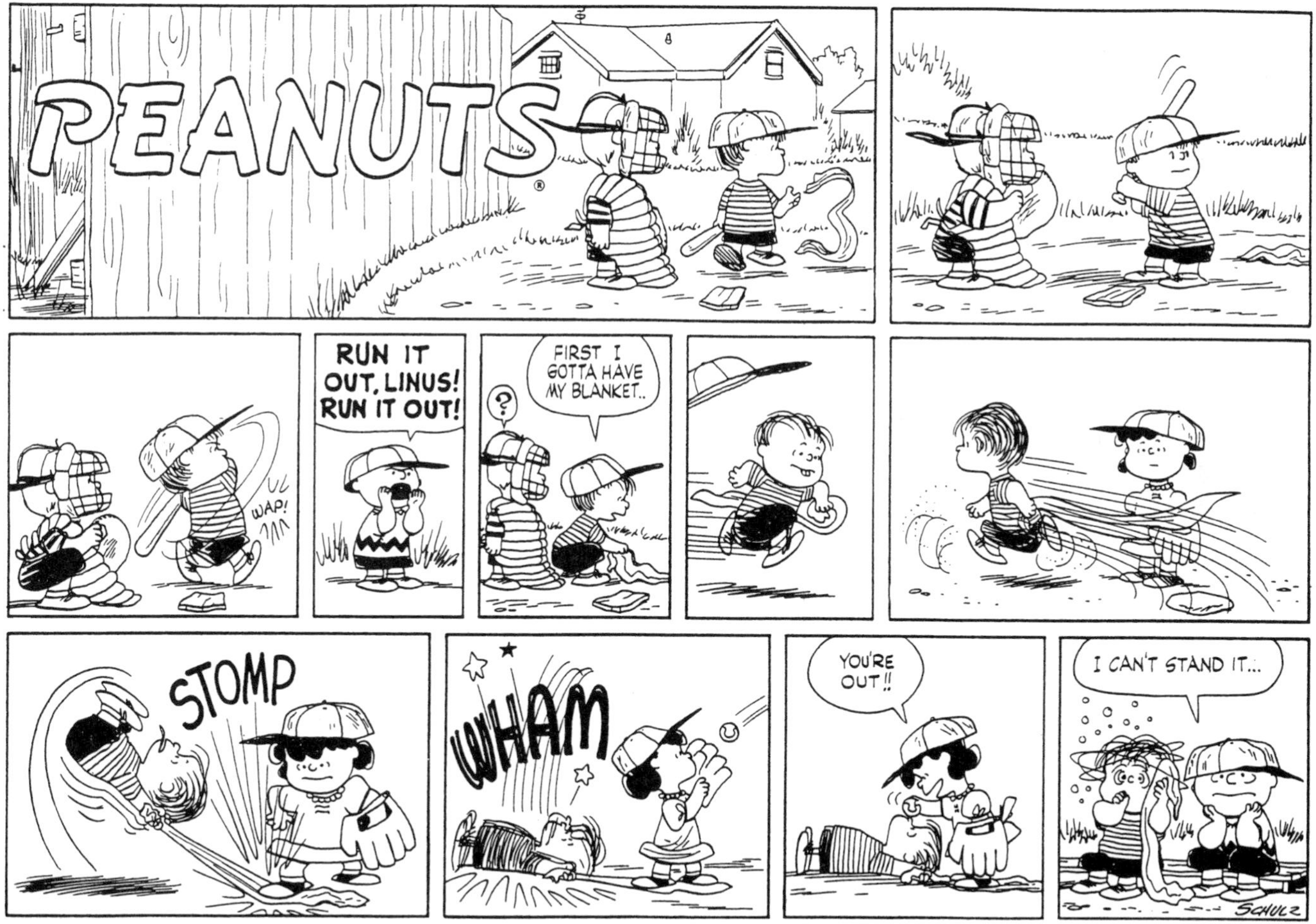

PEANUTS
RUN IT OUT, LINUS! RUN IT OUT!
?
FIRST I GOTTA HAVE MY BLANKET..
STOMP
WHAM
YOU'RE OUT!!
I CAN'T STAND IT...
SCHULZ

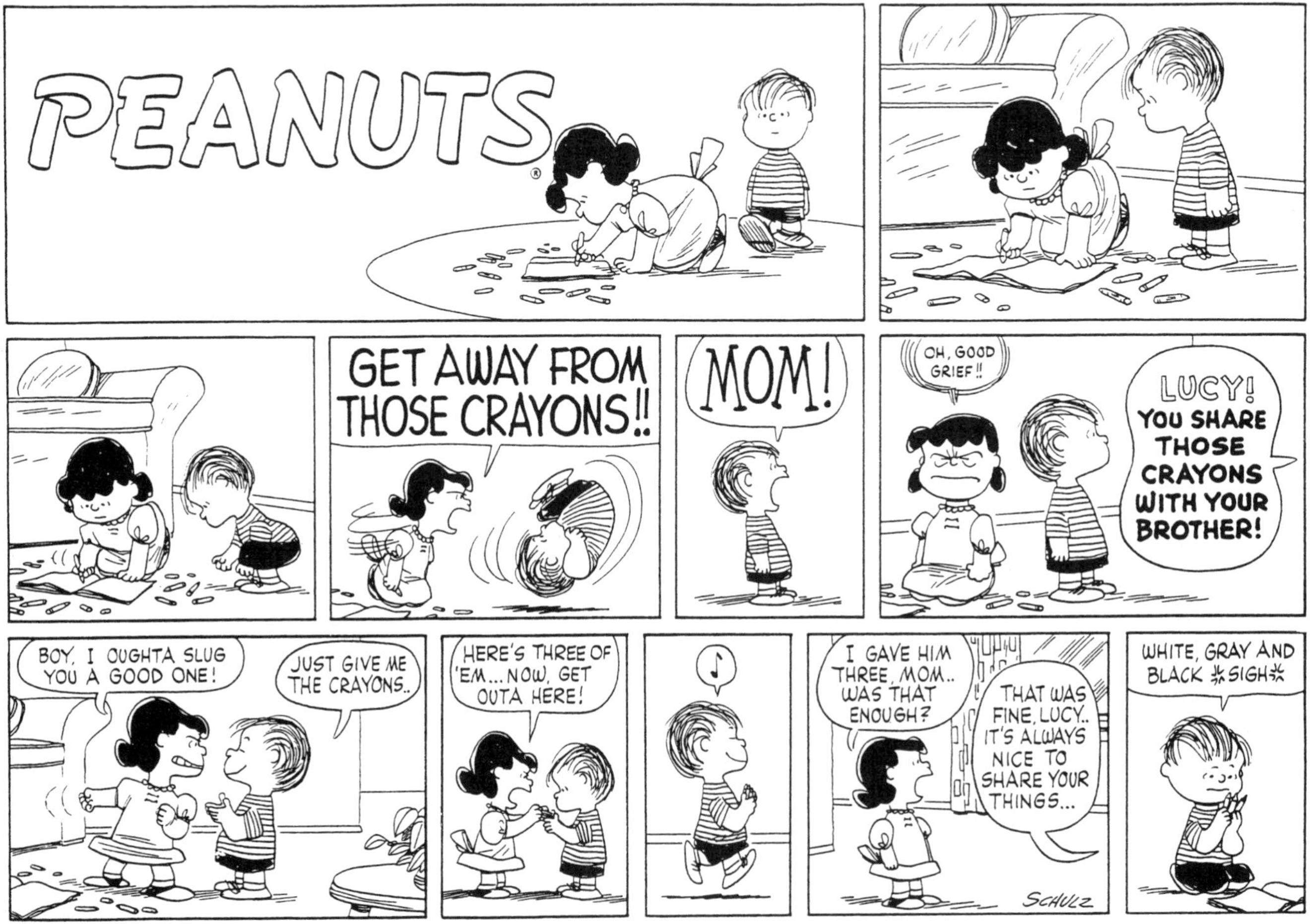
PEANUTS
GET AWAY FROM THOSE CRAYONS!!
MOM!
OH, GOOD GRIEF!!
LUCY! YOU SHARE THOSE CRAYONS WITH YOUR BROTHER!
BOY, I OUGHTA SLUG YOU A GOOD ONE!
JUST GIVE ME THE CRAYONS..
HERE'S THREE OF 'EM... NOW, GET OUTA HERE!
♪
I GAVE HIM THREE, MOM.. WAS THAT ENOUGH?
THAT WAS FINE, LUCY.. IT'S ALWAYS NICE TO SHARE YOUR THINGS...
SCHULZ
WHITE, GRAY AND BLACK *SIGH*

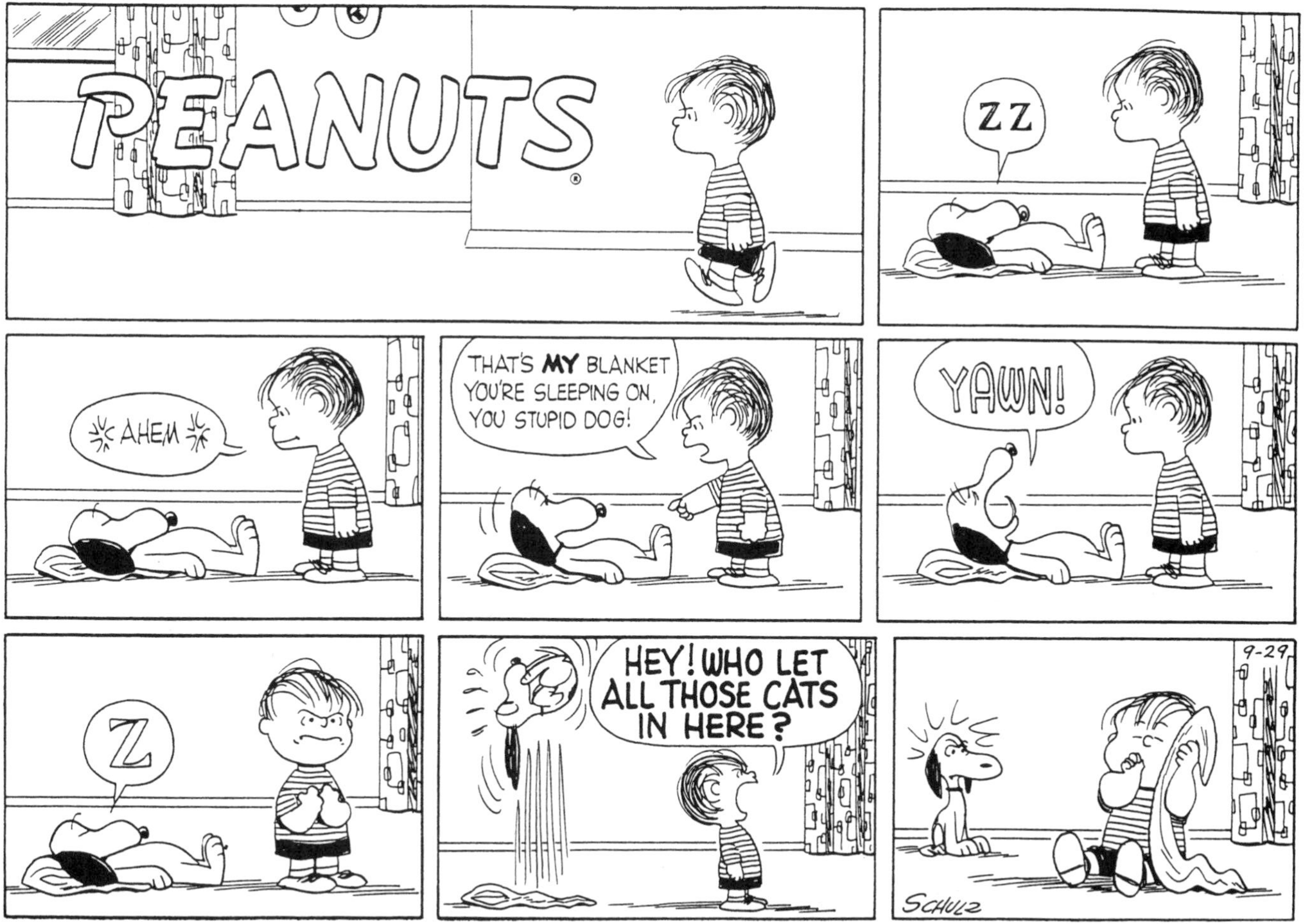
PEANUTS
ZZ
AHEM
THAT'S MY BLANKET YOU'RE SLEEPING ON, YOU STUPID DOG!
YAWN!
Z
HEY! WHO LET ALL THOSE CATS IN HERE?
9-29
SCHULZ

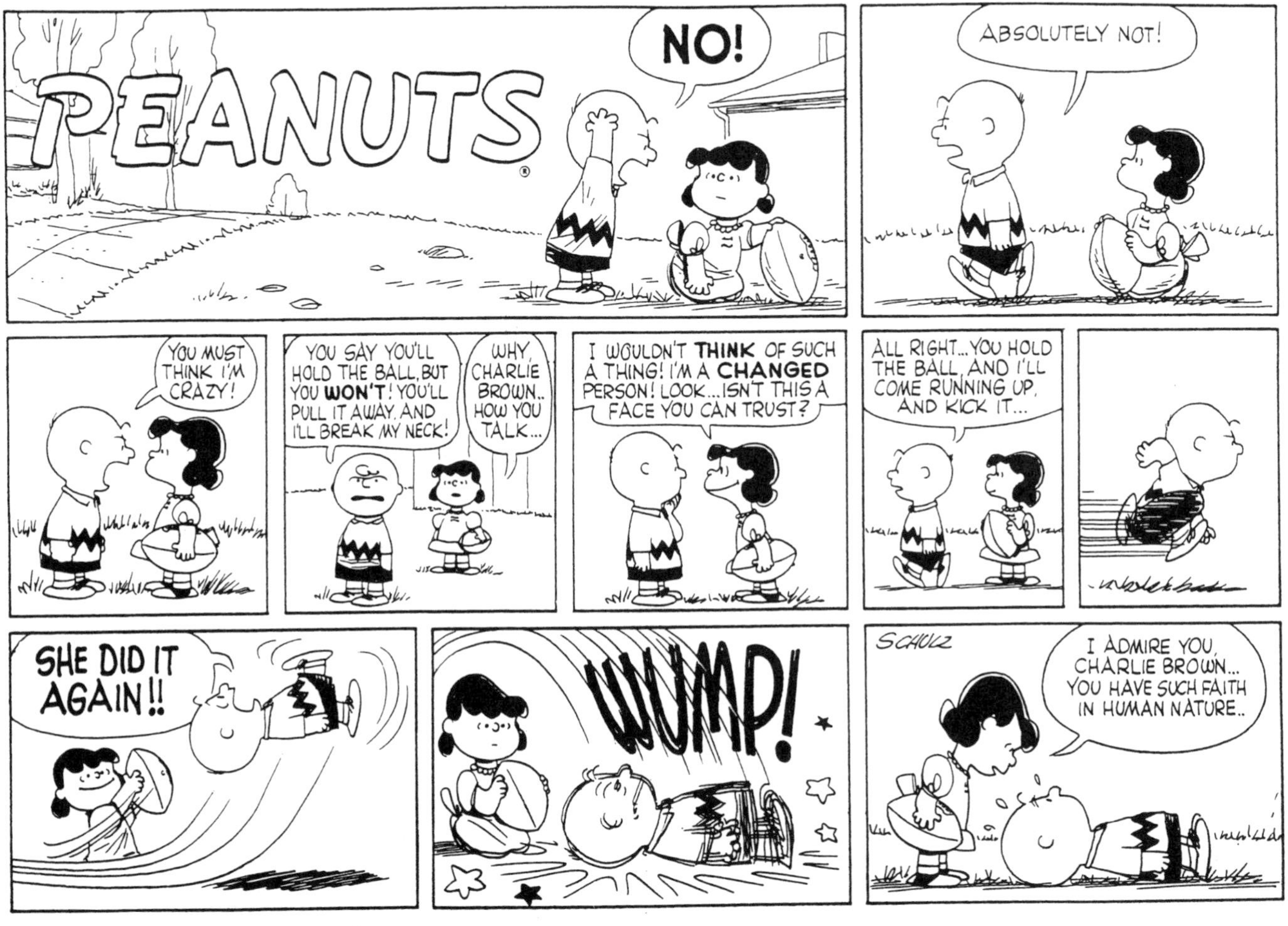
PEANUTS
NO!
ABSOLUTELY NOT!
YOU MUST THINK I'M CRAZY!
YOU SAY YOU'LL HOLD THE BALL, BUT YOU **WON'T**! YOU'LL PULL IT AWAY, AND I'LL BREAK MY NECK!
WHY, CHARLIE BROWN.. HOW YOU TALK...
I WOULDN'T **THINK** OF SUCH A THING! I'M A **CHANGED** PERSON! LOOK...ISN'T THIS A FACE YOU CAN TRUST?
ALL RIGHT...YOU HOLD THE BALL, AND I'LL COME RUNNING UP, AND KICK IT...
SHE DID IT AGAIN!!
WUMP!
SCHULZ
I ADMIRE YOU, CHARLIE BROWN... YOU HAVE SUCH FAITH IN HUMAN NATURE..

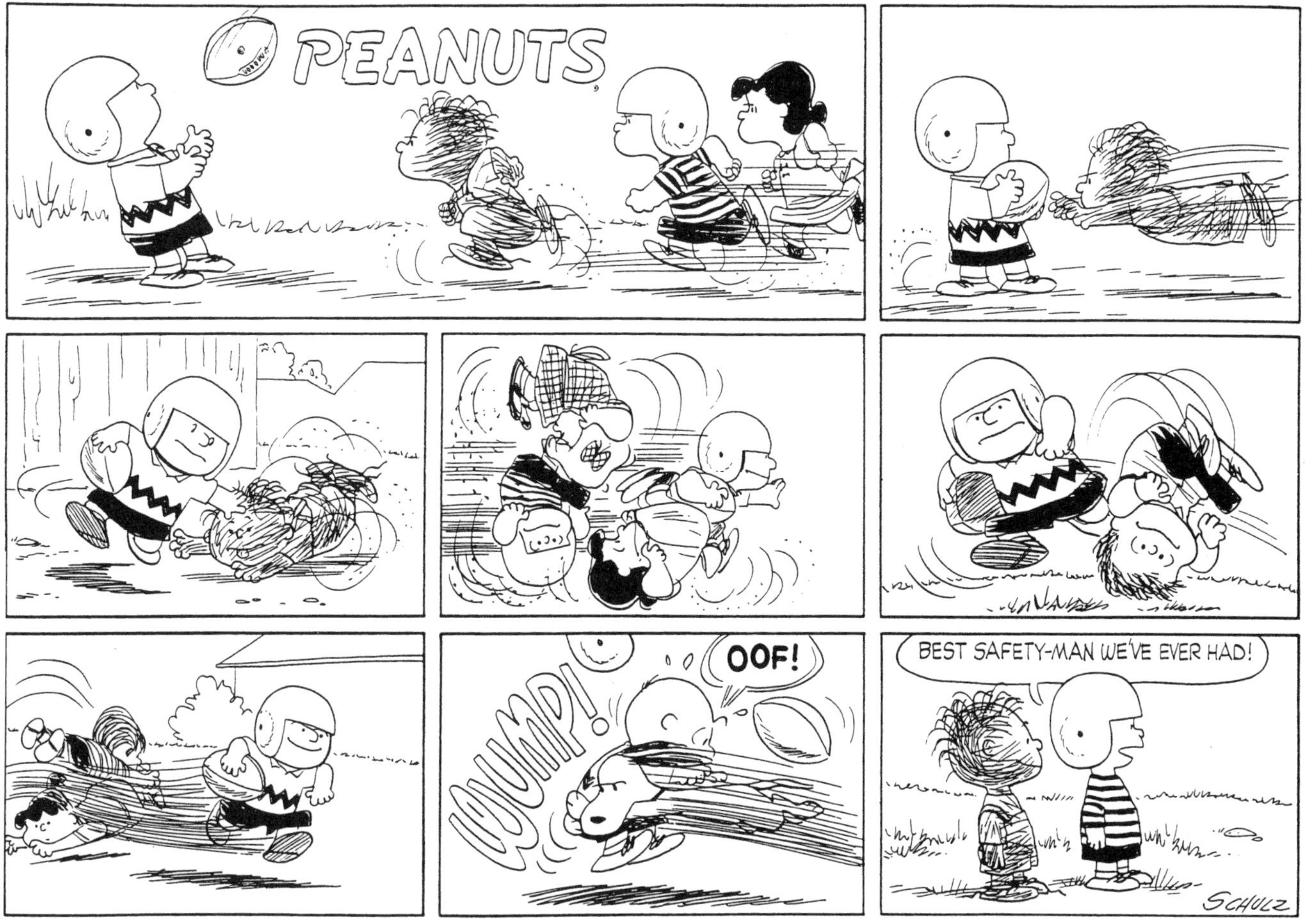

PEANUTS
WUMP!
OOF!
BEST SAFETY-MAN WE'VE EVER HAD!
SCHULZ

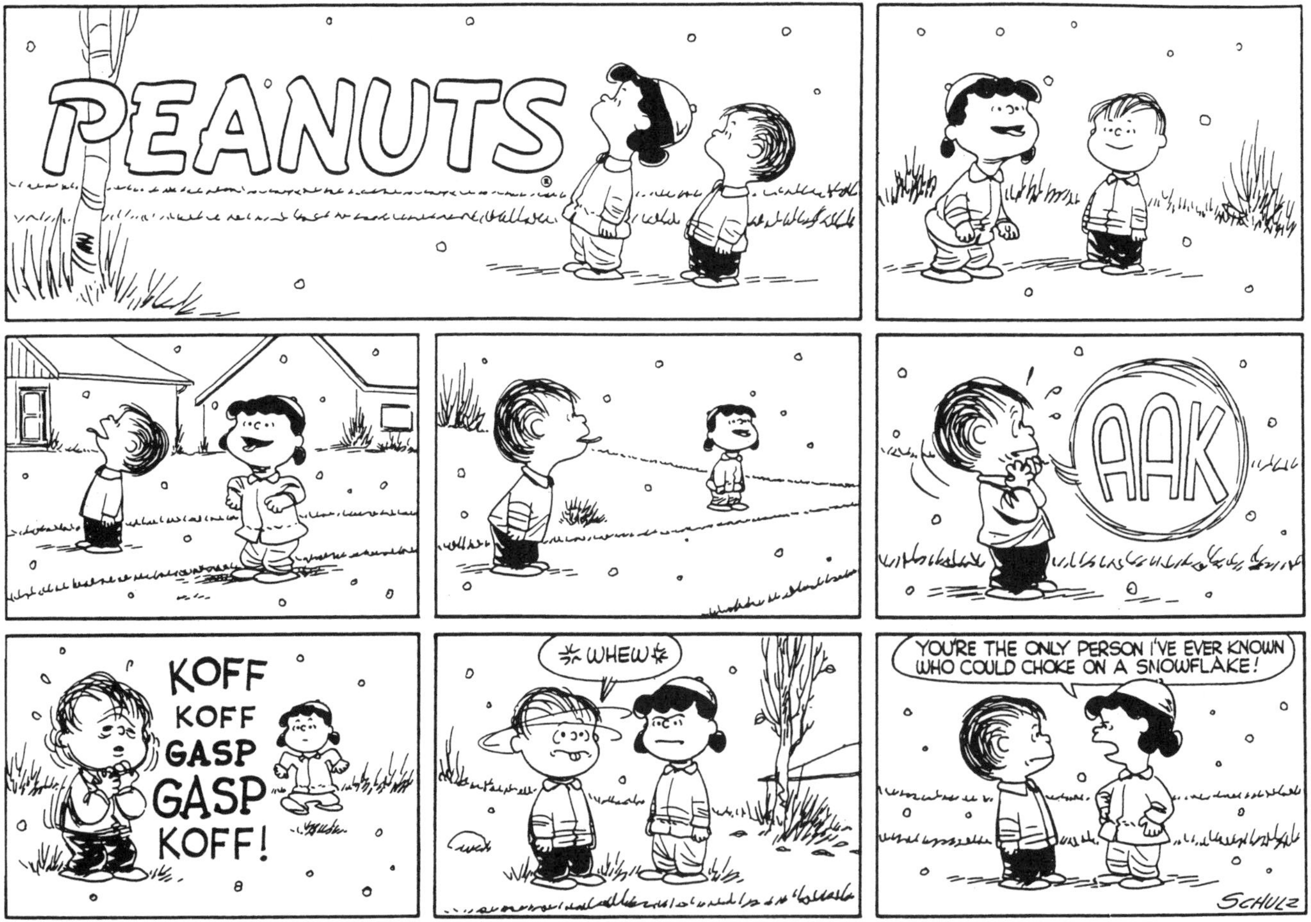
PEANUTS
AAK
KOFF
KOFF
GASP
GASP
KOFF!
WHEW
YOU'RE THE ONLY PERSON I'VE EVER KNOWN WHO COULD CHOKE ON A SNOWFLAKE!
SCHULZ

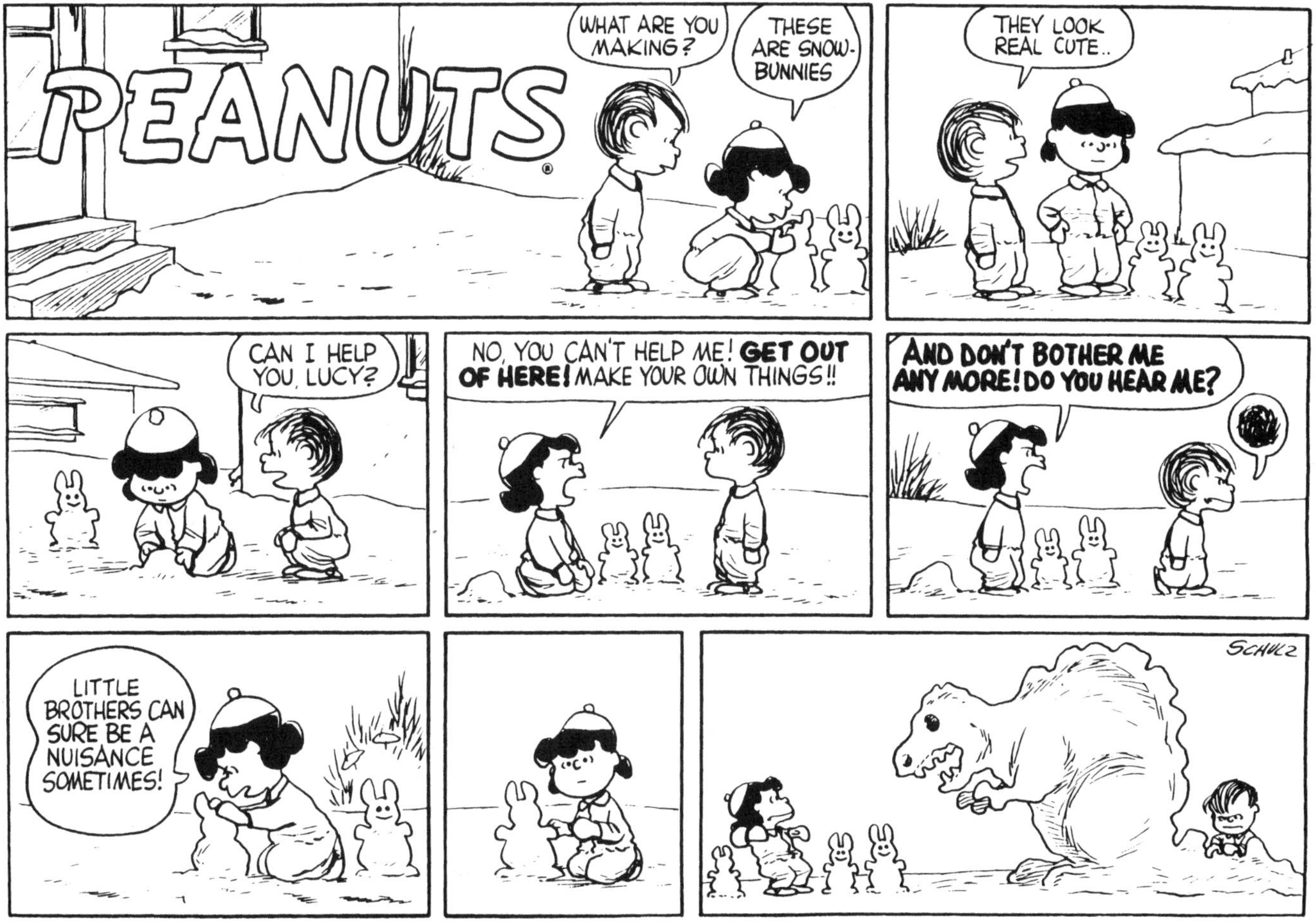
PEANUTS
WHAT ARE YOU MAKING?
THESE ARE SNOW-BUNNIES
THEY LOOK REAL CUTE..
CAN I HELP YOU, LUCY?
NO, YOU CAN'T HELP ME! GET OUT OF HERE! MAKE YOUR OWN THINGS!!
AND DON'T BOTHER ME ANY MORE! DO YOU HEAR ME?
LITTLE BROTHERS CAN SURE BE A NUISANCE SOMETIMES!
SCHULZ

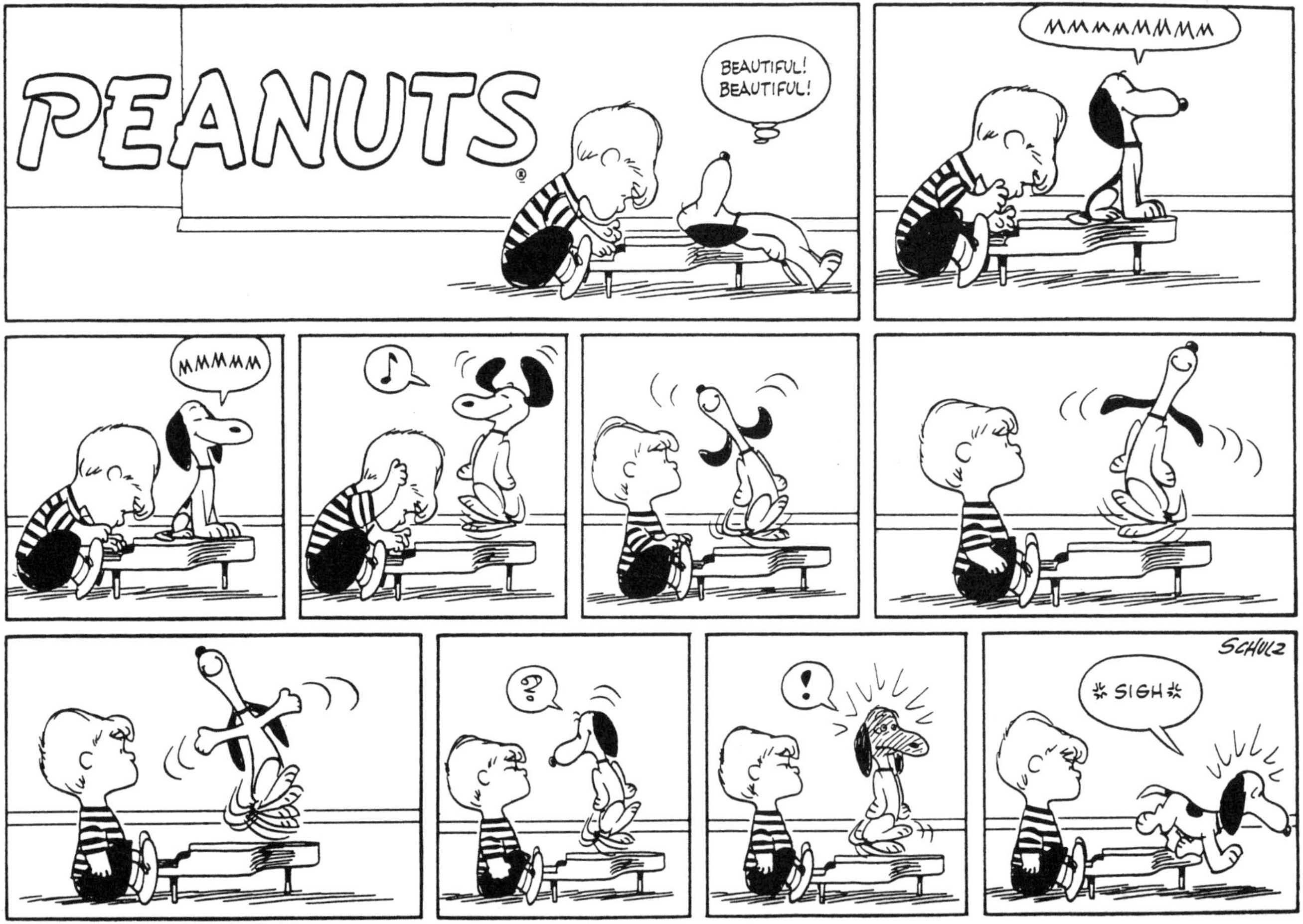
PEANUTS
BEAUTIFUL! BEAUTIFUL!
MMMMMMMMM
MMMMM
♪
?
!
SIGH
SCHULZ

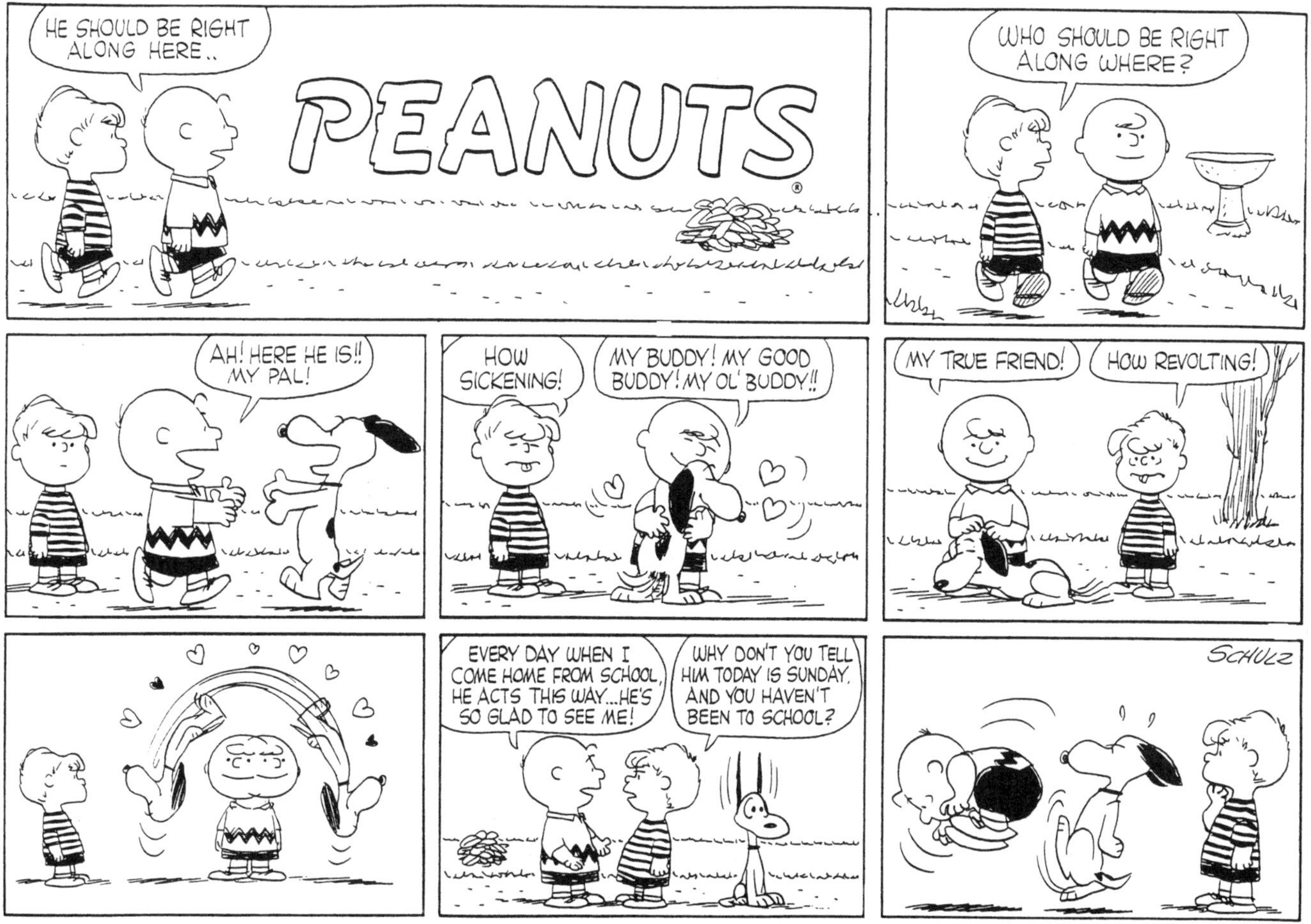
HE SHOULD BE RIGHT ALONG HERE..
PEANUTS
WHO SHOULD BE RIGHT ALONG WHERE?
AH! HERE HE IS!! MY PAL!
HOW SICKENING!
MY BUDDY! MY GOOD BUDDY! MY OL' BUDDY!!
MY TRUE FRIEND!
HOW REVOLTING!
EVERY DAY WHEN I COME HOME FROM SCHOOL, HE ACTS THIS WAY...HE'S SO GLAD TO SEE ME!
WHY DON'T YOU TELL HIM TODAY IS SUNDAY, AND YOU HAVEN'T BEEN TO SCHOOL?
SCHULZ

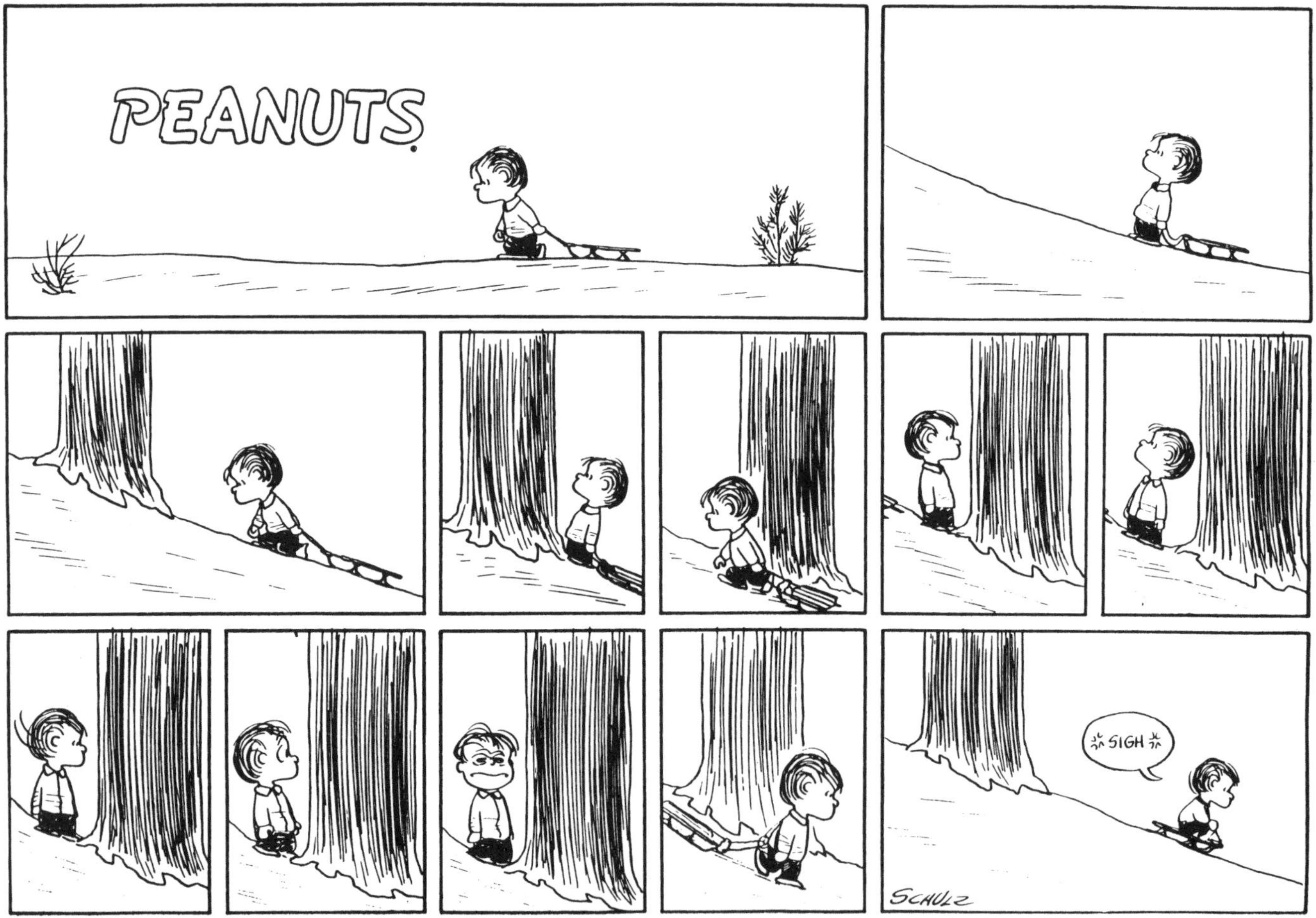
PEANUTS
SIGH
SCHULZ

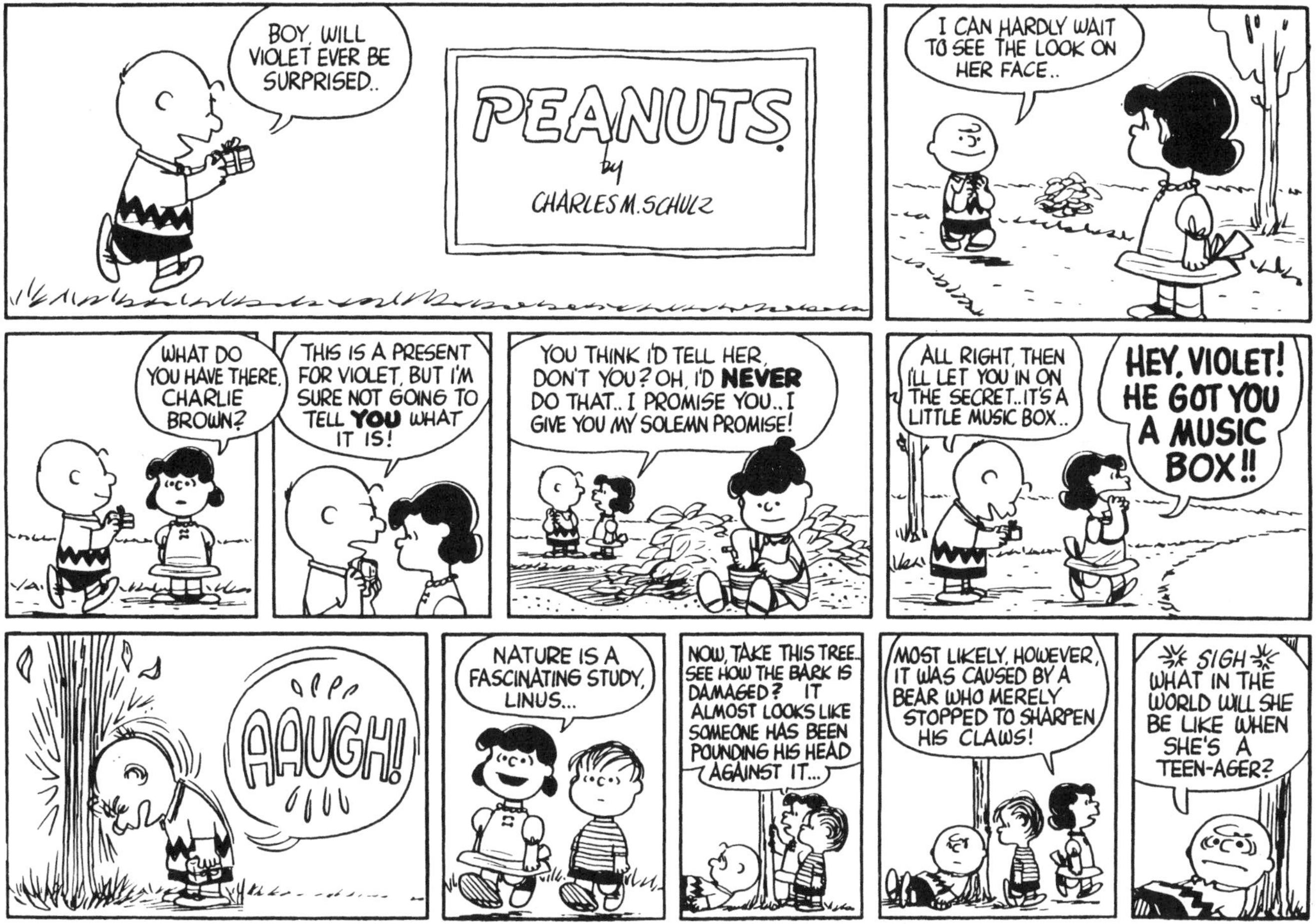
BOY, WILL VIOLET EVER BE SURPRISED..
PEANUTS
by
CHARLES M. SCHULZ
I CAN HARDLY WAIT TO SEE THE LOOK ON HER FACE..
WHAT DO YOU HAVE THERE, CHARLIE BROWN?
THIS IS A PRESENT FOR VIOLET, BUT I'M SURE NOT GOING TO TELL YOU WHAT IT IS!
YOU THINK I'D TELL HER, DON'T YOU? OH, I'D NEVER DO THAT.. I PROMISE YOU.. I GIVE YOU MY SOLEMN PROMISE!
ALL RIGHT, THEN I'LL LET YOU IN ON THE SECRET..IT'S A LITTLE MUSIC BOX..
HEY, VIOLET! HE GOT YOU A MUSIC BOX!!
AAUGH!
NATURE IS A FASCINATING STUDY, LINUS...
NOW, TAKE THIS TREE.. SEE HOW THE BARK IS DAMAGED? IT ALMOST LOOKS LIKE SOMEONE HAS BEEN POUNDING HIS HEAD AGAINST IT...
MOST LIKELY, HOWEVER, IT WAS CAUSED BY A BEAR WHO MERELY STOPPED TO SHARPEN HIS CLAWS!
SIGH
WHAT IN THE WORLD WILL SHE BE LIKE WHEN SHE'S A TEEN-AGER?

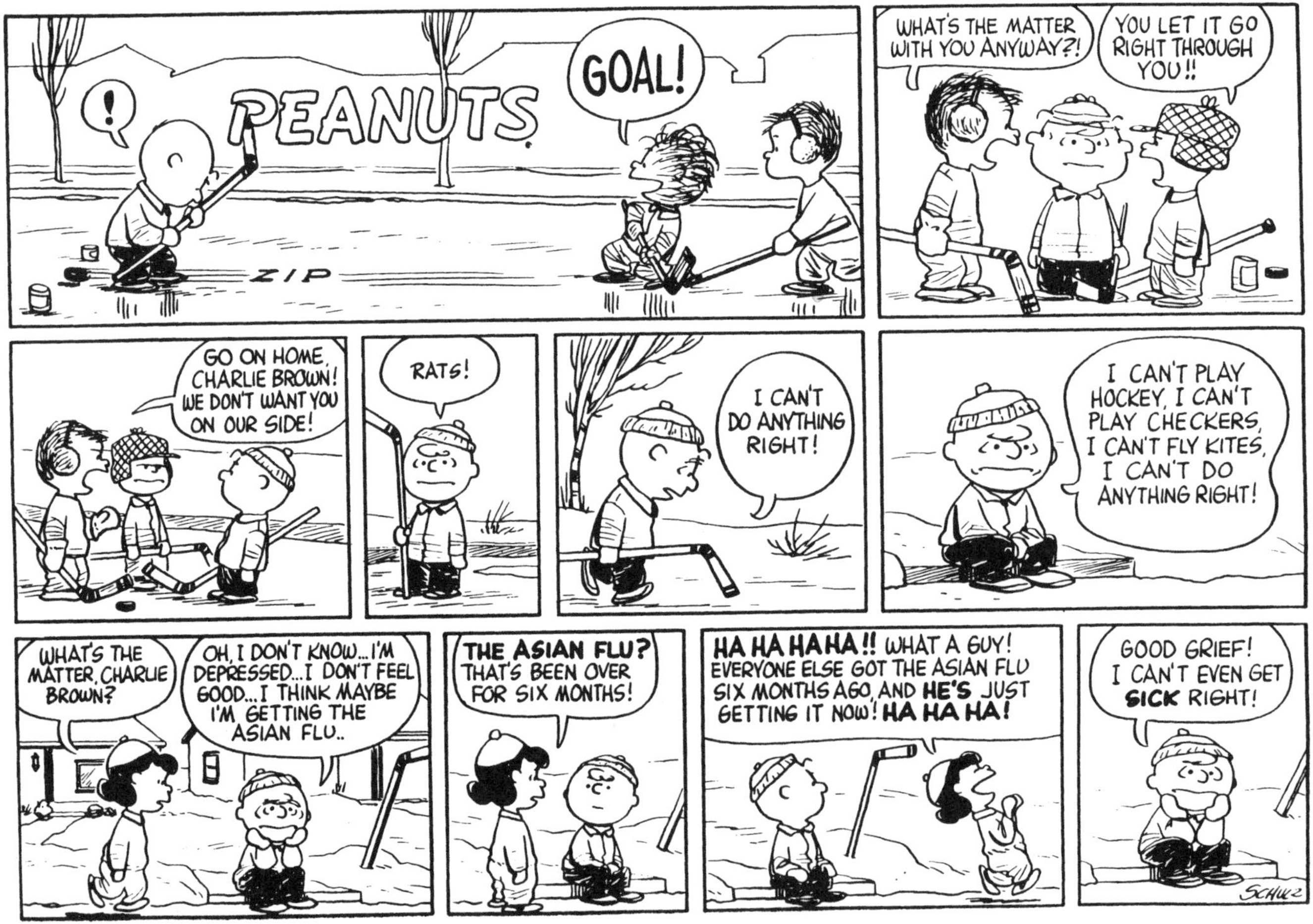
PEANUTS
!
ZIP
GOAL!
WHAT'S THE MATTER WITH YOU ANYWAY?!
YOU LET IT GO RIGHT THROUGH YOU!!
GO ON HOME, CHARLIE BROWN! WE DON'T WANT YOU ON OUR SIDE!
RATS!
I CAN'T DO ANYTHING RIGHT!
I CAN'T PLAY HOCKEY, I CAN'T PLAY CHECKERS, I CAN'T FLY KITES, I CAN'T DO ANYTHING RIGHT!
WHAT'S THE MATTER, CHARLIE BROWN?
OH, I DON'T KNOW...I'M DEPRESSED...I DON'T FEEL GOOD...I THINK MAYBE I'M GETTING THE ASIAN FLU..
THE ASIAN FLU? THAT'S BEEN OVER FOR SIX MONTHS!
HA HA HA HA!! WHAT A GUY! EVERYONE ELSE GOT THE ASIAN FLU SIX MONTHS AGO, AND HE'S JUST GETTING IT NOW! HA HA HA!
GOOD GRIEF! I CAN'T EVEN GET SICK RIGHT!
SCHULZ

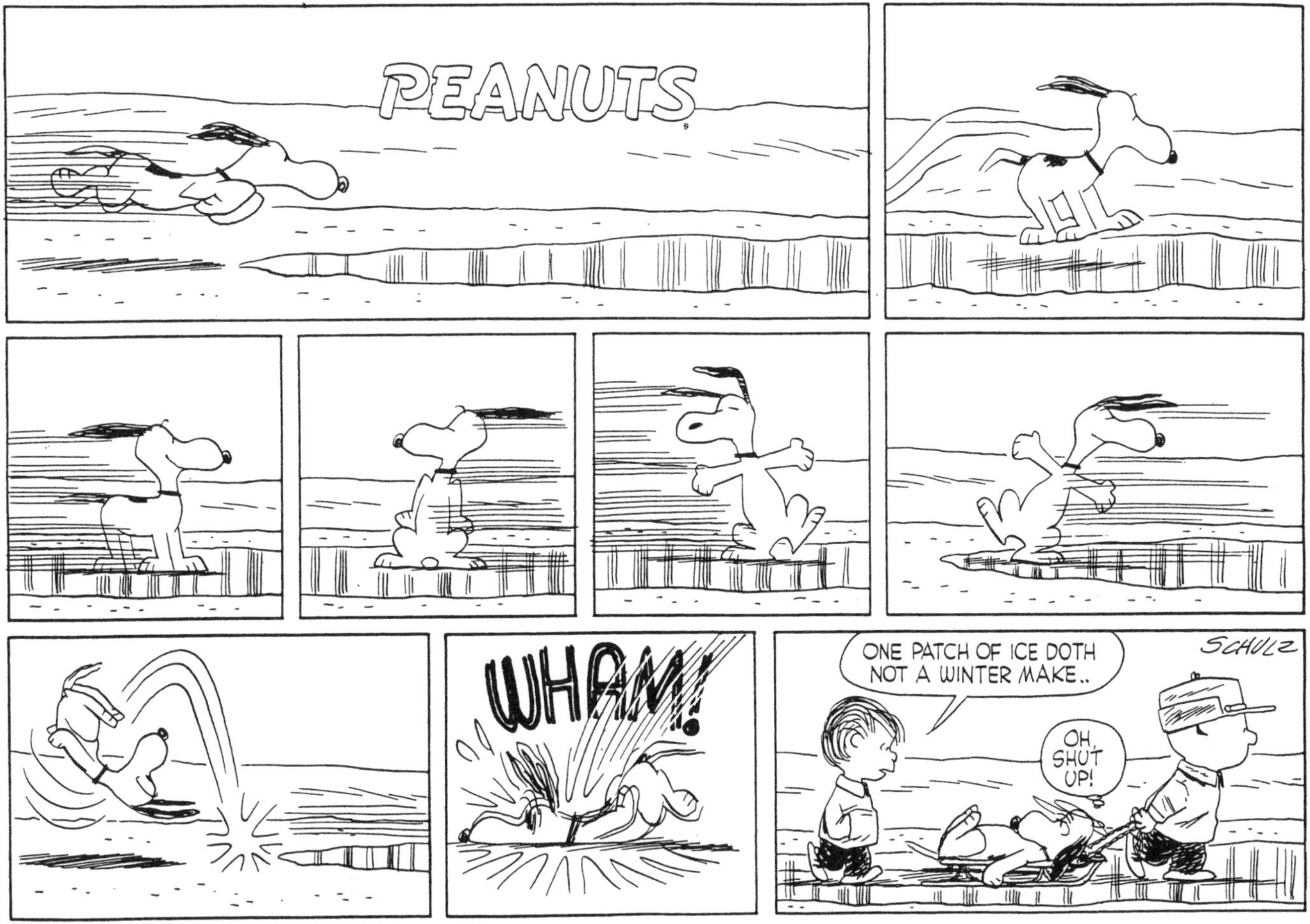
PEANUTS
WHAM!
ONE PATCH OF ICE DOTH NOT A WINTER MAKE..
OH, SHUT UP!
SCHULZ

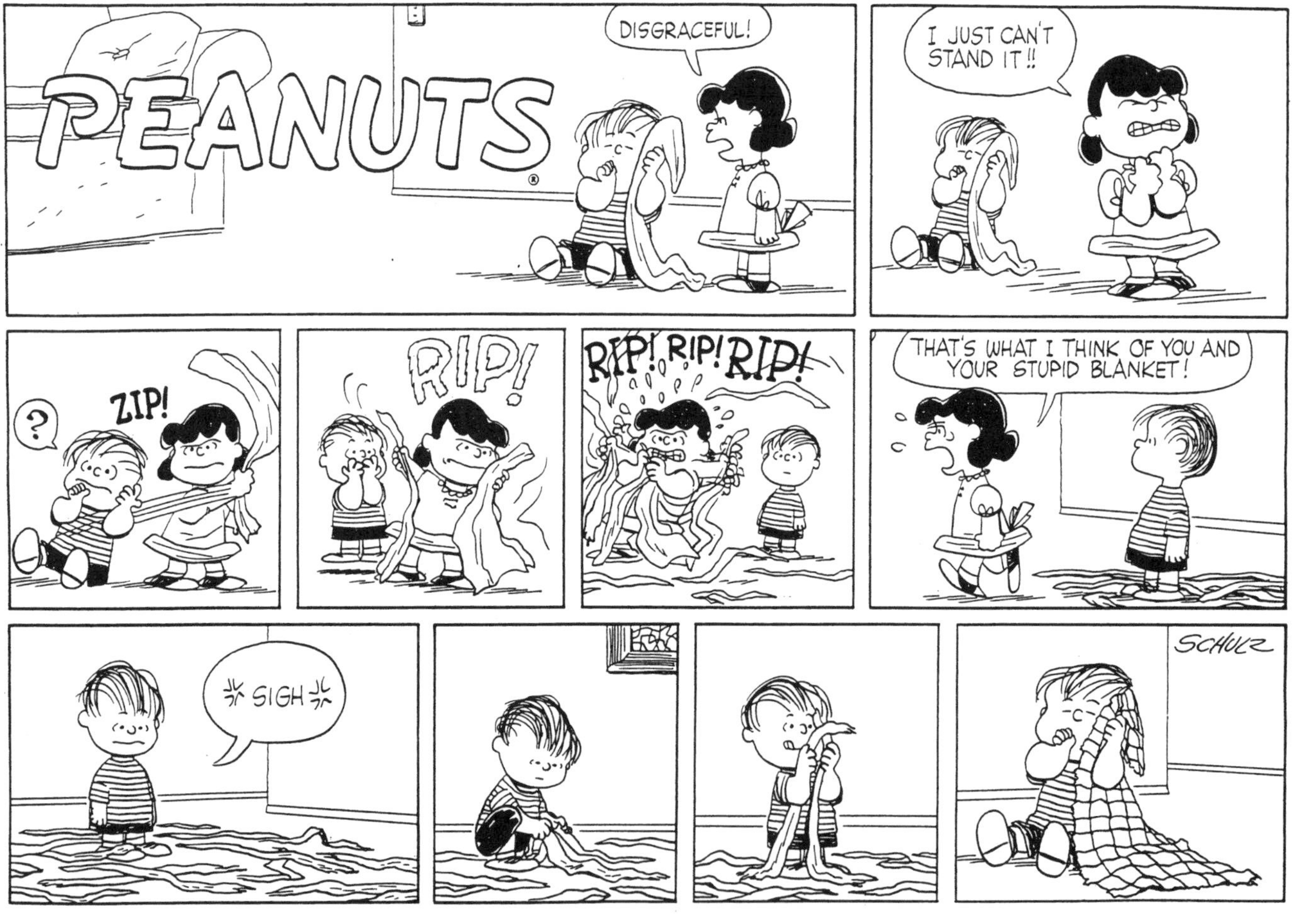

PEANUTS
DISGRACEFUL!
I JUST CAN'T STAND IT!!
?
ZIP!
RIP!
RIP! RIP! RIP!
THAT'S WHAT I THINK OF YOU AND YOUR STUPID BLANKET!
SIGH
SCHULZ

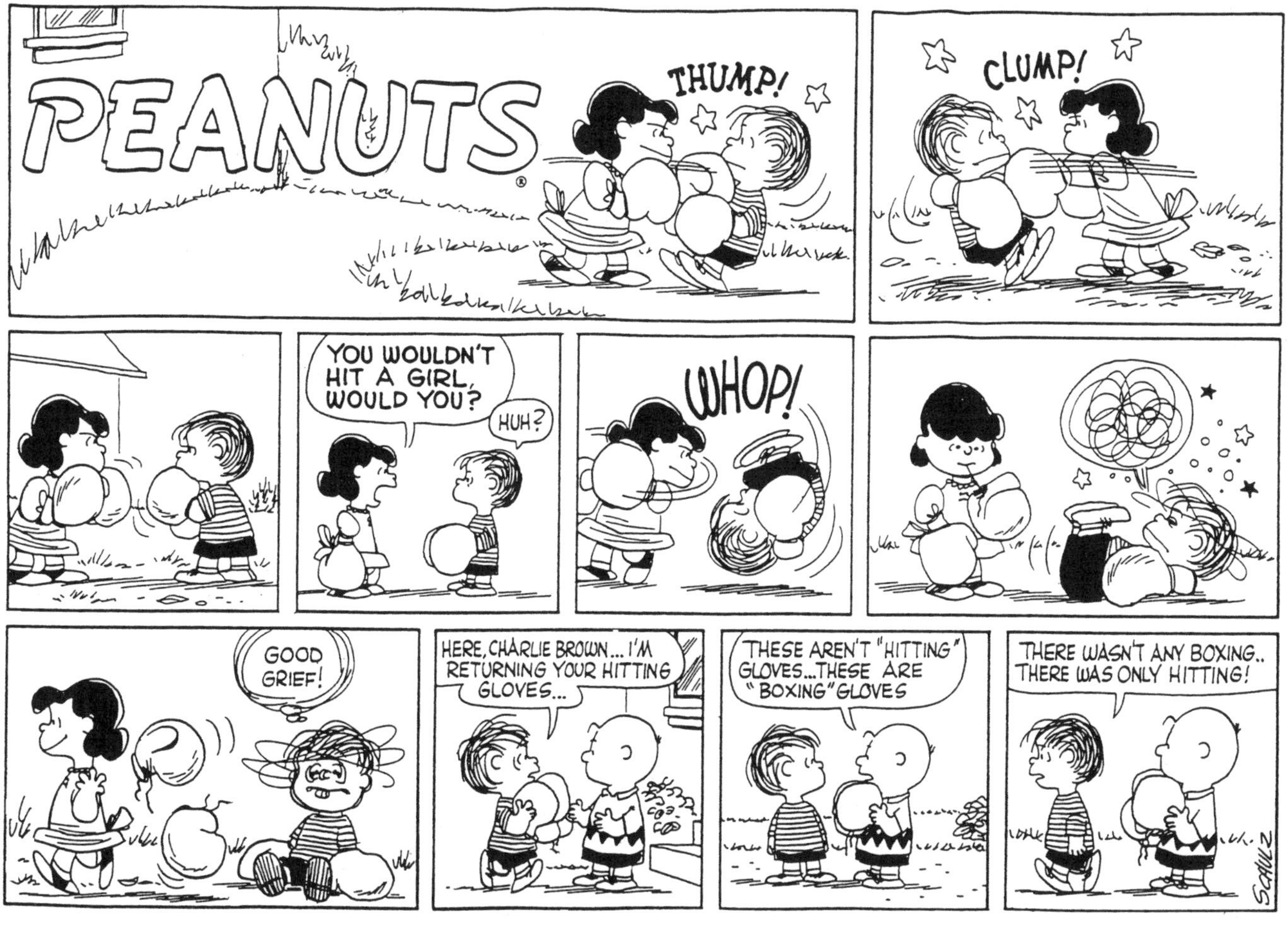
PEANUTS
THUMP!
CLUMP!
YOU WOULDN'T HIT A GIRL, WOULD YOU?
HUH?
WHOP!
GOOD GRIEF!
HERE, CHARLIE BROWN... I'M RETURNING YOUR HITTING GLOVES...
THESE AREN'T "HITTING" GLOVES...THESE ARE "BOXING" GLOVES
THERE WASN'T ANY BOXING.. THERE WAS ONLY HITTING!
SCHULZ

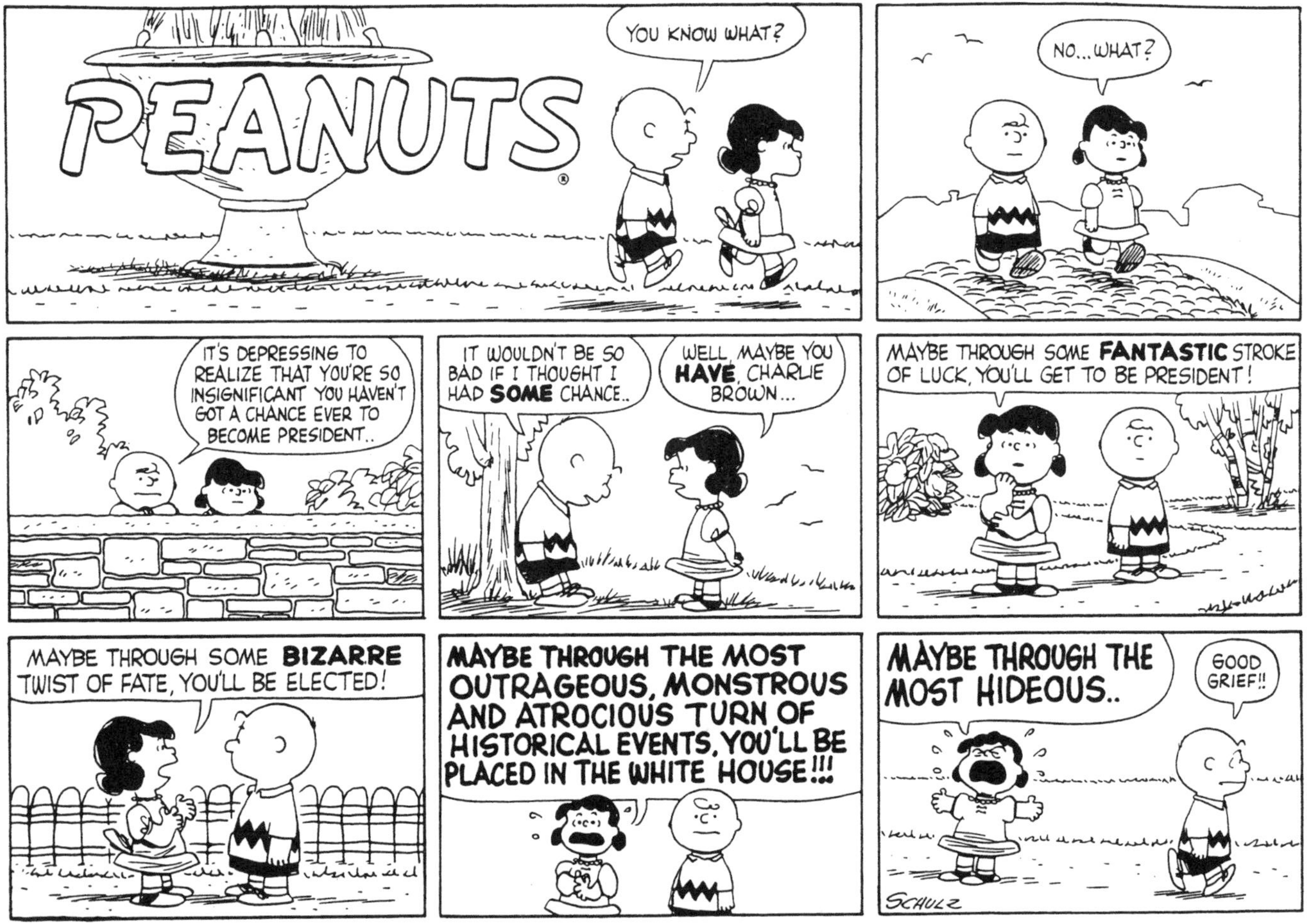
PEANUTS
YOU KNOW WHAT?
NO... WHAT?
IT'S DEPRESSING TO REALIZE THAT YOU'RE SO INSIGNIFICANT YOU HAVEN'T GOT A CHANCE EVER TO BECOME PRESIDENT..
IT WOULDN'T BE SO BAD IF I THOUGHT I HAD **SOME** CHANCE..
WELL, MAYBE YOU **HAVE**, CHARLIE BROWN...
MAYBE THROUGH SOME **FANTASTIC** STROKE OF LUCK, YOU'LL GET TO BE PRESIDENT!
MAYBE THROUGH SOME **BIZARRE** TWIST OF FATE, YOU'LL BE ELECTED!
MAYBE THROUGH THE MOST OUTRAGEOUS, MONSTROUS AND ATROCIOUS TURN OF HISTORICAL EVENTS, YOU'LL BE PLACED IN THE WHITE HOUSE!!!
MAYBE THROUGH THE MOST HIDEOUS..
GOOD GRIEF!!
SCHULZ

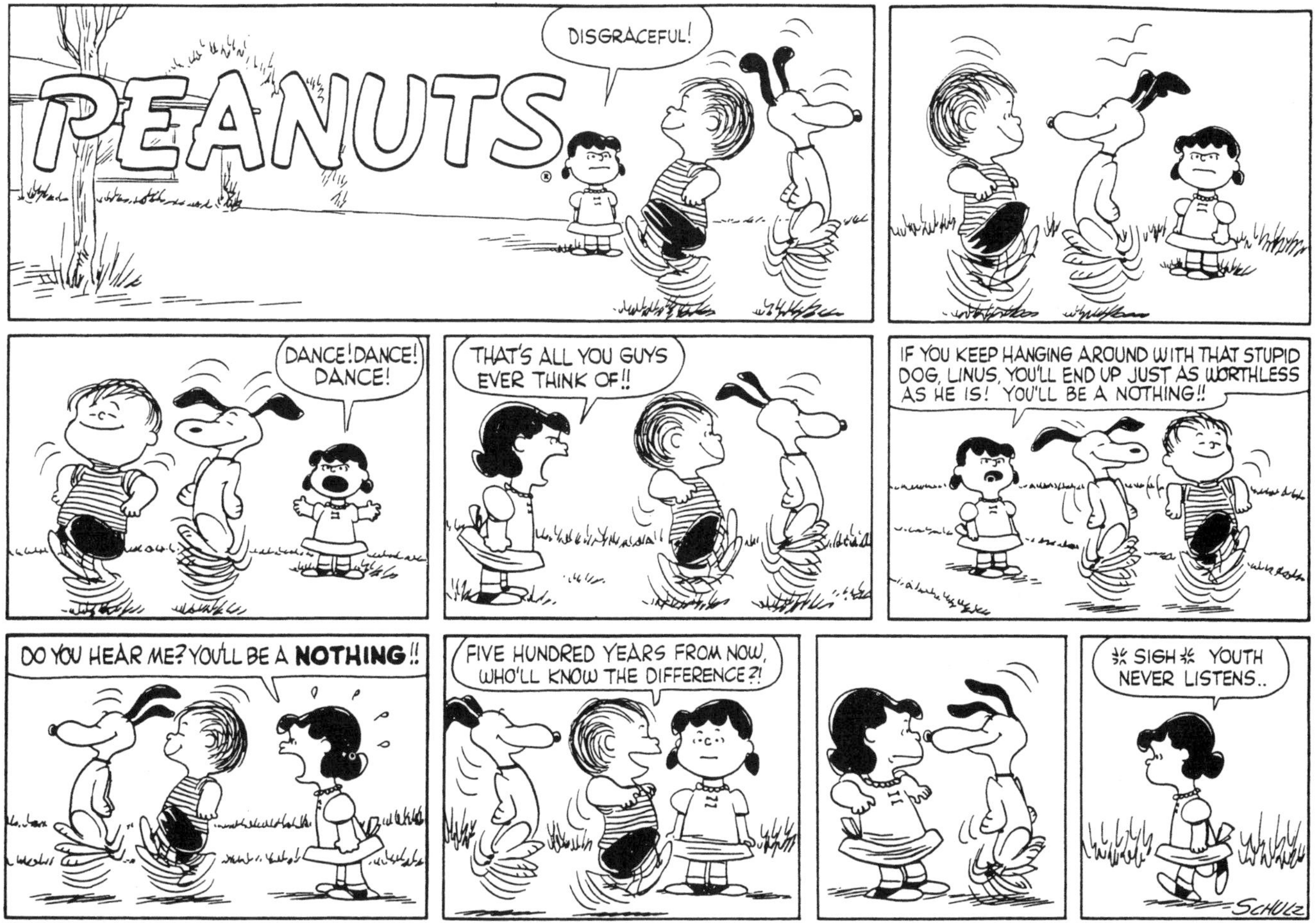
PEANUTS
DISGRACEFUL!
DANCE! DANCE! DANCE!
THAT'S ALL YOU GUYS EVER THINK OF!!
IF YOU KEEP HANGING AROUND WITH THAT STUPID DOG, LINUS, YOU'LL END UP JUST AS WORTHLESS AS HE IS! YOU'LL BE A NOTHING!!
DO YOU HEAR ME? YOU'LL BE A **NOTHING**!!
FIVE HUNDRED YEARS FROM NOW, WHO'LL KNOW THE DIFFERENCE?!
SIGH YOUTH NEVER LISTENS..
SCHULZ

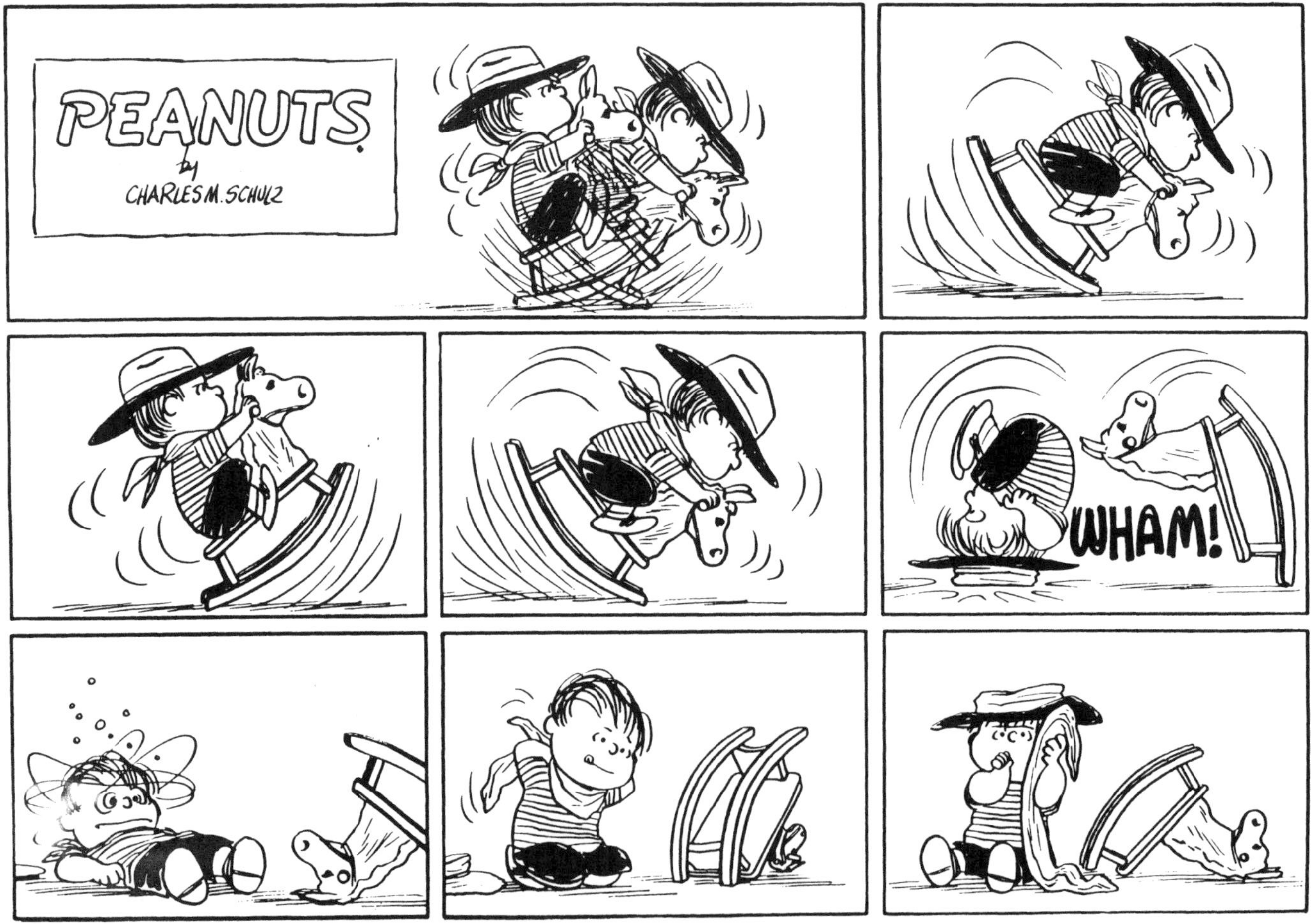
PEANUTS
by
CHARLES M. SCHULZ
WHAM!

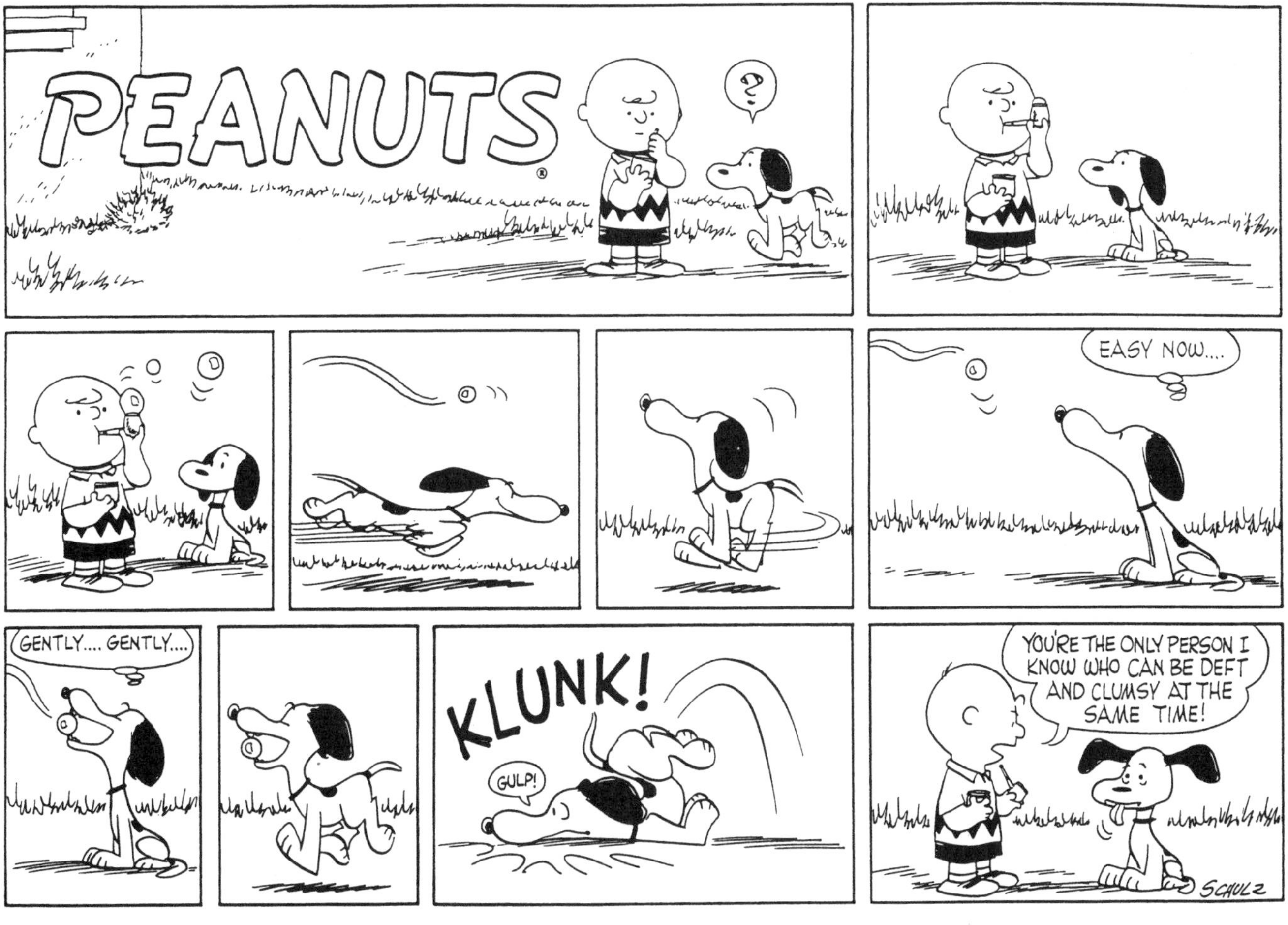
PEANUTS
?
EASY NOW....
GENTLY.... GENTLY....
KLUNK!
GULP!
YOU'RE THE ONLY PERSON I KNOW WHO CAN BE DEFT AND CLUMSY AT THE SAME TIME!
SCHULZ

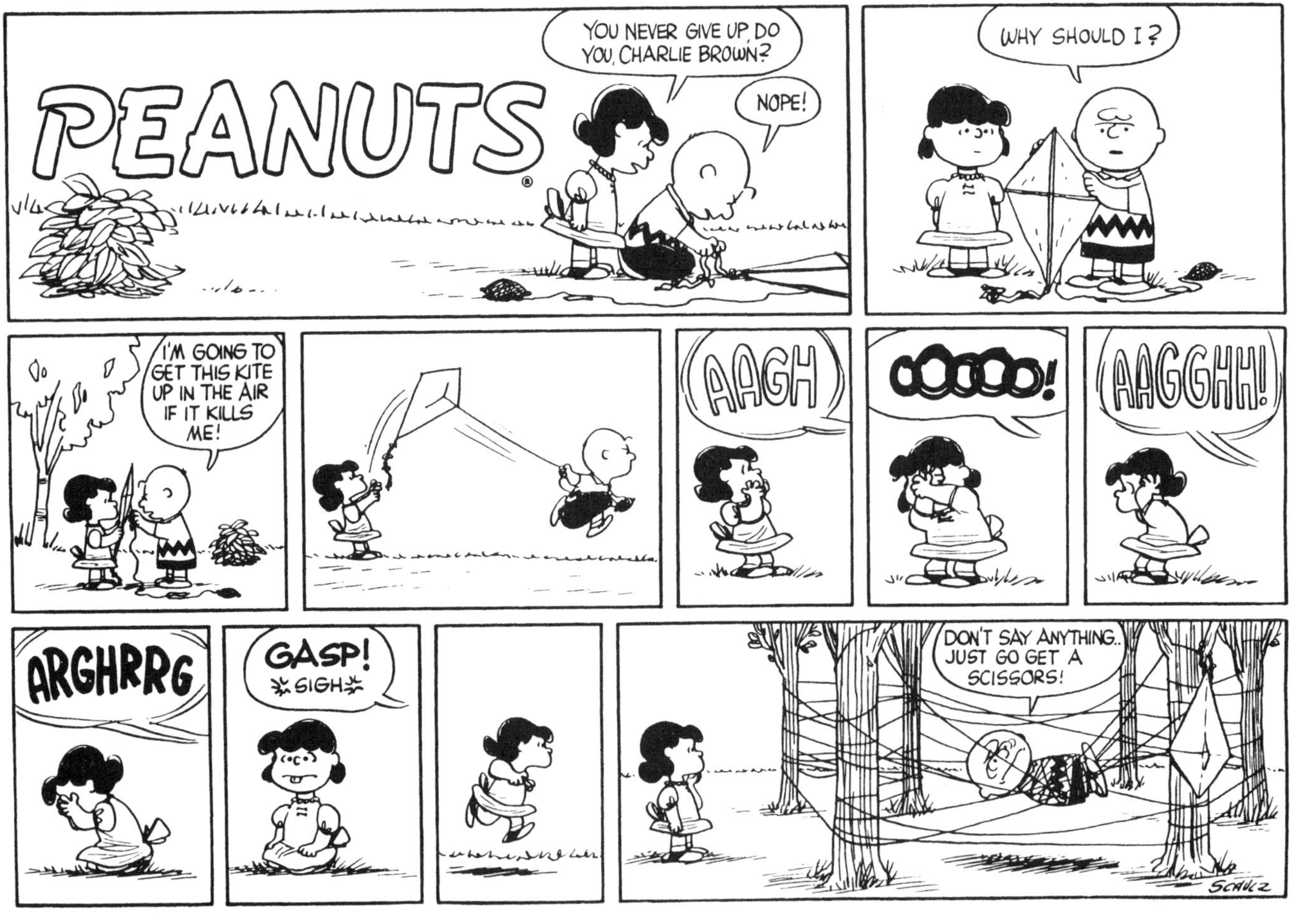
PEANUTS
YOU NEVER GIVE UP, DO YOU, CHARLIE BROWN?
NOPE!
WHY SHOULD I?
I'M GOING TO GET THIS KITE UP IN THE AIR IF IT KILLS ME!
AAGH
OOOOO!
AAGGHH!
ARGHRRG
GASP!
SIGH
DON'T SAY ANYTHING.. JUST GO GET A SCISSORS!
SCHULZ

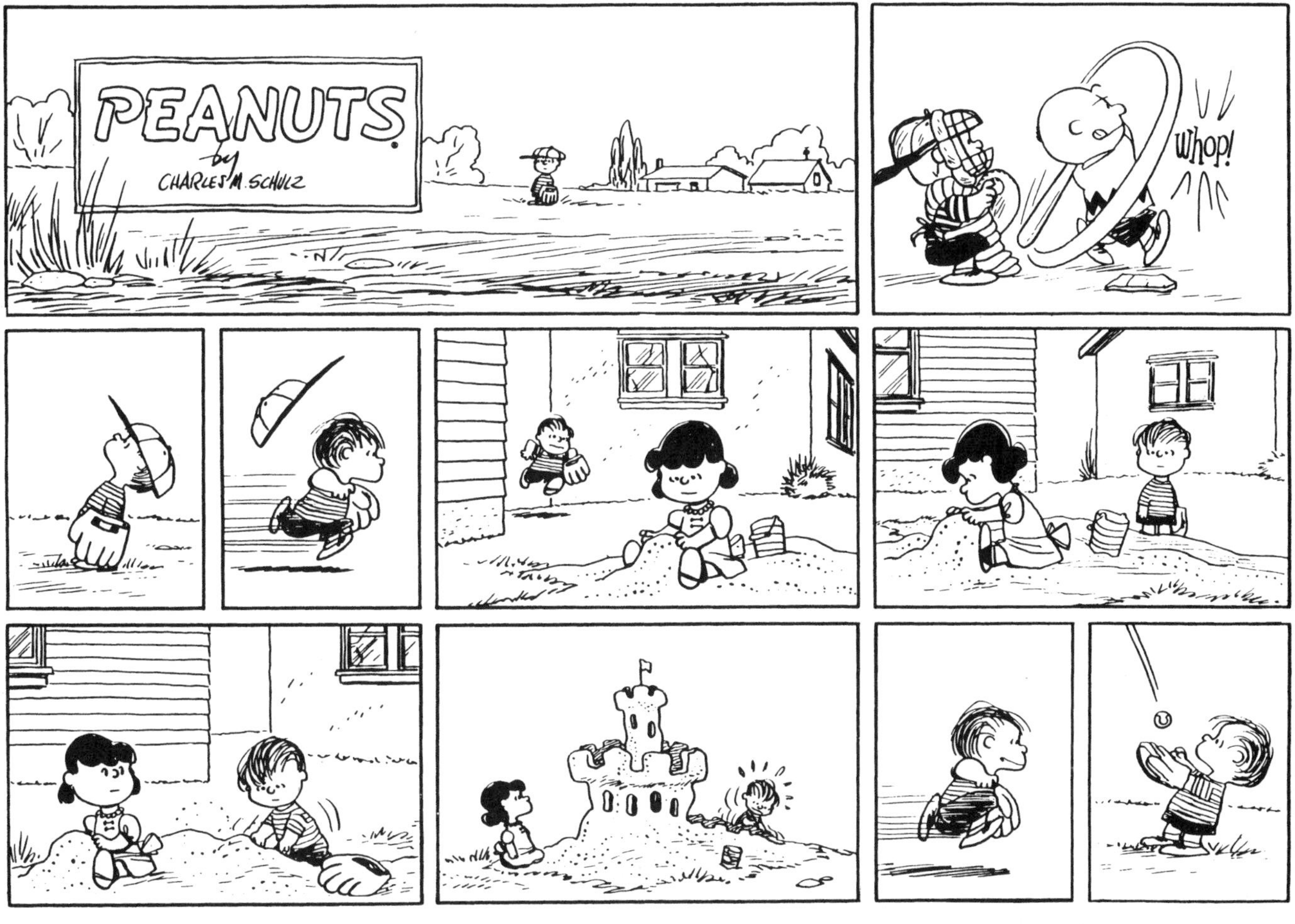
PEANUTS
by CHARLES M. SCHULZ
WHOP!

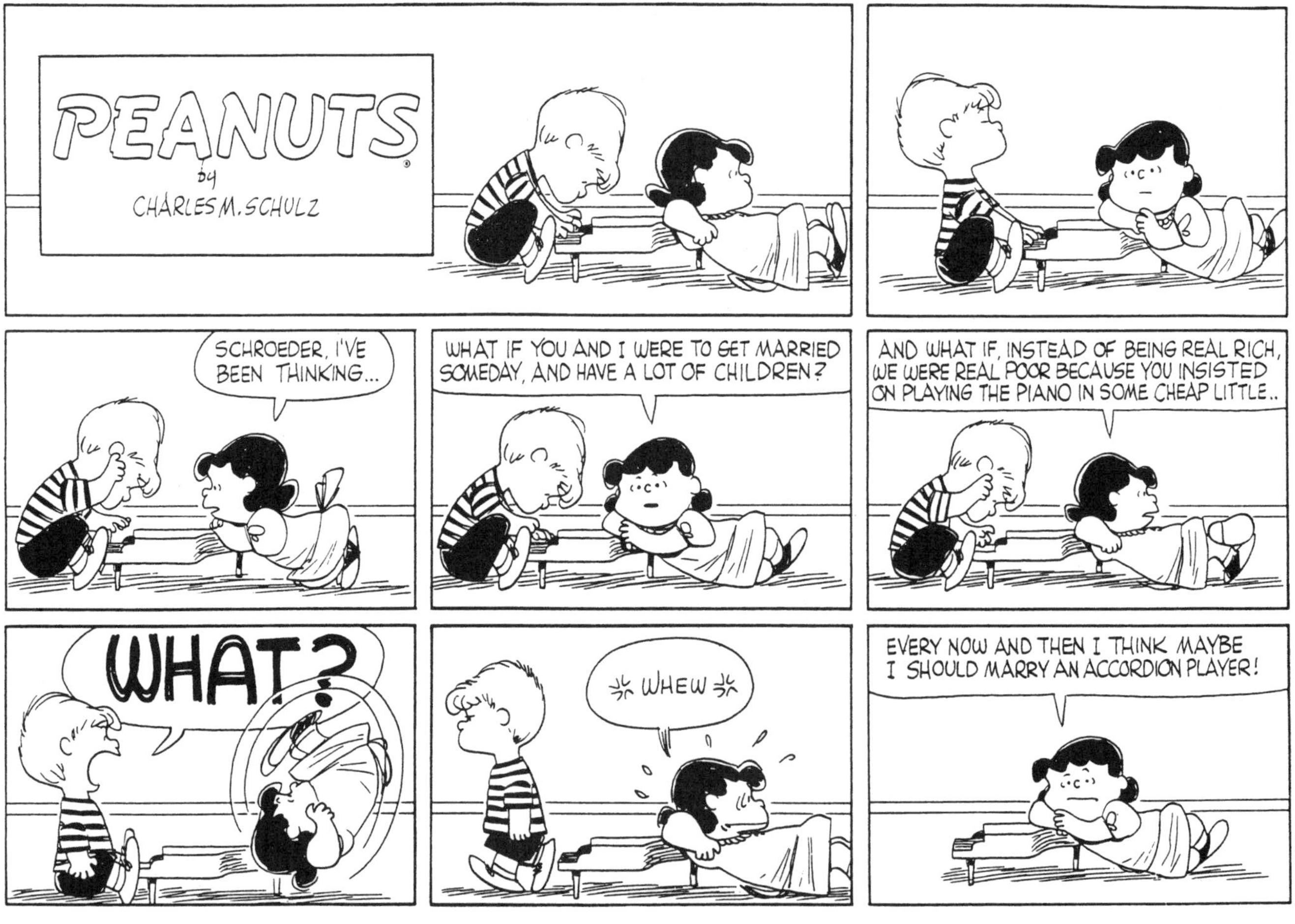
PEANUTS
by CHARLES M. SCHULZ
SCHROEDER, I'VE BEEN THINKING...
WHAT IF YOU AND I WERE TO GET MARRIED SOMEDAY, AND HAVE A LOT OF CHILDREN?
AND WHAT IF, INSTEAD OF BEING REAL RICH, WE WERE REAL POOR BECAUSE YOU INSISTED ON PLAYING THE PIANO IN SOME CHEAP LITTLE..
WHAT?
WHEW
EVERY NOW AND THEN I THINK MAYBE I SHOULD MARRY AN ACCORDION PLAYER!

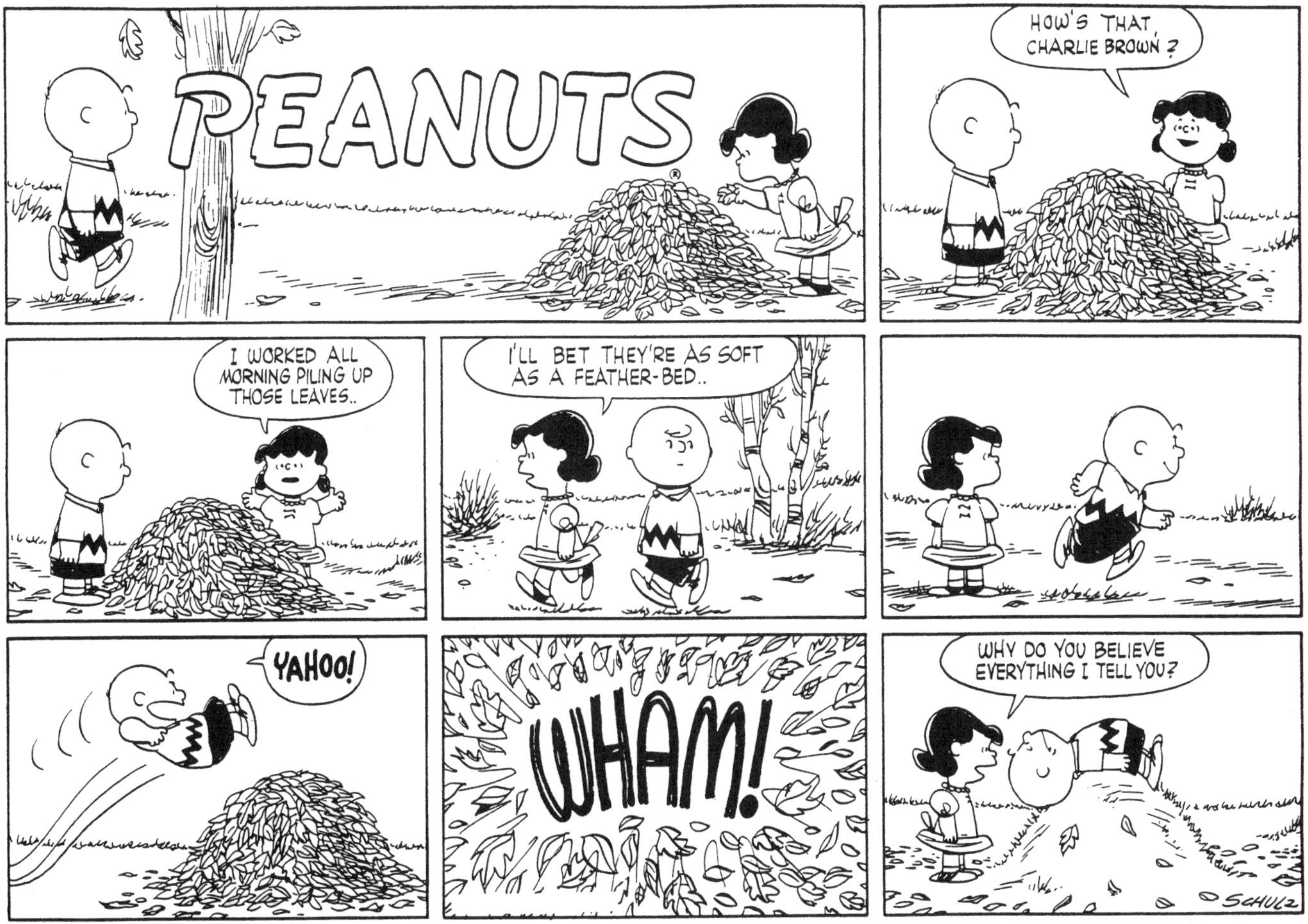
PEANUTS
HOW'S THAT, CHARLIE BROWN?
I WORKED ALL MORNING PILING UP THOSE LEAVES..
I'LL BET THEY'RE AS SOFT AS A FEATHER-BED..
YAHOO!
WHAM!
WHY DO YOU BELIEVE EVERYTHING I TELL YOU?
SCHULZ

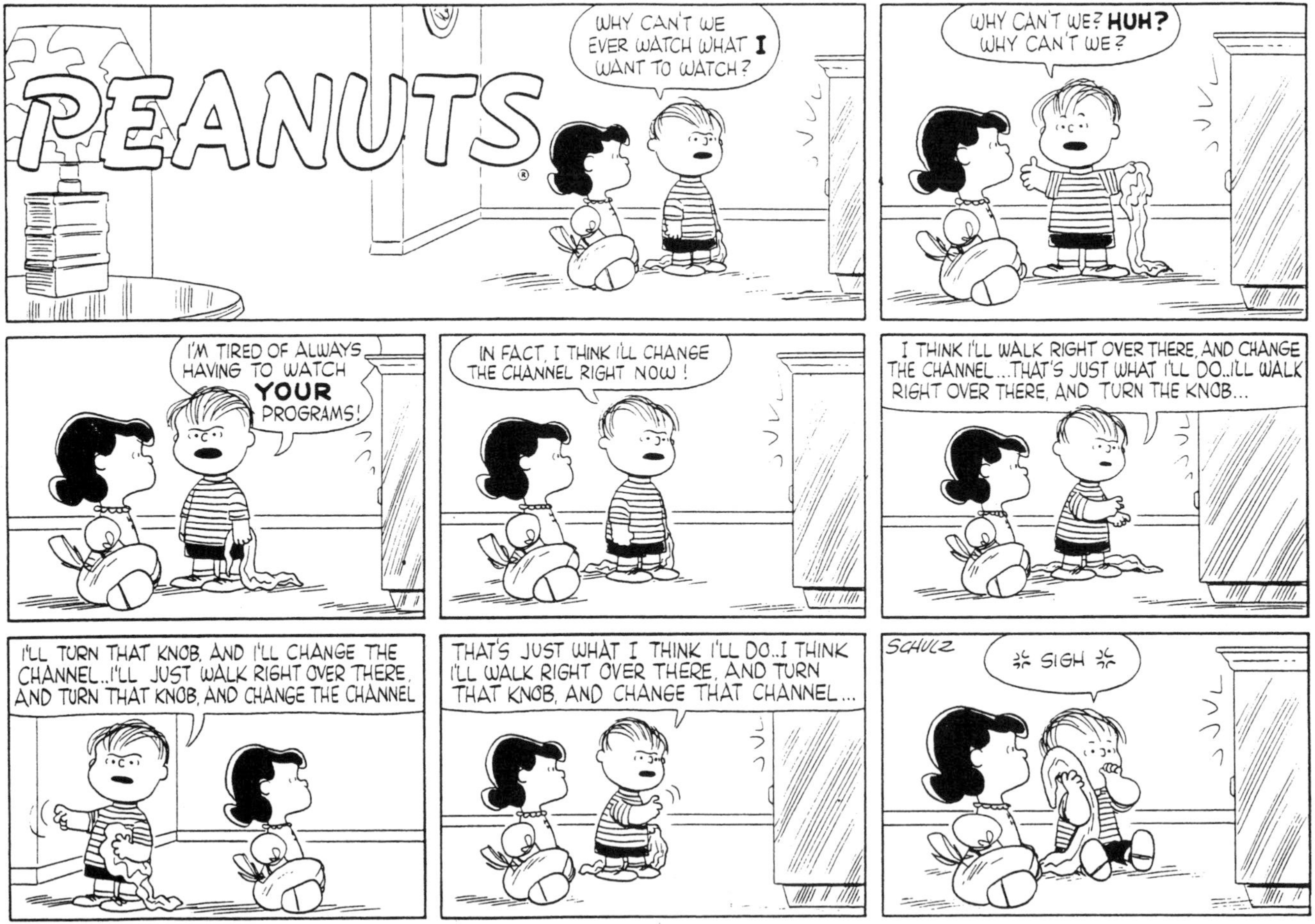
PEANUTS®
WHY CAN'T WE EVER WATCH WHAT I WANT TO WATCH?
WHY CAN'T WE? HUH? WHY CAN'T WE?
I'M TIRED OF ALWAYS HAVING TO WATCH YOUR PROGRAMS!
IN FACT, I THINK I'LL CHANGE THE CHANNEL RIGHT NOW!
I THINK I'LL WALK RIGHT OVER THERE, AND CHANGE THE CHANNEL...THAT'S JUST WHAT I'LL DO..I'LL WALK RIGHT OVER THERE, AND TURN THE KNOB...
I'LL TURN THAT KNOB, AND I'LL CHANGE THE CHANNEL..I'LL JUST WALK RIGHT OVER THERE, AND TURN THAT KNOB, AND CHANGE THE CHANNEL
THAT'S JUST WHAT I THINK I'LL DO..I THINK I'LL WALK RIGHT OVER THERE, AND TURN THAT KNOB, AND CHANGE THAT CHANNEL...
SCHULZ
SIGH

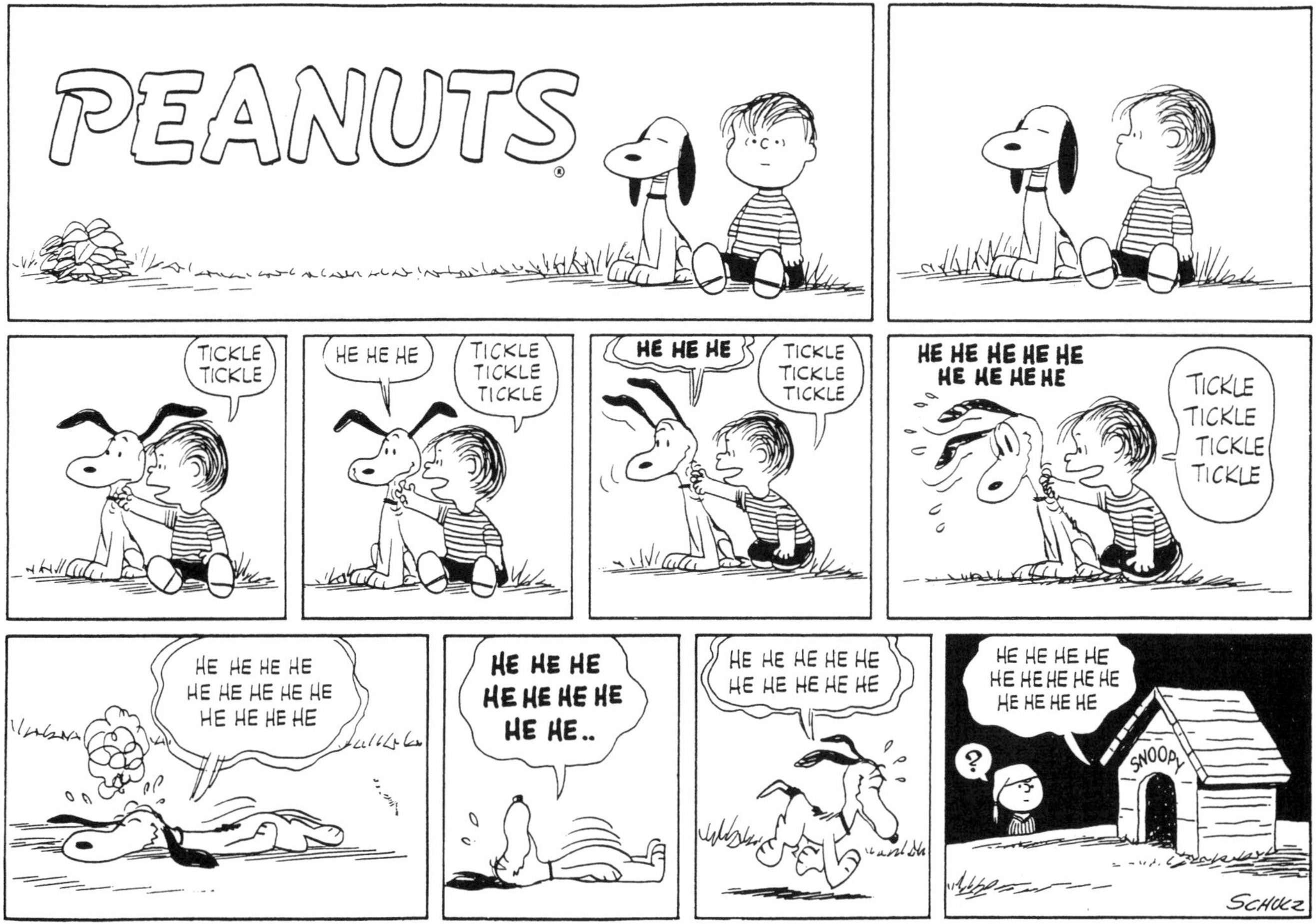
PEANUTS
TICKLE TICKLE
HE HE HE
TICKLE TICKLE TICKLE
HE HE HE
TICKLE TICKLE TICKLE
HE HE HE HE HE HE HE HE HE
TICKLE TICKLE TICKLE TICKLE
HE HE HE HE HE HE HE HE HE HE HE HE HE
HE HE HE HE HE HE HE HE HE HE..
HE HE HE HE HE HE HE HE HE HE
?
HE HE HE HE HE HE HE HE HE HE HE HE HE
SNOOPY
SCHULZ

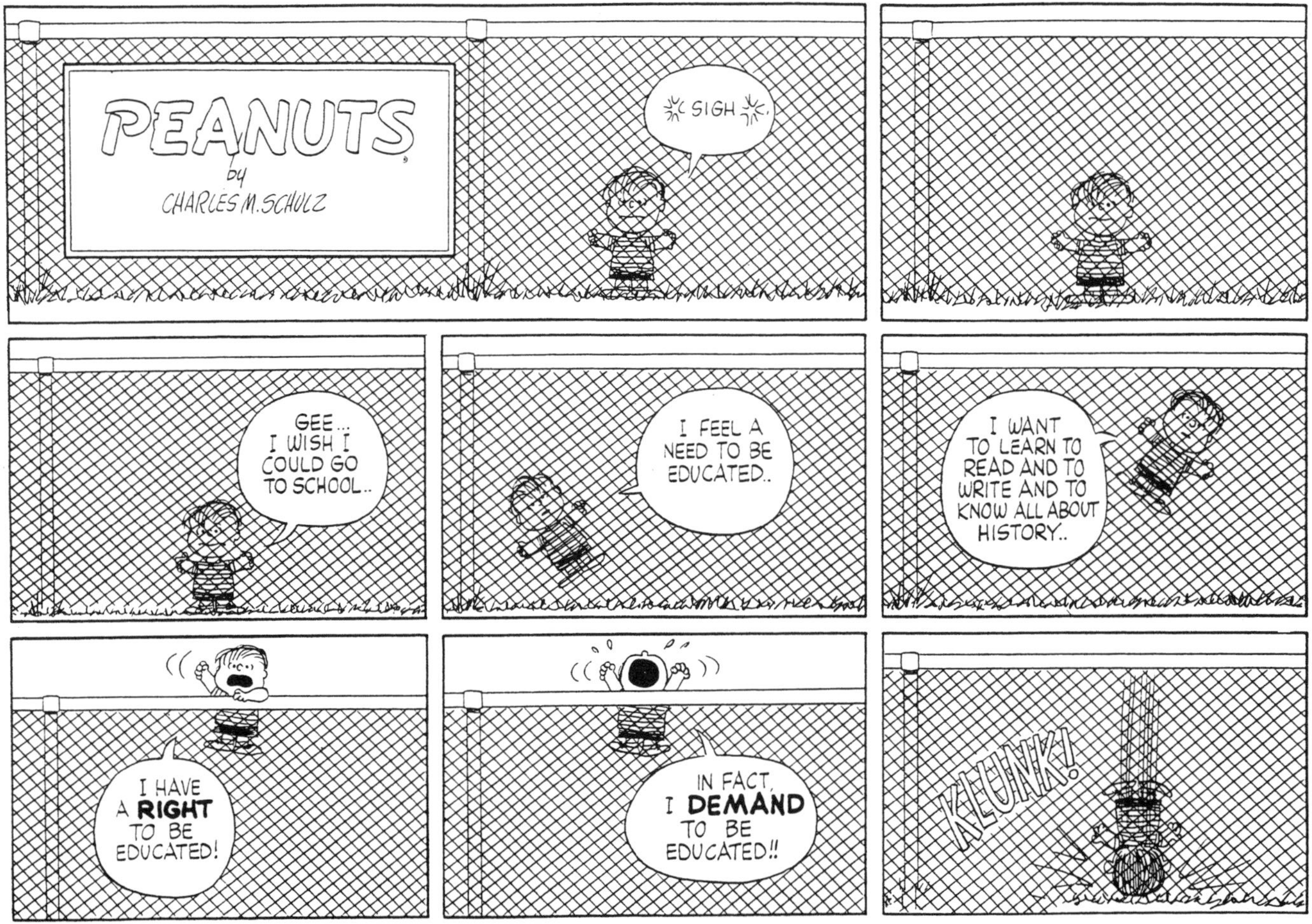
PEANUTS
by
CHARLES M. SCHULZ
SIGH
GEE... I WISH I COULD GO TO SCHOOL..
I FEEL A NEED TO BE EDUCATED..
I WANT TO LEARN TO READ AND TO WRITE AND TO KNOW ALL ABOUT HISTORY..
I HAVE A **RIGHT** TO BE EDUCATED!
IN FACT, I **DEMAND** TO BE EDUCATED!!
KLUNK!

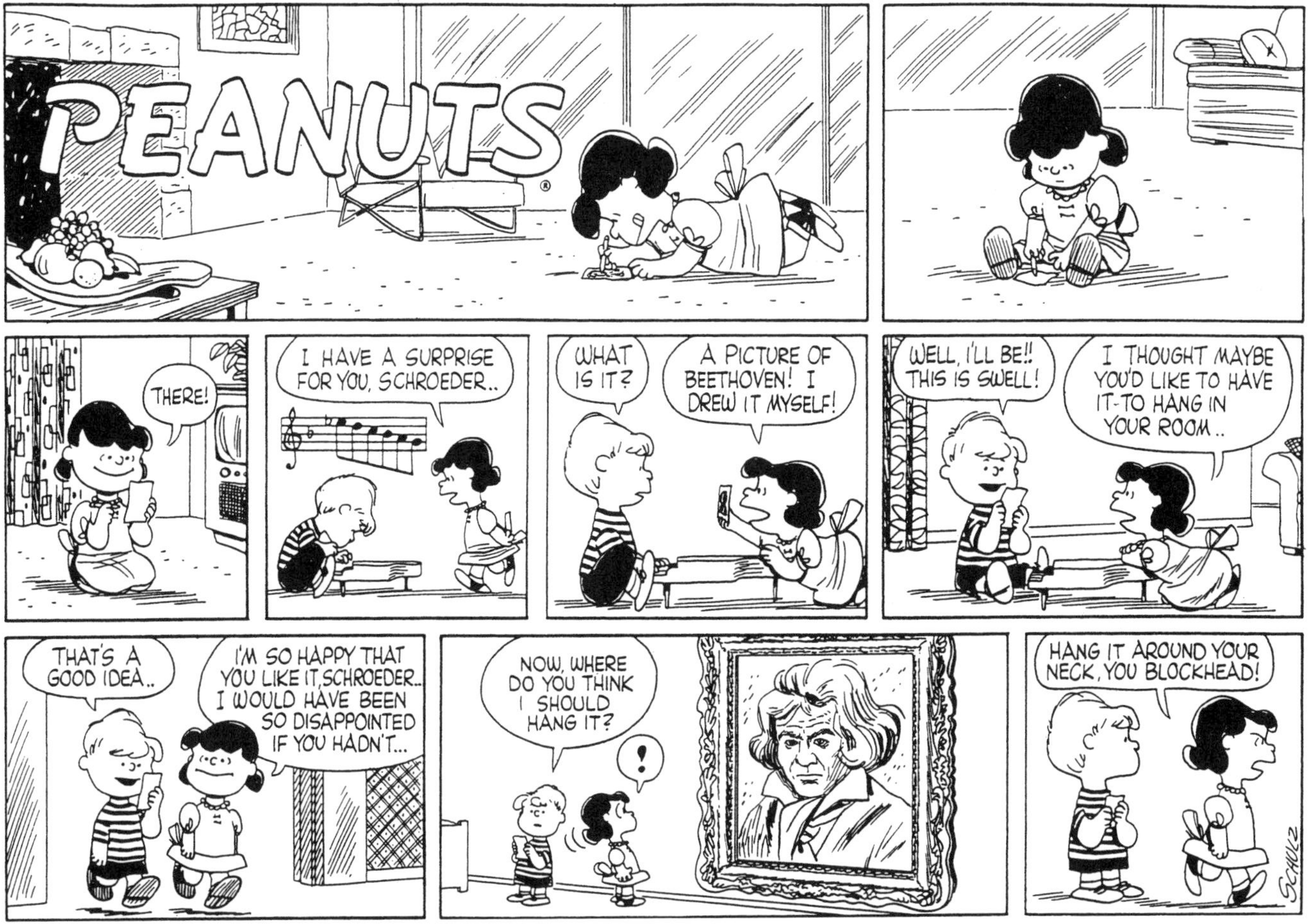
PEANUTS
THERE!
I HAVE A SURPRISE FOR YOU, SCHROEDER..
WHAT IS IT?
A PICTURE OF BEETHOVEN! I DREW IT MYSELF!
WELL, I'LL BE!! THIS IS SWELL!
I THOUGHT MAYBE YOU'D LIKE TO HAVE IT-TO HANG IN YOUR ROOM..
THAT'S A GOOD IDEA..
I'M SO HAPPY THAT YOU LIKE IT, SCHROEDER.. I WOULD HAVE BEEN SO DISAPPOINTED IF YOU HADN'T...
NOW, WHERE DO YOU THINK I SHOULD HANG IT?
!
HANG IT AROUND YOUR NECK, YOU BLOCKHEAD!
SCHULZ

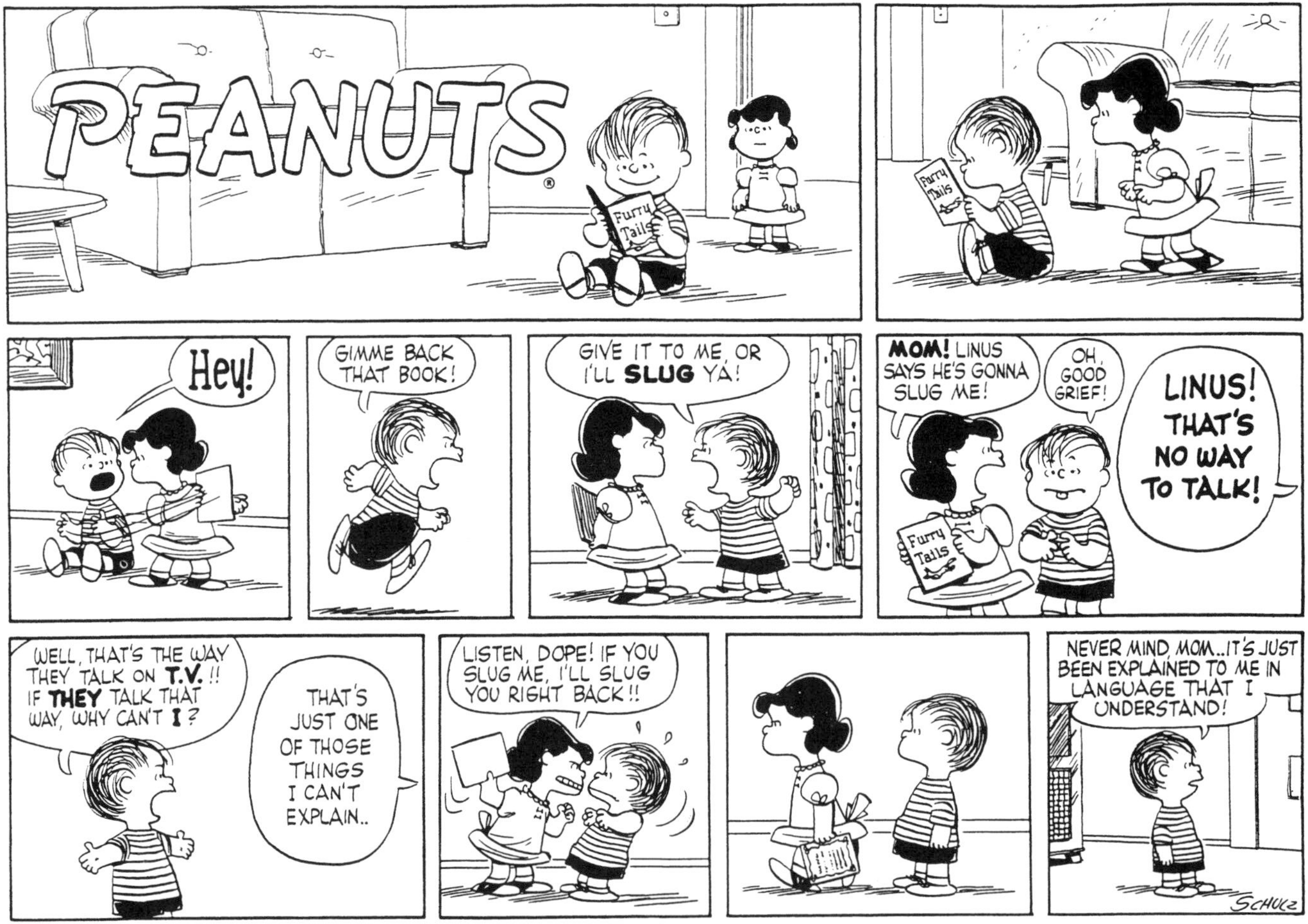
PEANUTS
Furry Tails
Hey!
GIMME BACK THAT BOOK!
GIVE IT TO ME, OR I'LL SLUG YA!
MOM! LINUS SAYS HE'S GONNA SLUG ME!
OH, GOOD GRIEF!
LINUS! THAT'S NO WAY TO TALK!
WELL, THAT'S THE WAY THEY TALK ON T.V.!! IF THEY TALK THAT WAY, WHY CAN'T I?
THAT'S JUST ONE OF THOSE THINGS I CAN'T EXPLAIN..
LISTEN, DOPE! IF YOU SLUG ME, I'LL SLUG YOU RIGHT BACK!!
NEVER MIND MOM..IT'S JUST BEEN EXPLAINED TO ME IN LANGUAGE THAT I UNDERSTAND!
SCHULZ

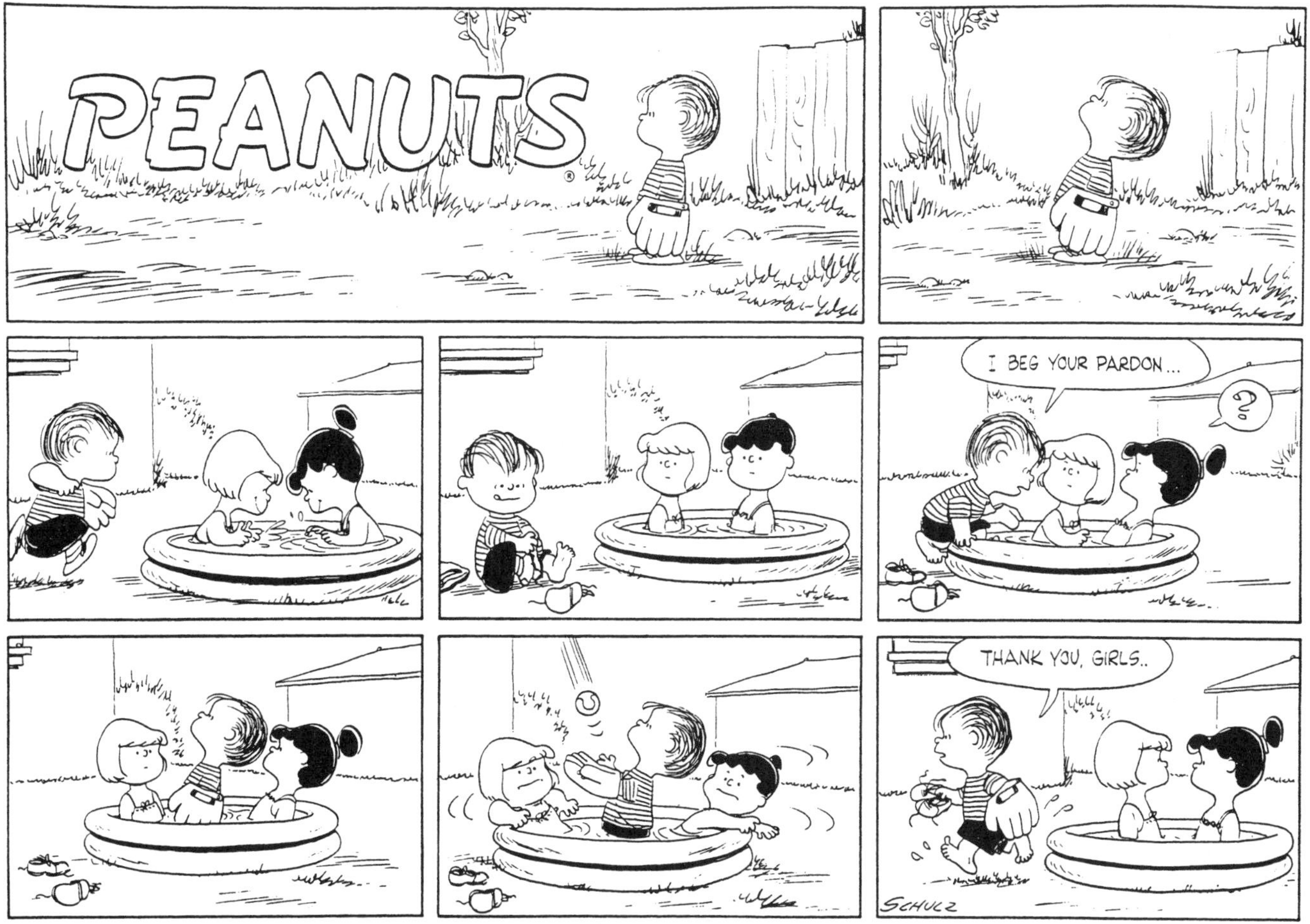
PEANUTS
I BEG YOUR PARDON...
?
THANK YOU, GIRLS..
SCHULZ

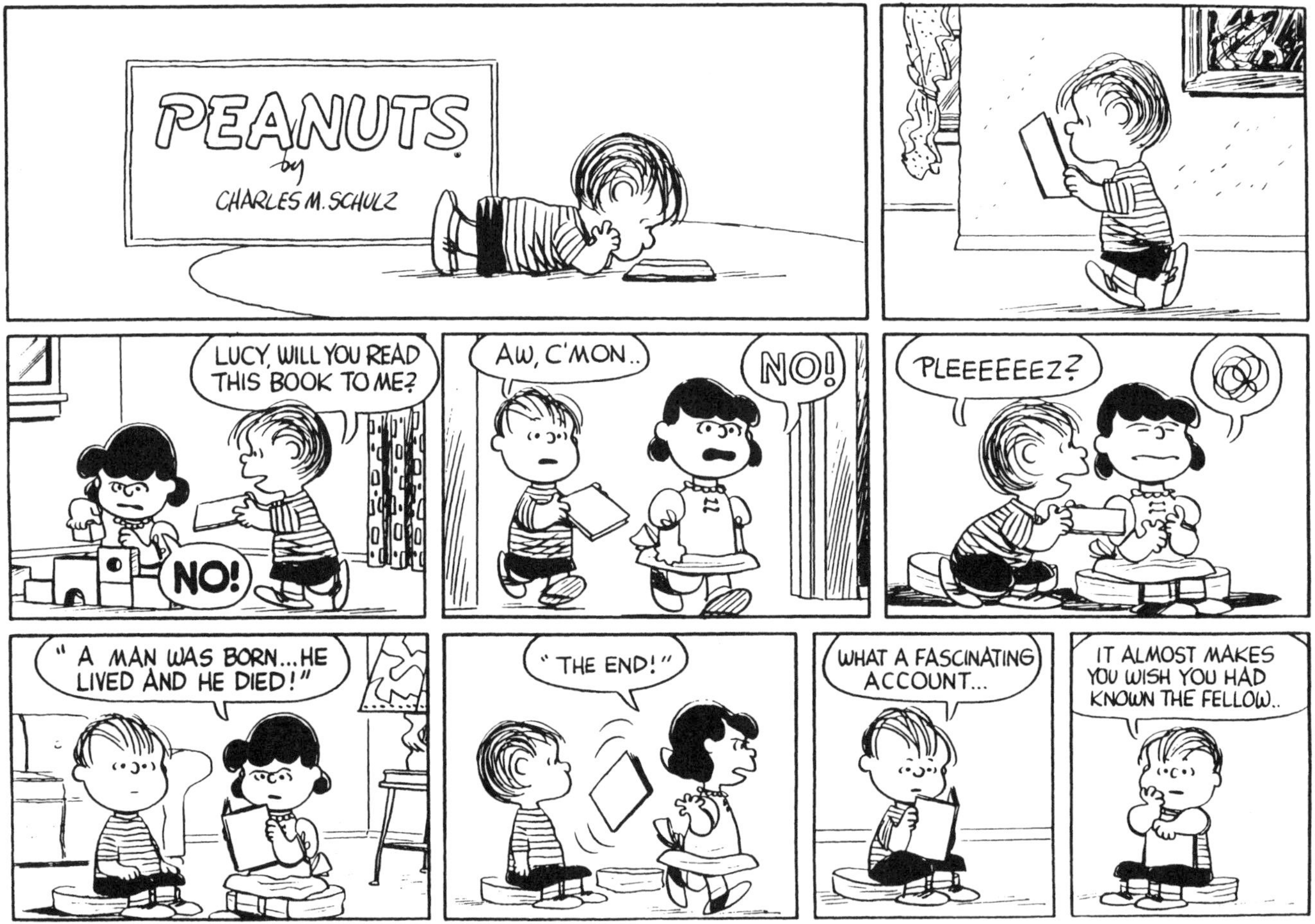
PEANUTS
by
CHARLES M. SCHULZ
LUCY, WILL YOU READ THIS BOOK TO ME?
NO!
AW, C'MON..
NO!
PLEEEEEEEZ?
" A MAN WAS BORN...HE LIVED AND HE DIED!"
" THE END!"
WHAT A FASCINATING ACCOUNT...
IT ALMOST MAKES YOU WISH YOU HAD KNOWN THE FELLOW..

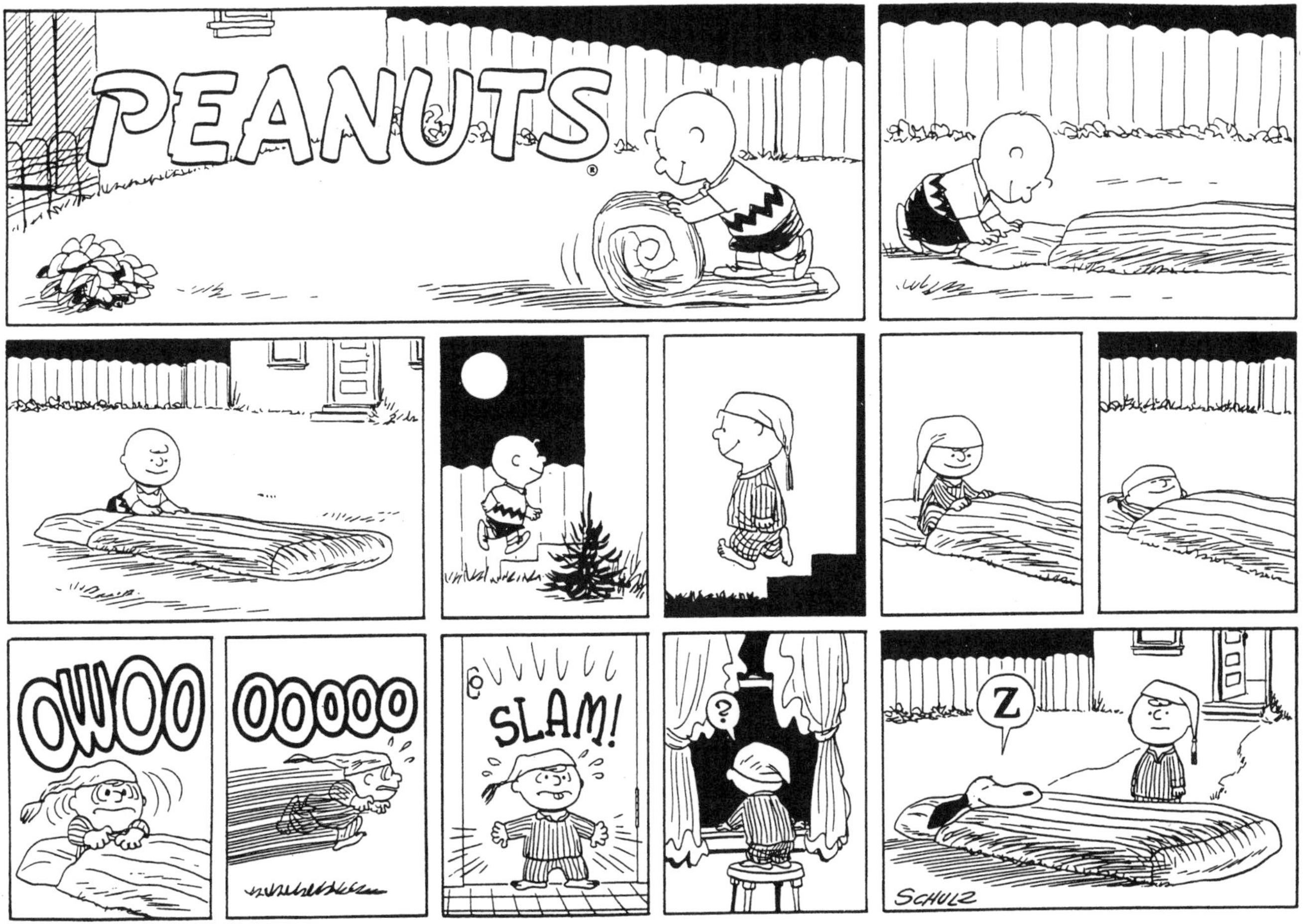
PEANUTS
OWOO
OOOOO
SLAM!
?
Z
SCHULZ

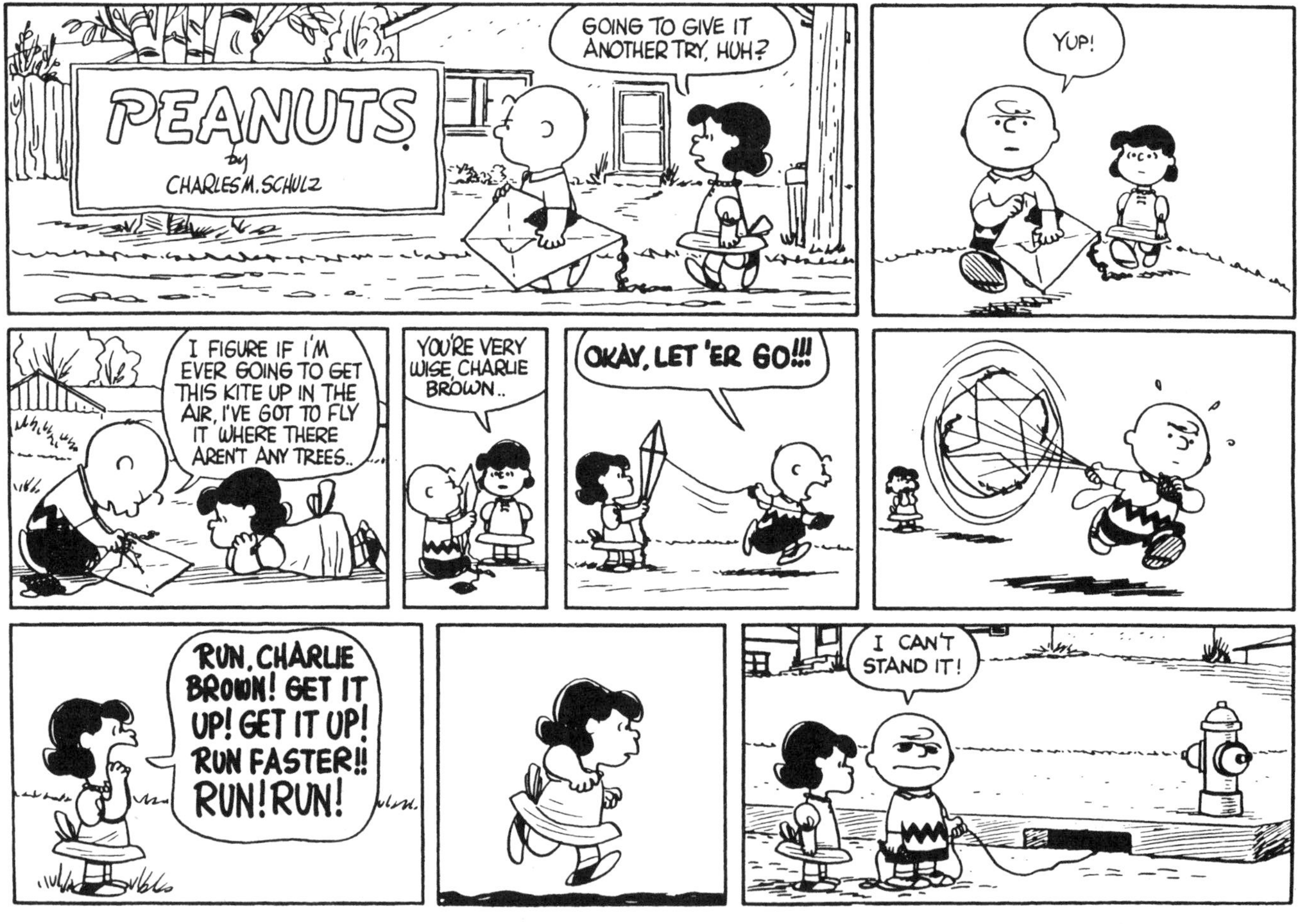
PEANUTS
by
CHARLES M. SCHULZ
GOING TO GIVE IT ANOTHER TRY, HUH?
YUP!
I FIGURE IF I'M EVER GOING TO GET THIS KITE UP IN THE AIR, I'VE GOT TO FLY IT WHERE THERE AREN'T ANY TREES..
YOU'RE VERY WISE, CHARLIE BROWN..
OKAY, LET 'ER GO!!!
RUN, CHARLIE BROWN! GET IT UP! GET IT UP! RUN FASTER!! RUN! RUN!
I CAN'T STAND IT!

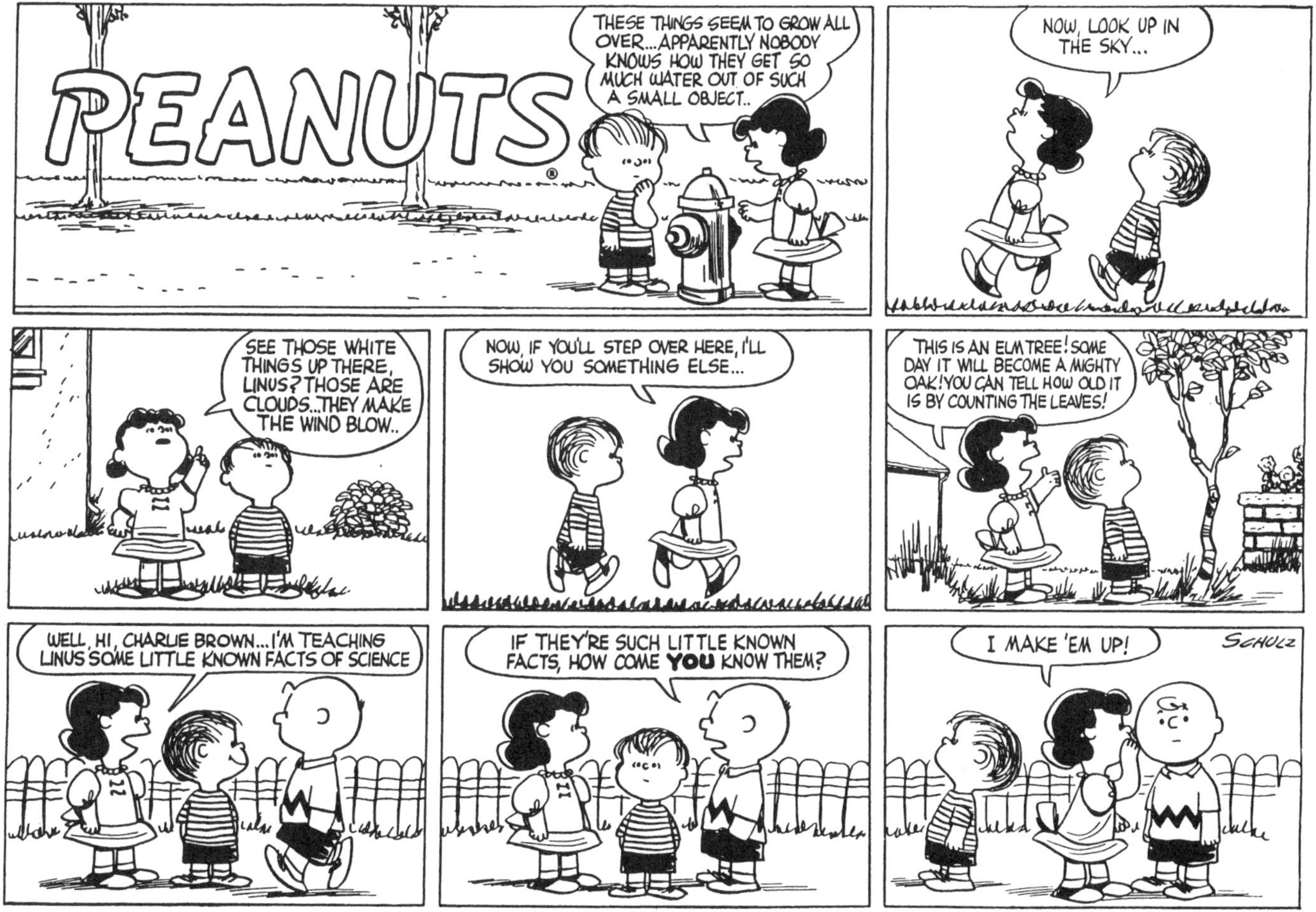
PEANUTS
THESE THINGS SEEM TO GROW ALL OVER...APPARENTLY NOBODY KNOWS HOW THEY GET SO MUCH WATER OUT OF SUCH A SMALL OBJECT..
NOW, LOOK UP IN THE SKY...
SEE THOSE WHITE THINGS UP THERE, LINUS? THOSE ARE CLOUDS...THEY MAKE THE WIND BLOW..
NOW, IF YOU'LL STEP OVER HERE, I'LL SHOW YOU SOMETHING ELSE...
THIS IS AN ELM TREE! SOME DAY IT WILL BECOME A MIGHTY OAK! YOU CAN TELL HOW OLD IT IS BY COUNTING THE LEAVES!
WELL, HI, CHARLIE BROWN...I'M TEACHING LINUS SOME LITTLE KNOWN FACTS OF SCIENCE
IF THEY'RE SUCH LITTLE KNOWN FACTS, HOW COME **YOU** KNOW THEM?
I MAKE 'EM UP!
SCHULZ

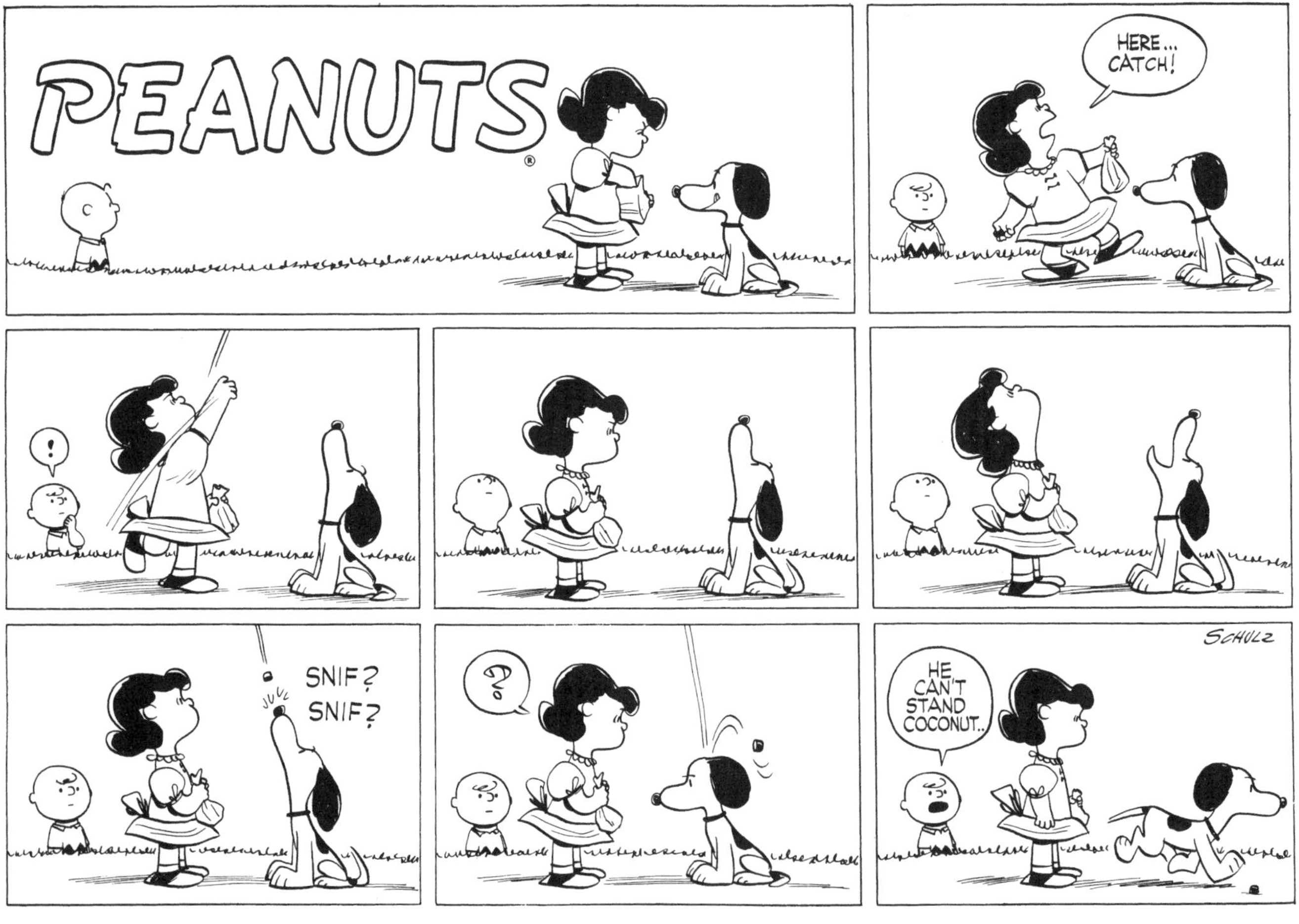
PEANUTS
HERE... CATCH!
!
SNIF? SNIF?
?
SCHULZ
HE CAN'T STAND COCONUT..

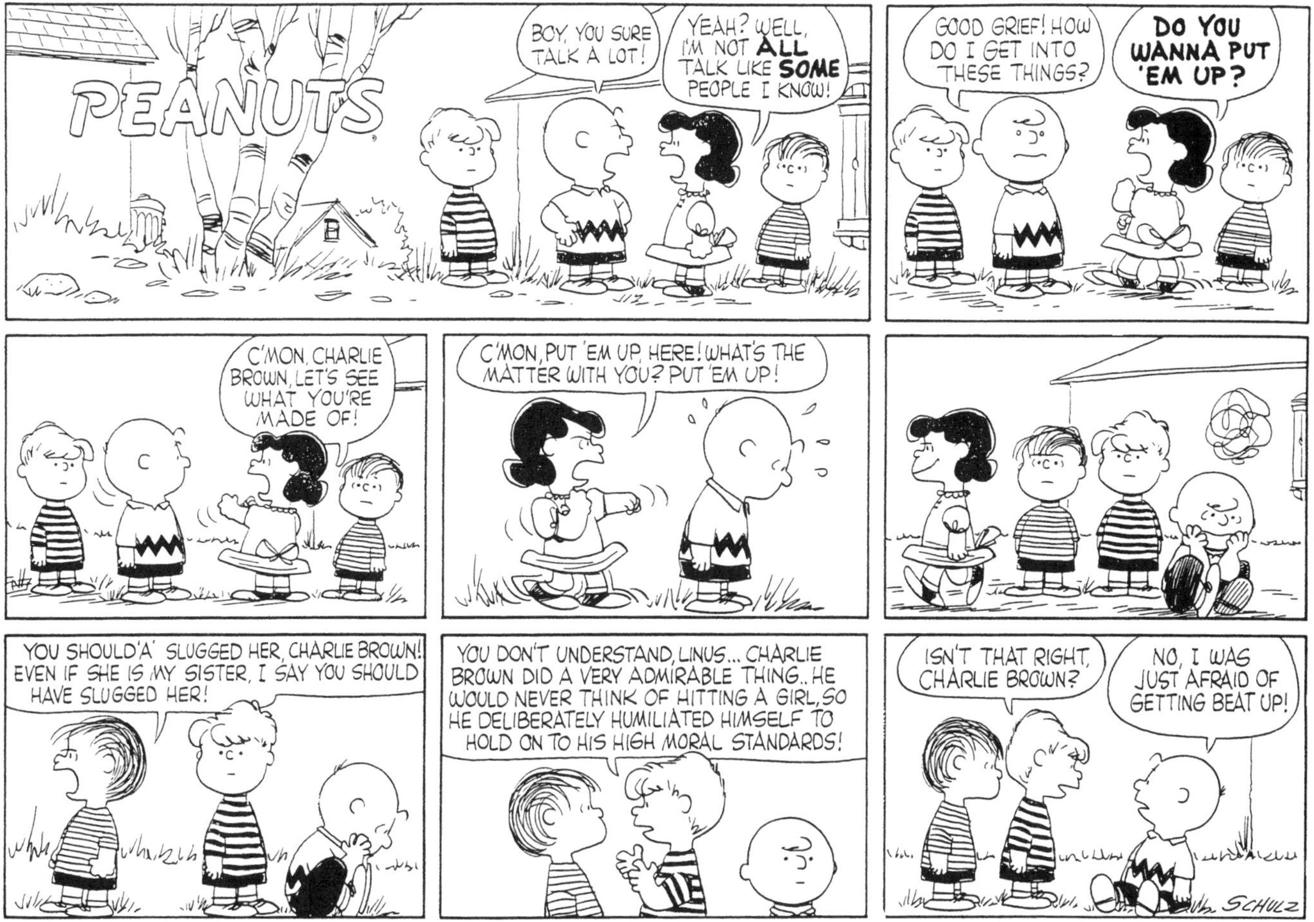
PEANUTS
BOY, YOU SURE TALK A LOT!
YEAH? WELL, I'M NOT ALL TALK LIKE SOME PEOPLE I KNOW!
GOOD GRIEF! HOW DO I GET INTO THESE THINGS?
DO YOU WANNA PUT 'EM UP?
C'MON, CHARLIE BROWN, LET'S SEE WHAT YOU'RE MADE OF!
C'MON, PUT 'EM UP, HERE! WHAT'S THE MATTER WITH YOU? PUT 'EM UP!
YOU SHOULD'A' SLUGGED HER, CHARLIE BROWN! EVEN IF SHE IS MY SISTER, I SAY YOU SHOULD HAVE SLUGGED HER!
YOU DON'T UNDERSTAND, LINUS... CHARLIE BROWN DID A VERY ADMIRABLE THING.. HE WOULD NEVER THINK OF HITTING A GIRL, SO HE DELIBERATELY HUMILIATED HIMSELF TO HOLD ON TO HIS HIGH MORAL STANDARDS!
ISN'T THAT RIGHT, CHARLIE BROWN?
NO, I WAS JUST AFRAID OF GETTING BEAT UP!
SCHULZ

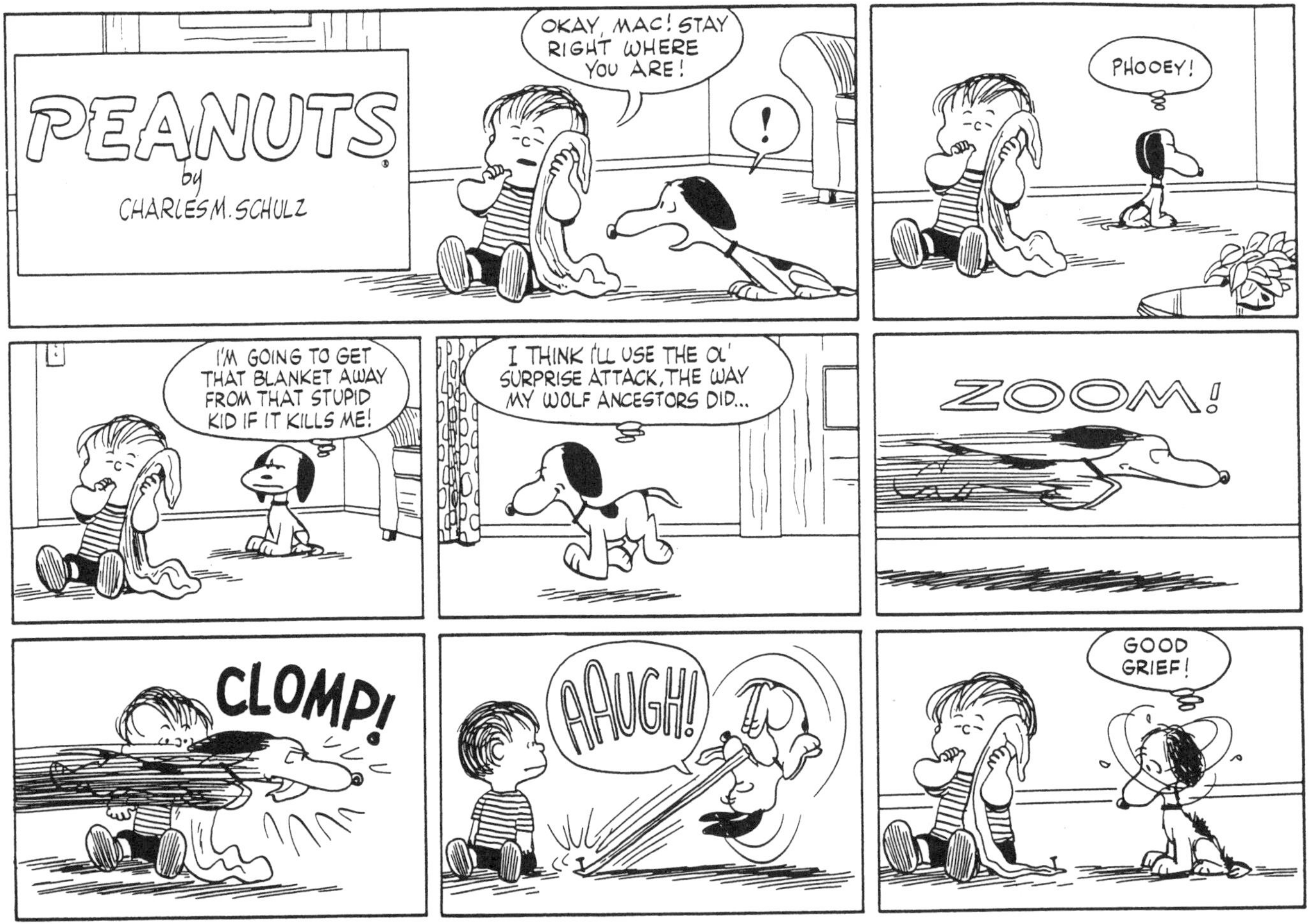
PEANUTS
by
CHARLES M. SCHULZ
OKAY, MAC! STAY RIGHT WHERE YOU ARE!
!
PHOOEY!
I'M GOING TO GET THAT BLANKET AWAY FROM THAT STUPID KID IF IT KILLS ME!
I THINK I'LL USE THE OL' SURPRISE ATTACK, THE WAY MY WOLF ANCESTORS DID...
ZOOM!
CLOMP!
AAUGH!
GOOD GRIEF!

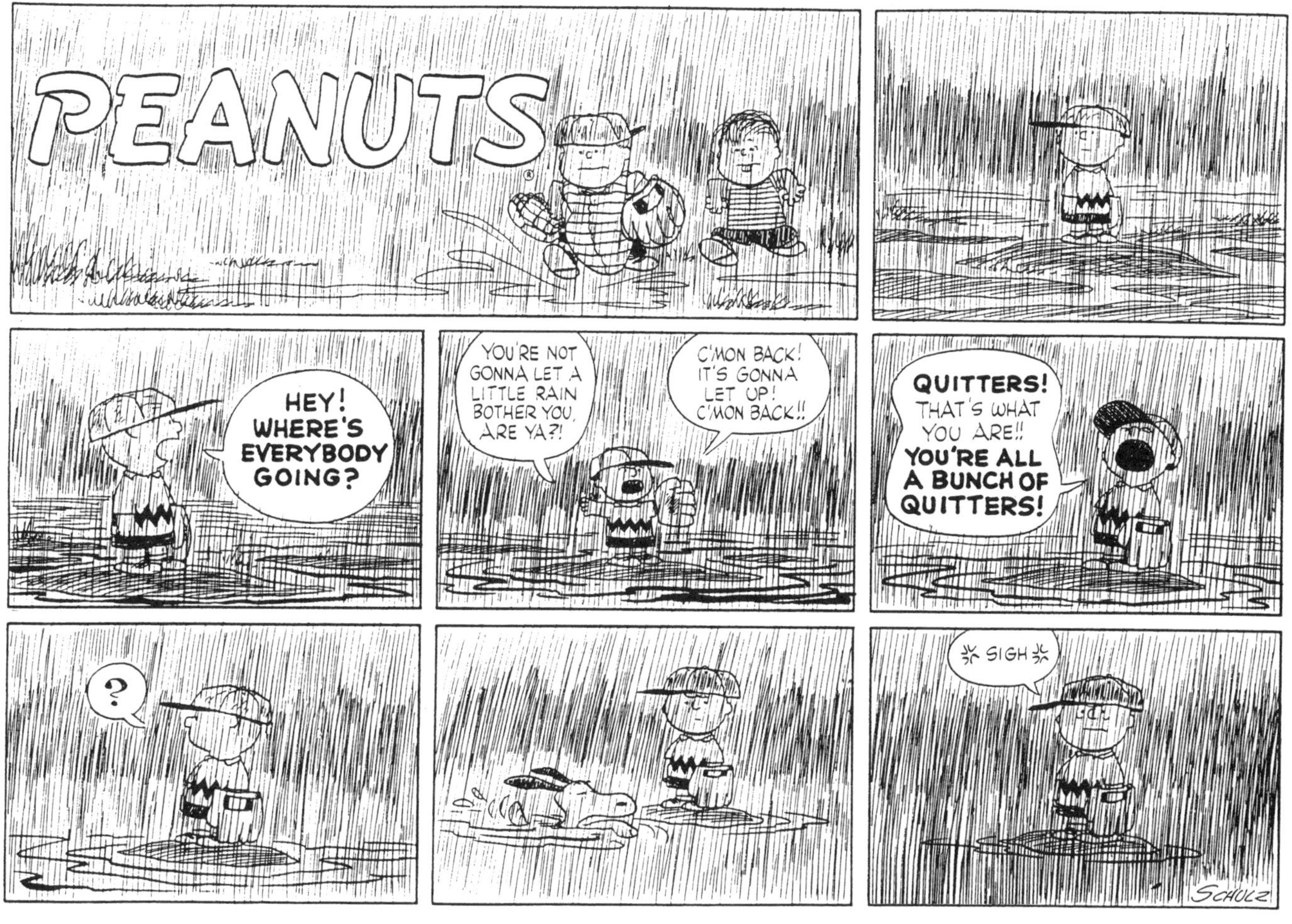
PEANUTS
HEY! WHERE'S EVERYBODY GOING?
YOU'RE NOT GONNA LET A LITTLE RAIN BOTHER YOU, ARE YA?!
C'MON BACK! IT'S GONNA LET UP! C'MON BACK!!
QUITTERS! THAT'S WHAT YOU ARE!! YOU'RE ALL A BUNCH OF QUITTERS!
?
SIGH
SCHULZ

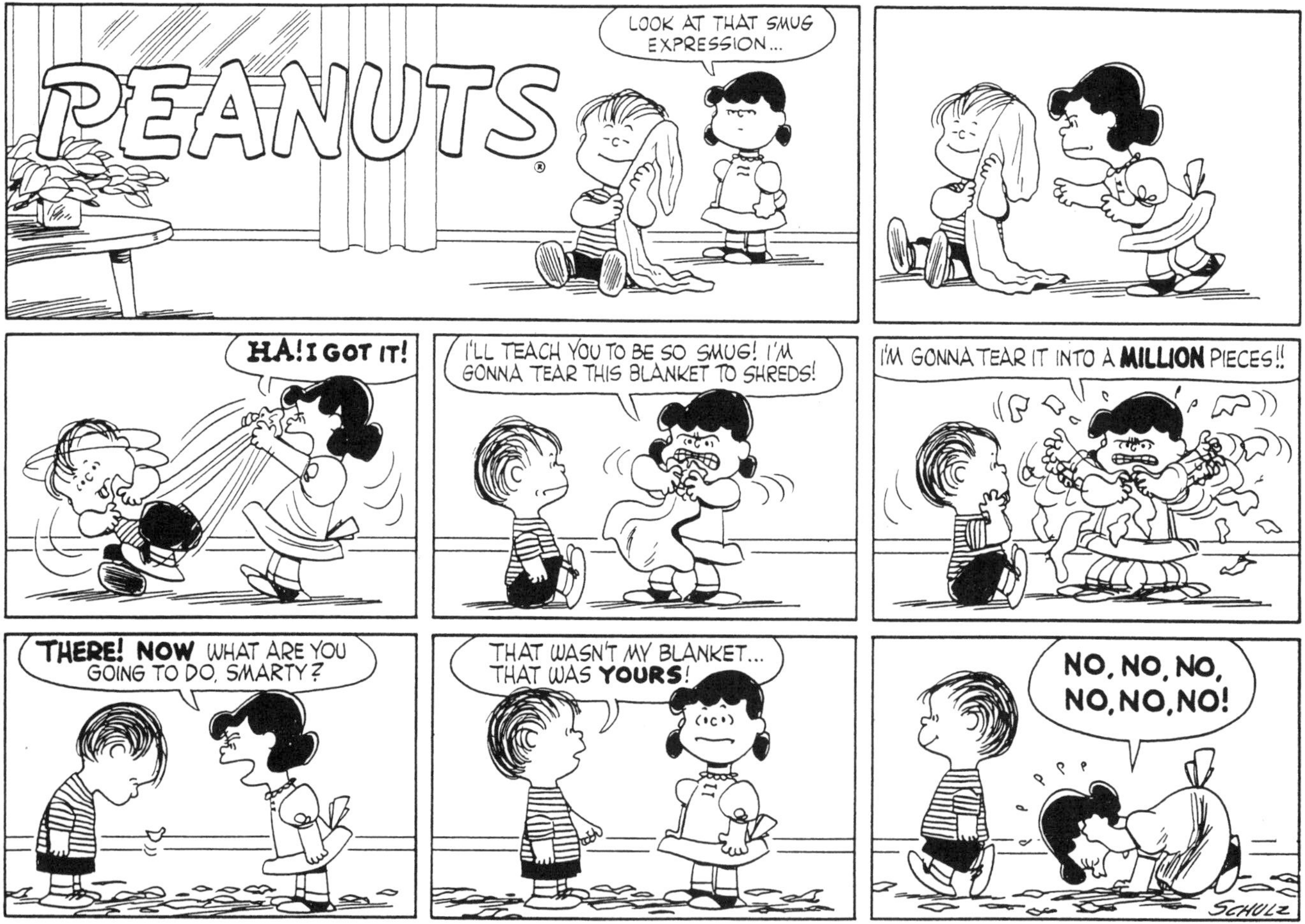
PEANUTS
LOOK AT THAT SMUG EXPRESSION...
HA! I GOT IT!
I'LL TEACH YOU TO BE SO SMUG! I'M GONNA TEAR THIS BLANKET TO SHREDS!
I'M GONNA TEAR IT INTO A MILLION PIECES!!
THERE! NOW WHAT ARE YOU GOING TO DO, SMARTY?
THAT WASN'T MY BLANKET... THAT WAS YOURS!
NO, NO, NO, NO, NO, NO!
SCHULZ

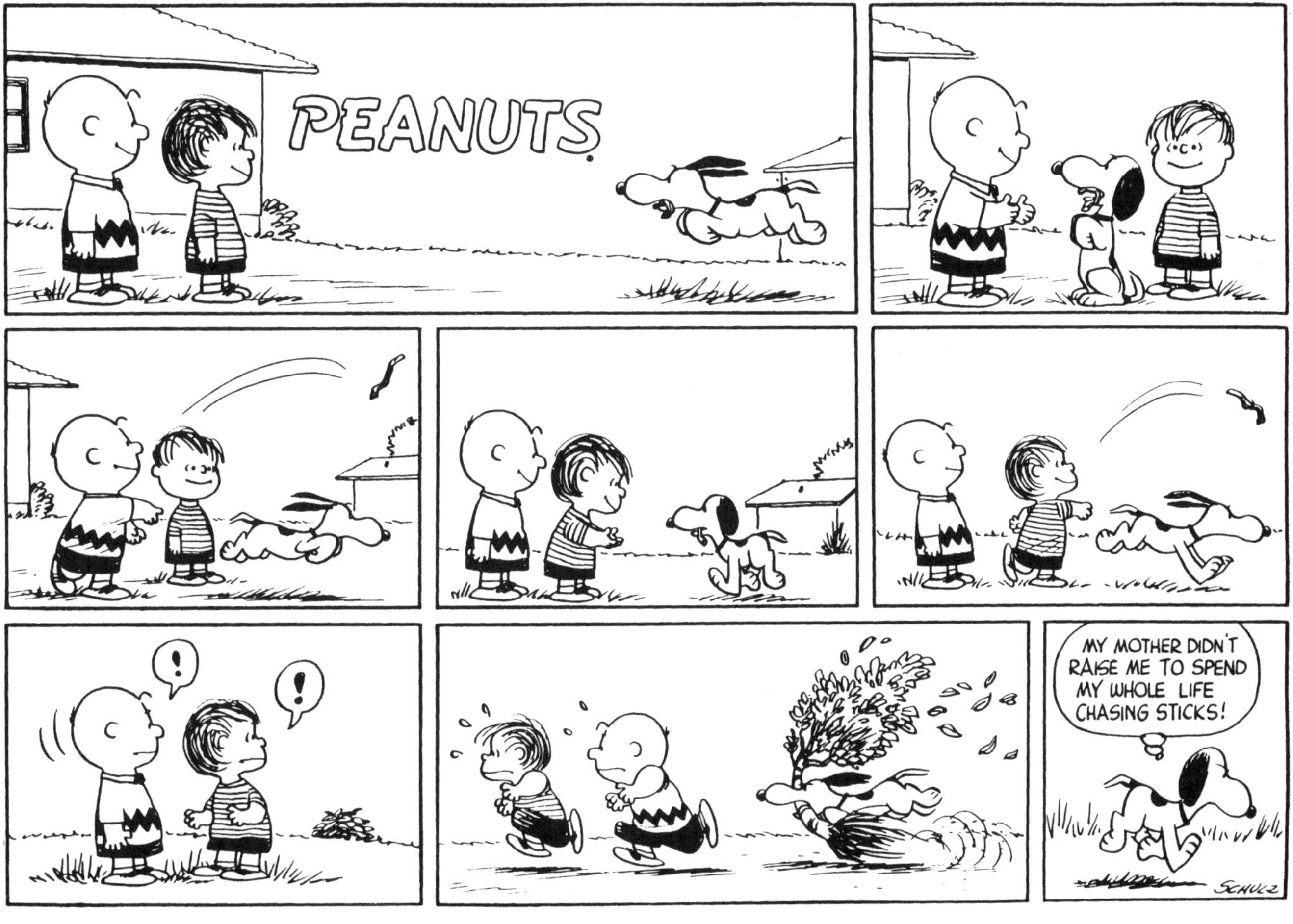
PEANUTS
!
!
MY MOTHER DIDN'T RAISE ME TO SPEND MY WHOLE LIFE CHASING STICKS!
SCHULZ

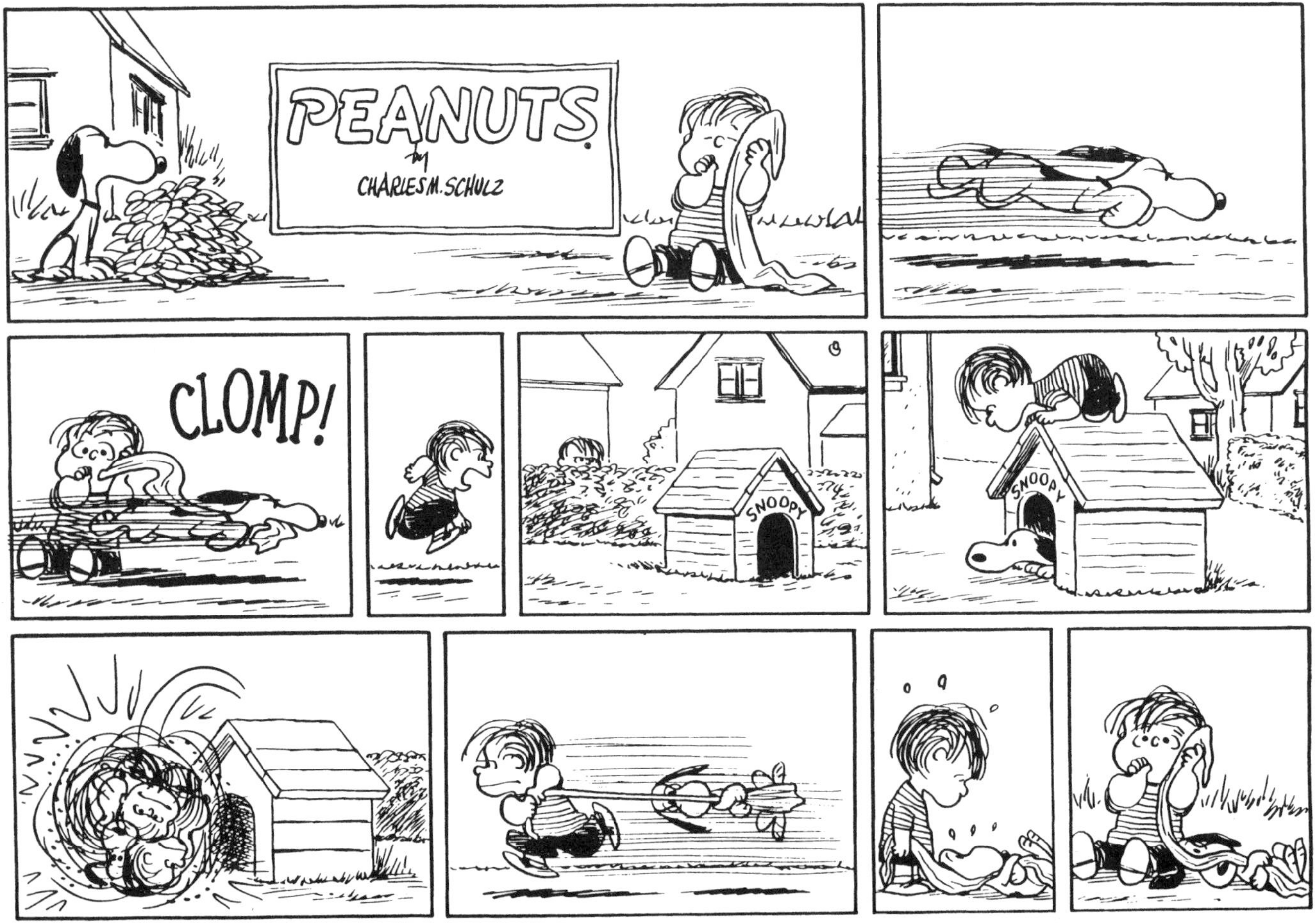
PEANUTS
by
CHARLES M. SCHULZ
CLOMP!
SNOOPY
SNOOPY

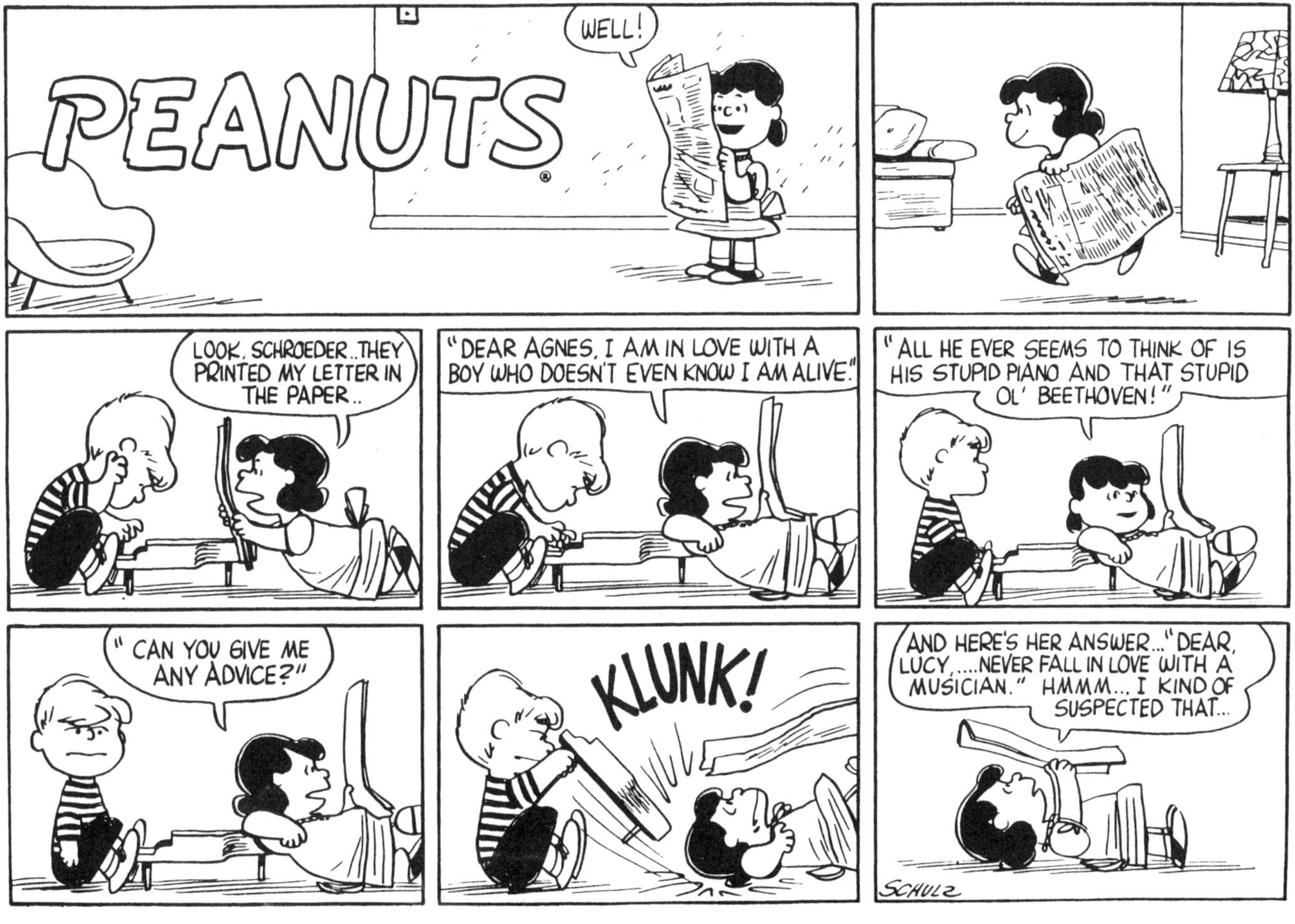
PEANUTS
WELL!
LOOK, SCHROEDER..THEY PRINTED MY LETTER IN THE PAPER..
"DEAR AGNES, I AM IN LOVE WITH A BOY WHO DOESN'T EVEN KNOW I AM ALIVE."
"ALL HE EVER SEEMS TO THINK OF IS HIS STUPID PIANO AND THAT STUPID OL' BEETHOVEN!"
" CAN YOU GIVE ME ANY ADVICE?"
KLUNK!
AND HERE'S HER ANSWER..."DEAR, LUCY,....NEVER FALL IN LOVE WITH A MUSICIAN." HMMM... I KIND OF SUSPECTED THAT...
SCHULZ

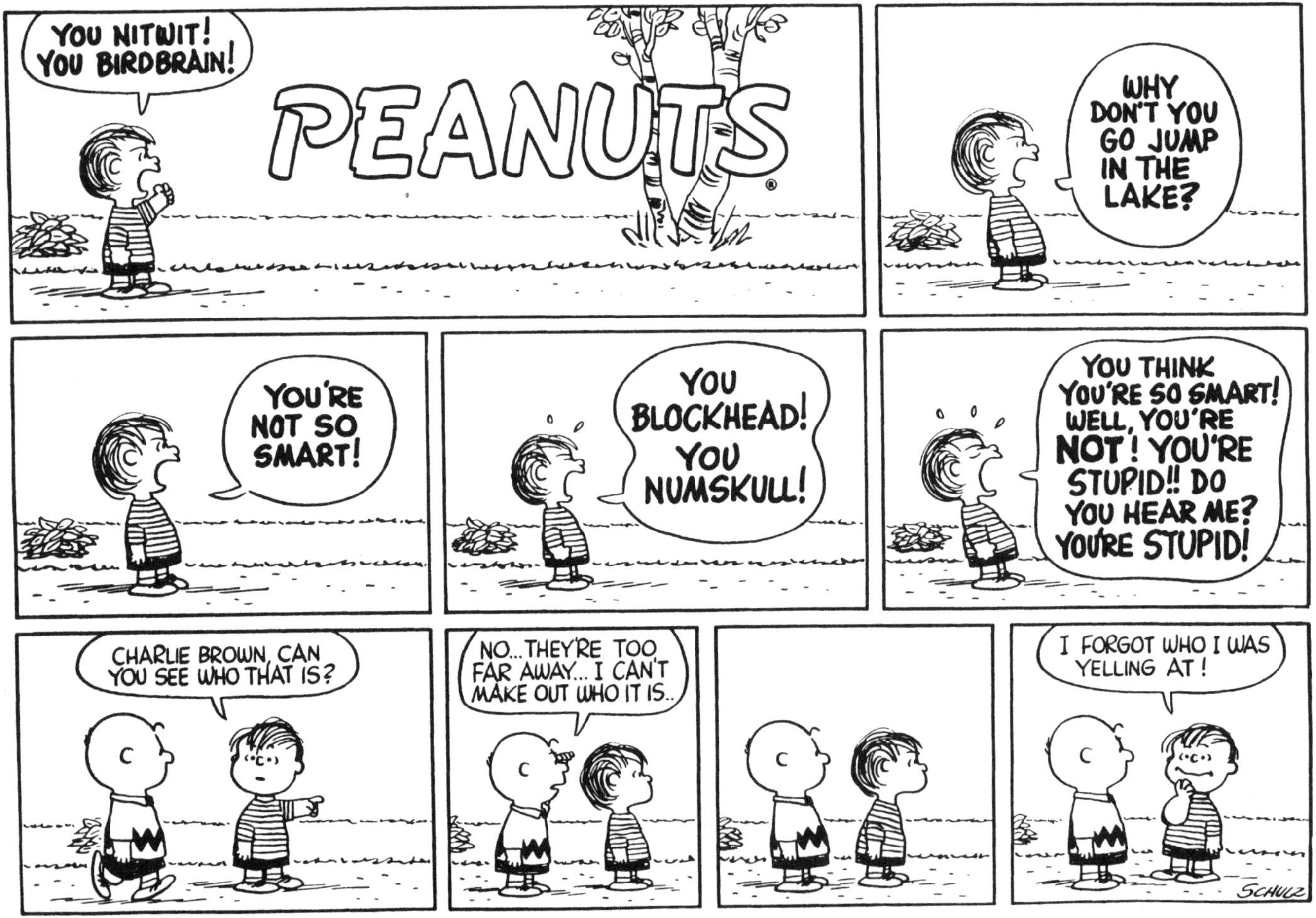
YOU NITWIT! YOU BIRDBRAIN!
PEANUTS®
WHY DON'T YOU GO JUMP IN THE LAKE?
YOU'RE NOT SO SMART!
YOU BLOCKHEAD! YOU NUMSKULL!
YOU THINK YOU'RE SO SMART! WELL, YOU'RE NOT! YOU'RE STUPID!! DO YOU HEAR ME? YOU'RE STUPID!
CHARLIE BROWN, CAN YOU SEE WHO THAT IS?
NO...THEY'RE TOO FAR AWAY... I CAN'T MAKE OUT WHO IT IS..
I FORGOT WHO I WAS YELLING AT!
SCHULZ

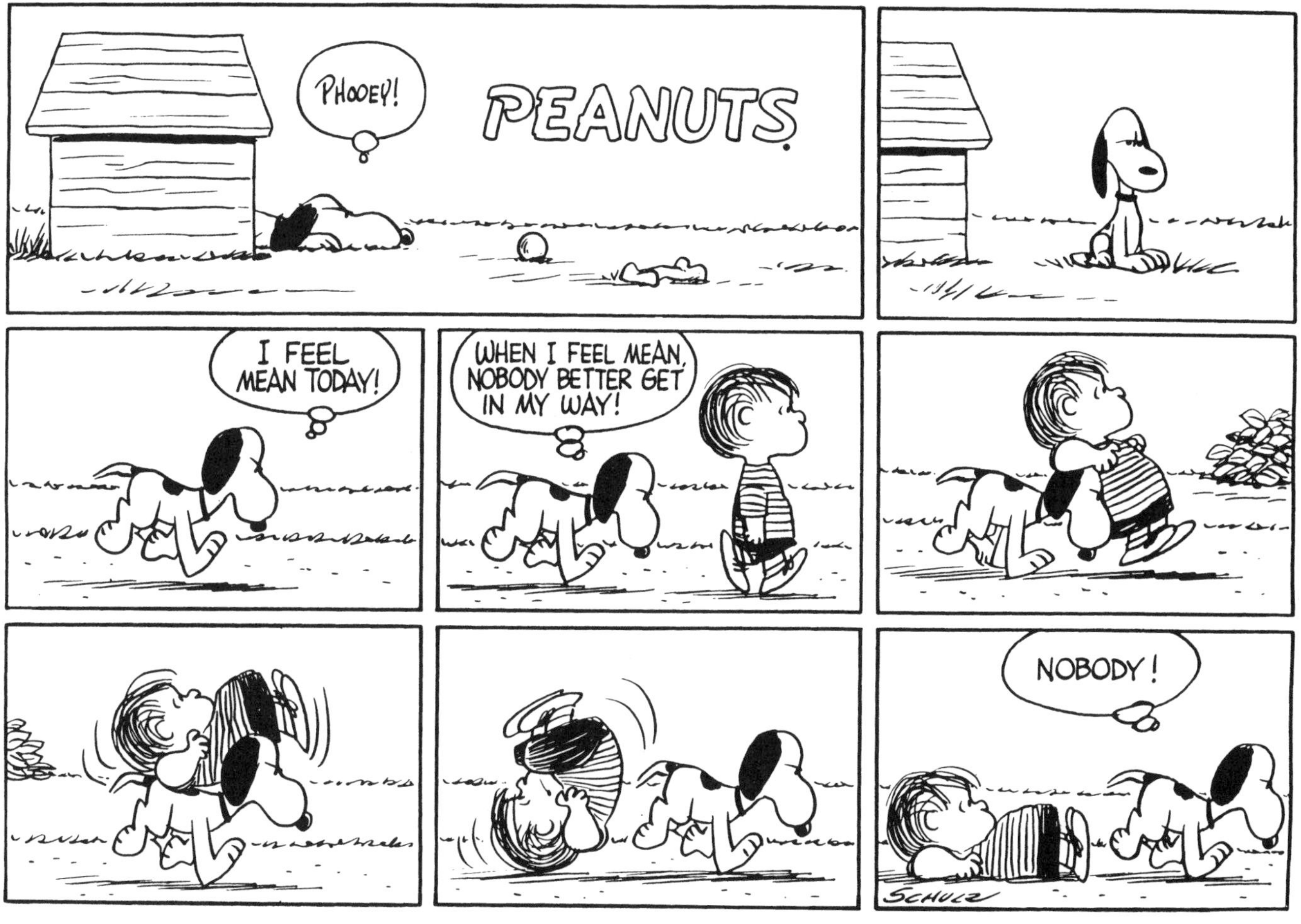
PHOOEY!
PEANUTS
I FEEL MEAN TODAY!
WHEN I FEEL MEAN, NOBODY BETTER GET IN MY WAY!
NOBODY!
SCHULZ

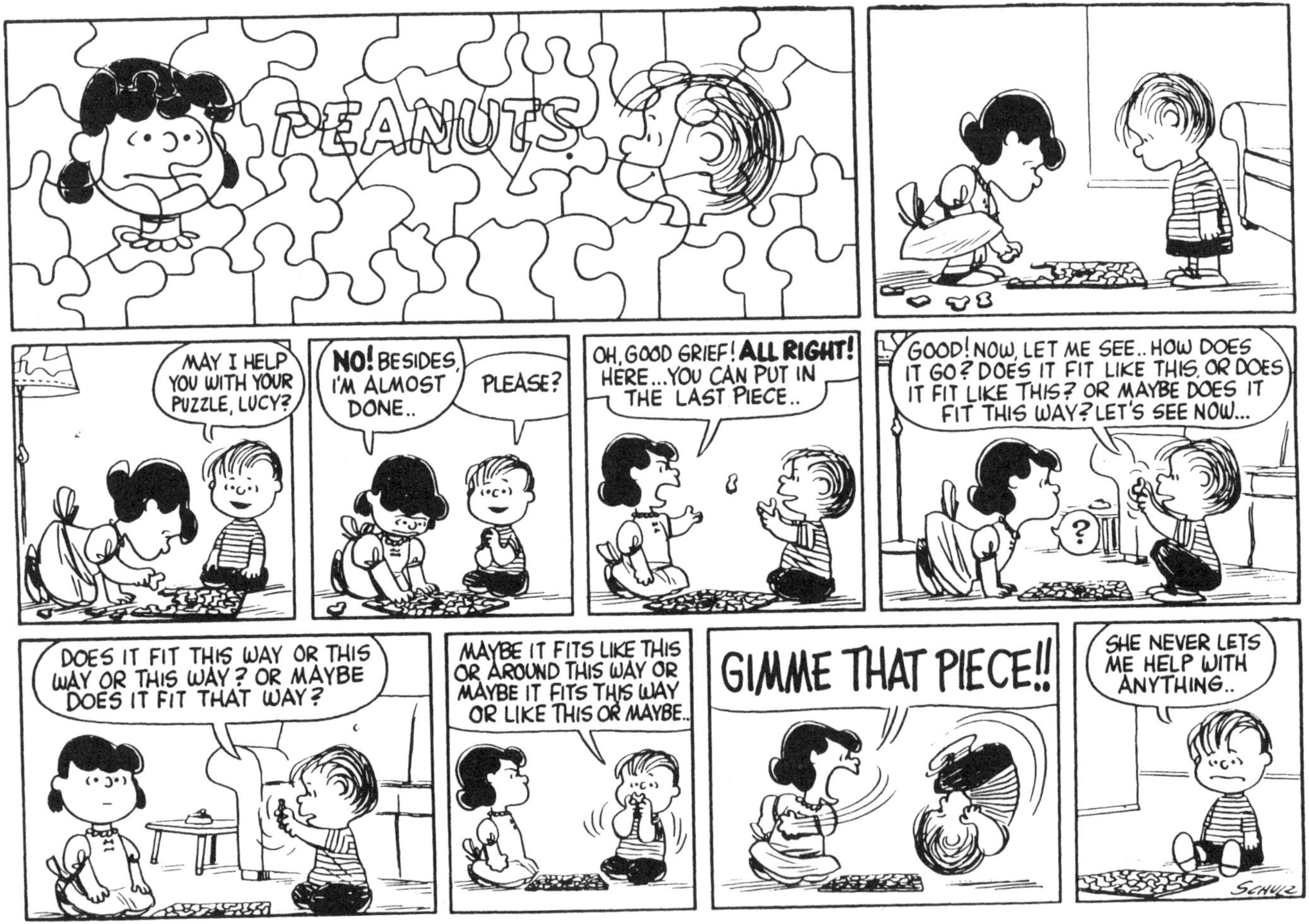
PEANUTS
MAY I HELP YOU WITH YOUR PUZZLE, LUCY?
NO! BESIDES, I'M ALMOST DONE..
PLEASE?
OH, GOOD GRIEF! ALL RIGHT! HERE...YOU CAN PUT IN THE LAST PIECE..
GOOD! NOW, LET ME SEE.. HOW DOES IT GO? DOES IT FIT LIKE THIS, OR DOES IT FIT LIKE THIS? OR MAYBE DOES IT FIT THIS WAY? LET'S SEE NOW...
?
DOES IT FIT THIS WAY OR THIS WAY OR THIS WAY? OR MAYBE DOES IT FIT THAT WAY?
MAYBE IT FITS LIKE THIS OR AROUND THIS WAY OR MAYBE IT FITS THIS WAY OR LIKE THIS OR MAYBE..
GIMME THAT PIECE!!
SHE NEVER LETS ME HELP WITH ANYTHING..
SCHULZ

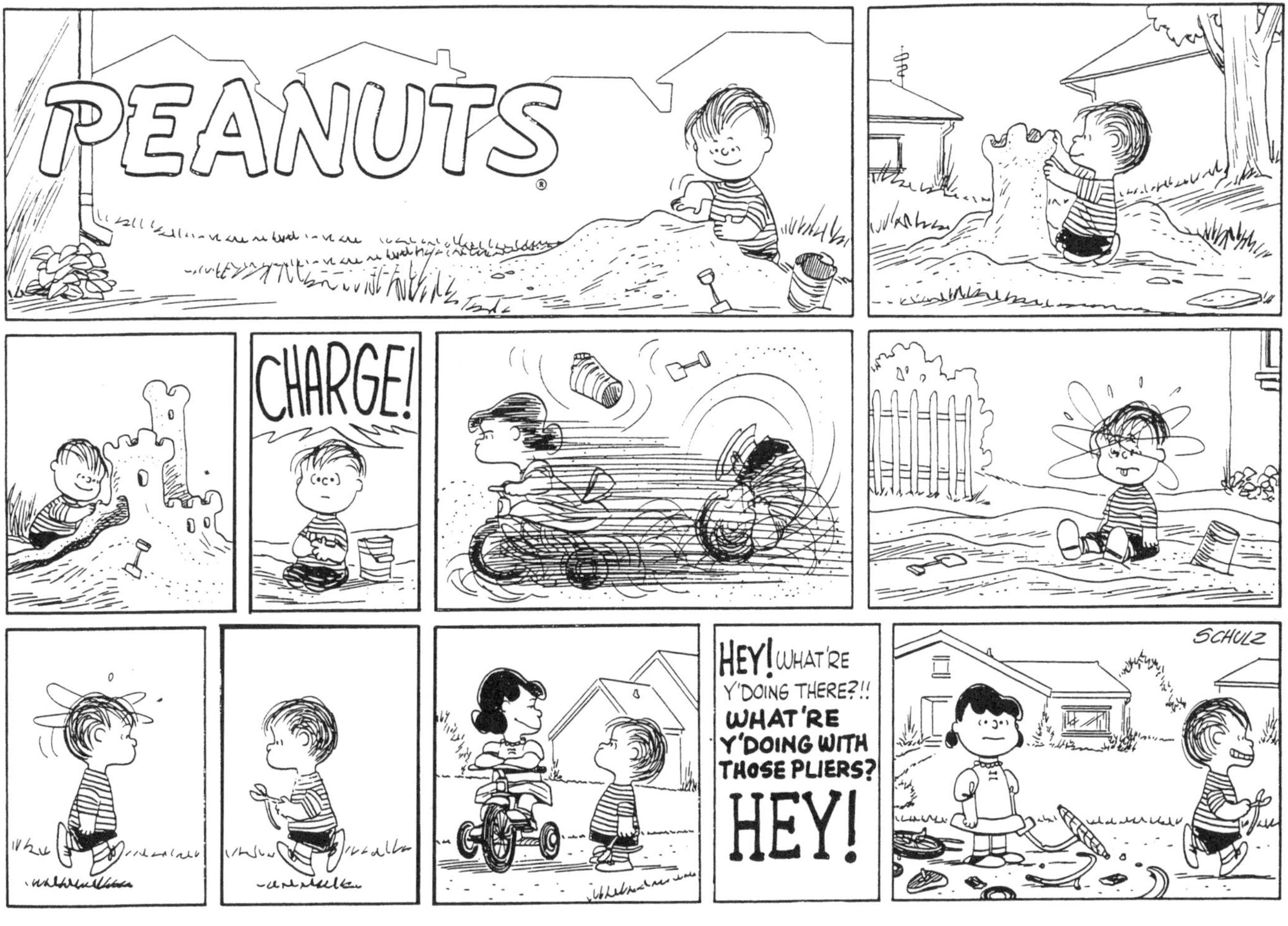
PEANUTS
CHARGE!
HEY! WHAT'RE Y'DOING THERE?!! WHAT'RE Y'DOING WITH THOSE PLIERS? HEY!
SCHULZ

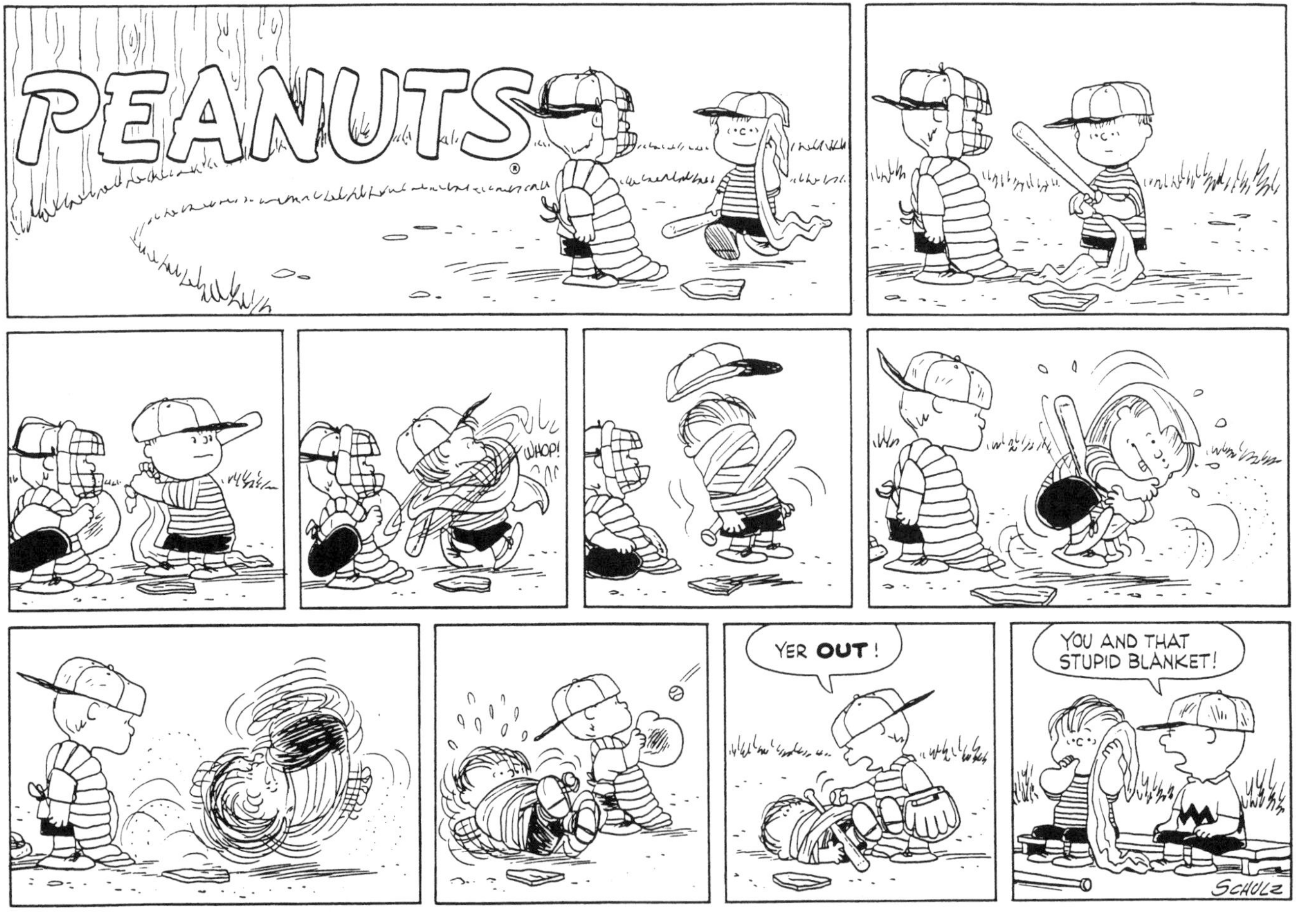
PEANUTS
WHOP!
YER OUT!
YOU AND THAT STUPID BLANKET!
SCHULZ

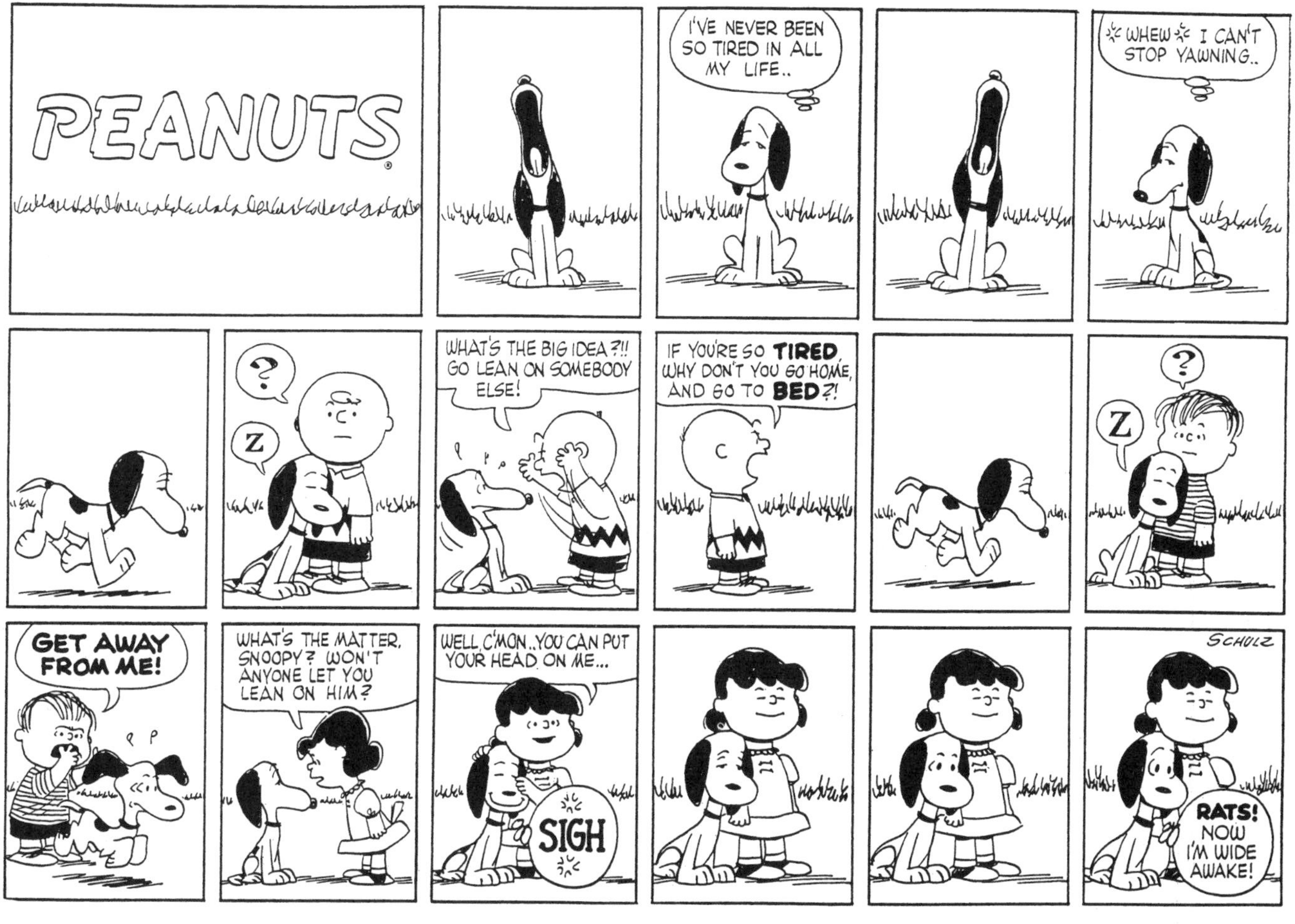
PEANUTS
I'VE NEVER BEEN SO TIRED IN ALL MY LIFE..
WHEW I CAN'T STOP YAWNING..
?
Z
WHAT'S THE BIG IDEA?!! GO LEAN ON SOMEBODY ELSE!
IF YOU'RE SO TIRED WHY DON'T YOU GO HOME, AND GO TO BED?!
Z
?
GET AWAY FROM ME!
WHAT'S THE MATTER, SNOOPY? WON'T ANYONE LET YOU LEAN ON HIM?
WELL, C'MON..YOU CAN PUT YOUR HEAD ON ME...
SIGH
SCHULZ
RATS! NOW I'M WIDE AWAKE!

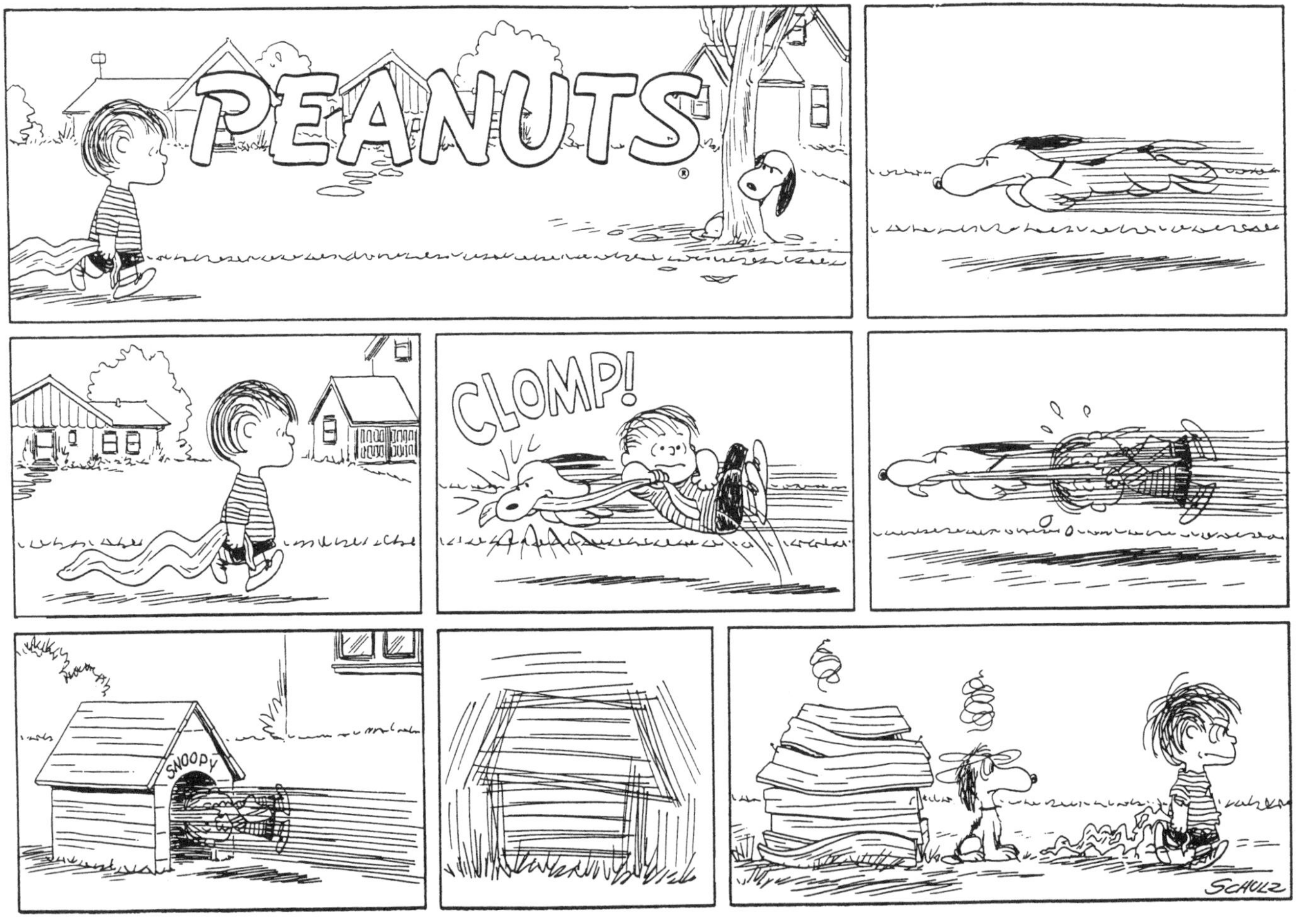
PEANUTS
CLOMP!
SNOOPY
SCHULZ

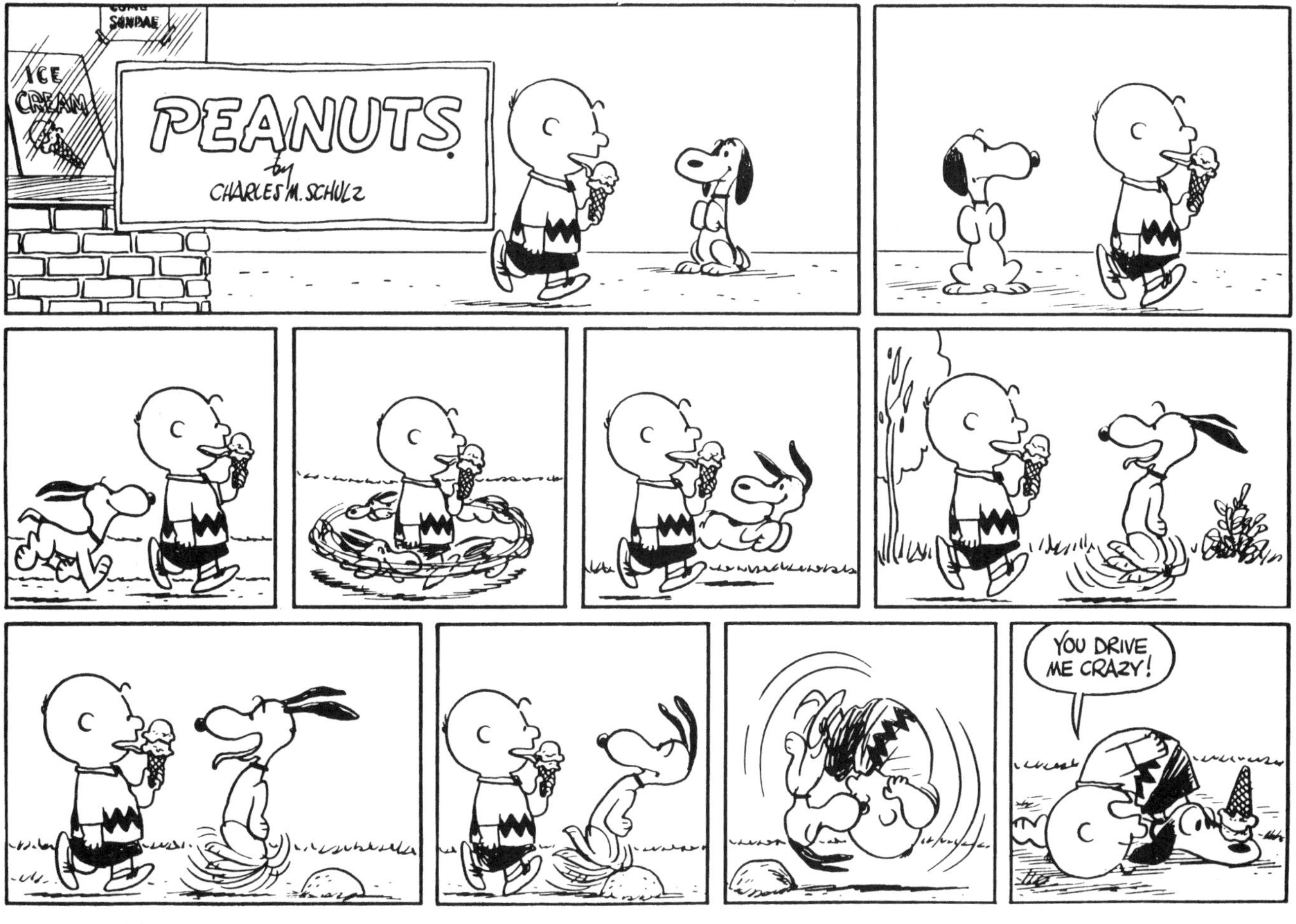
SUNDAE
ICE CREAM
PEANUTS
by
CHARLES M. SCHULZ
YOU DRIVE ME CRAZY!

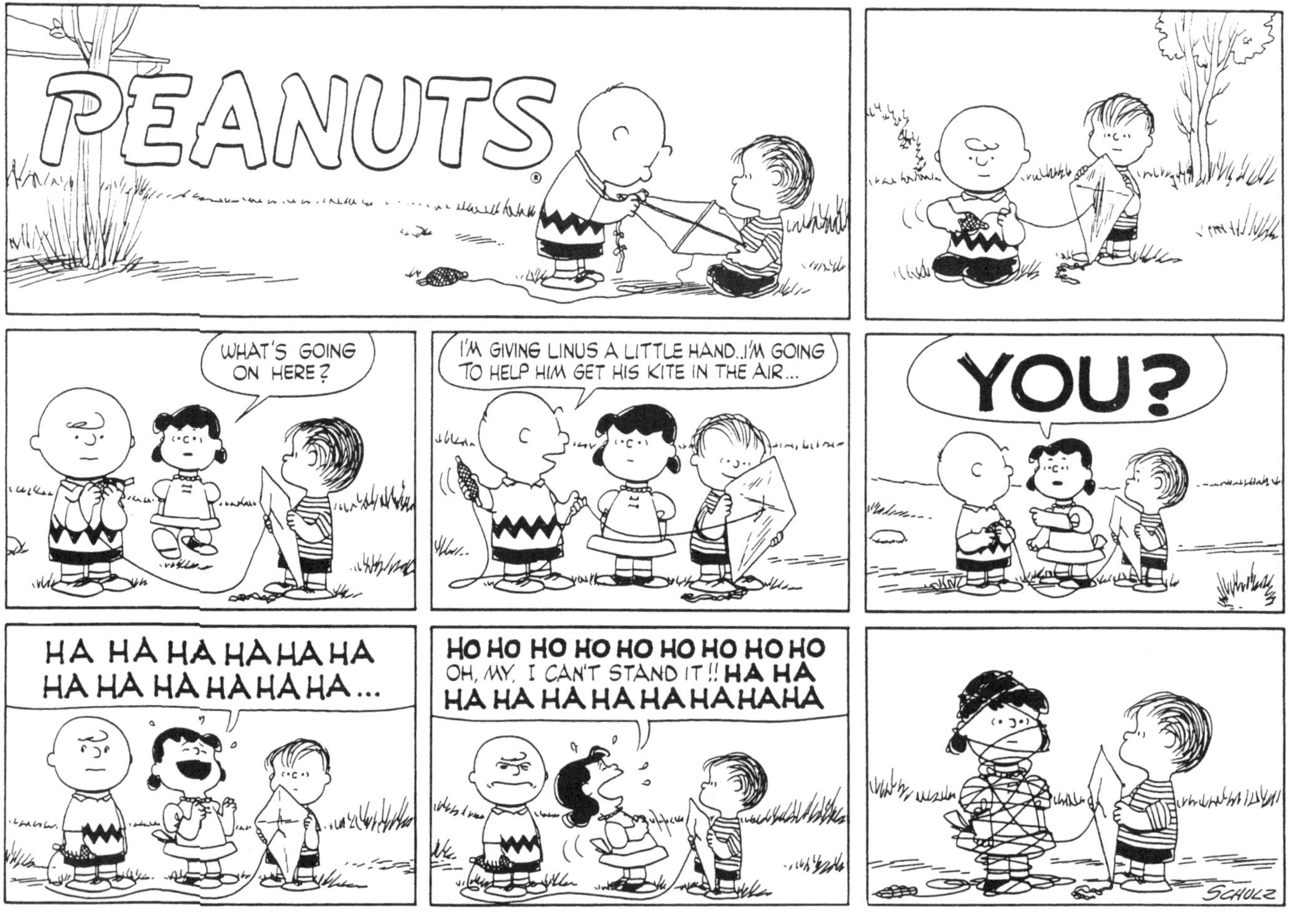
PEANUTS
WHAT'S GOING ON HERE?
I'M GIVING LINUS A LITTLE HAND..I'M GOING TO HELP HIM GET HIS KITE IN THE AIR...
YOU?
HA HA HA HA HA HA HA HA HA HA HA HA HA...
HO HO HO HO HO HO HO HO HO OH, MY, I CAN'T STAND IT!! HA HA HA HA HA HA HA HA HA HA
SCHULZ

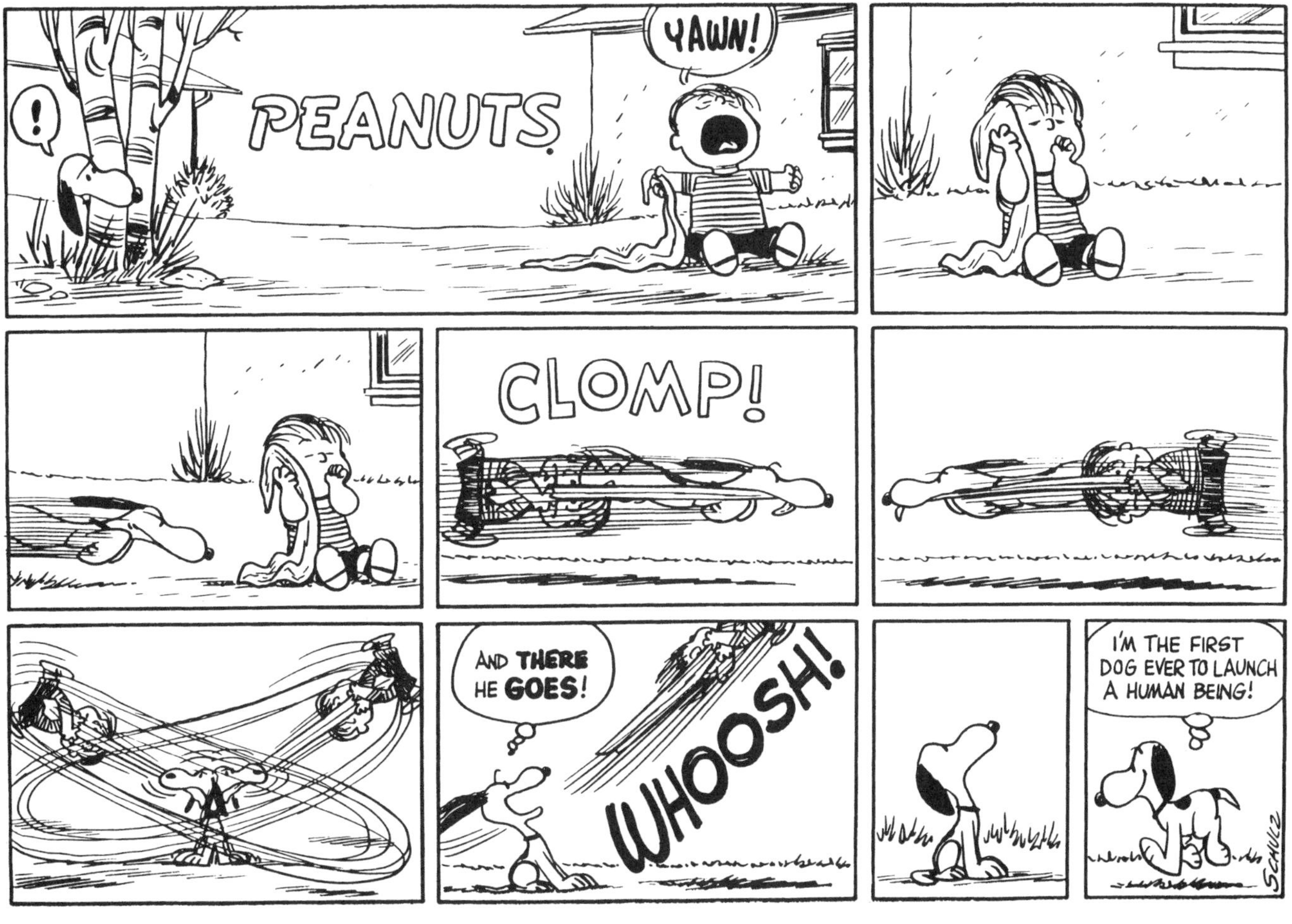
PEANUTS
!
YAWN!
CLOMP!
AND THERE HE GOES!
WHOOSH!
I'M THE FIRST DOG EVER TO LAUNCH A HUMAN BEING!
SCHULZ

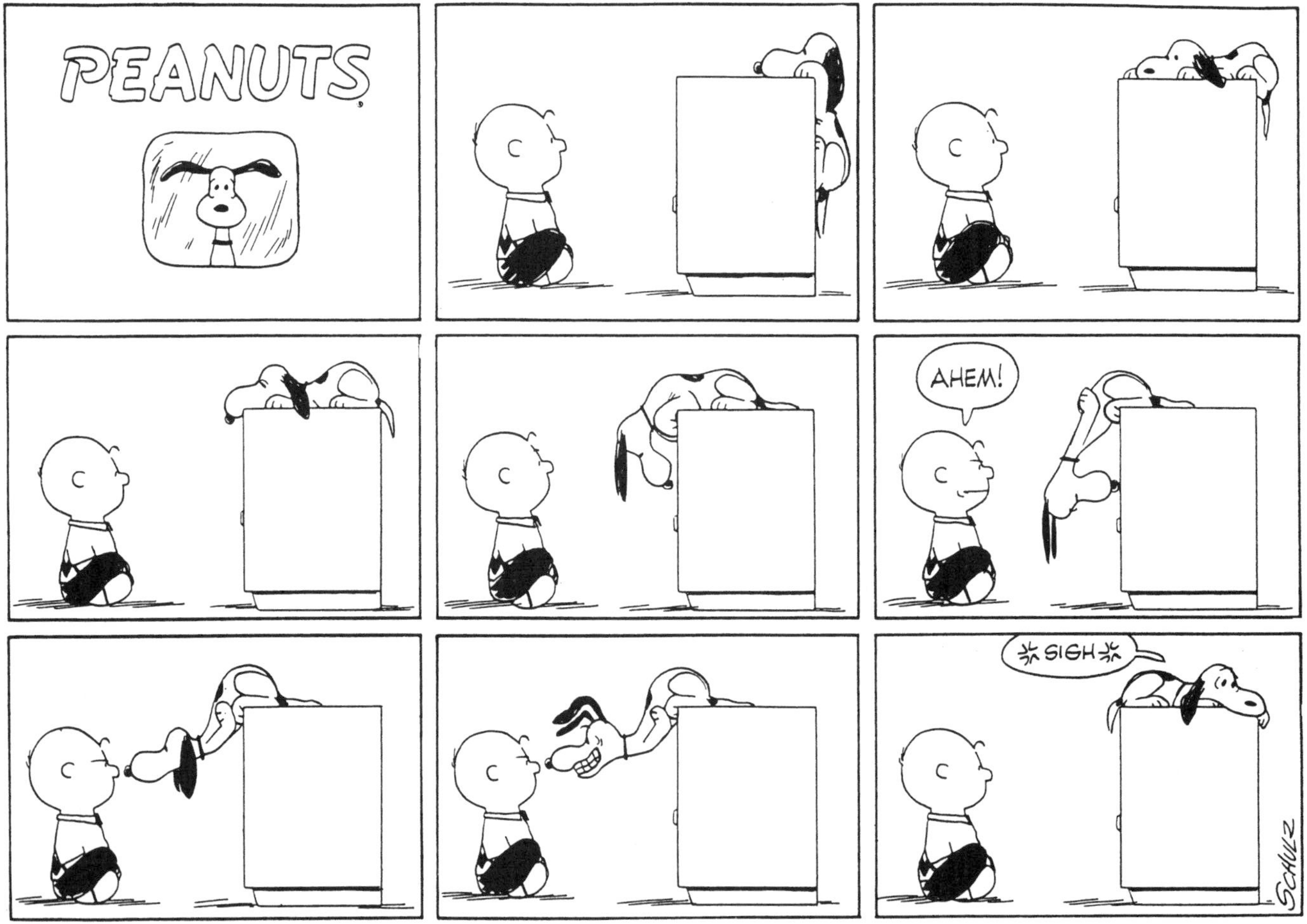
PEANUTS
AHEM!
SIGH
SCHULZ

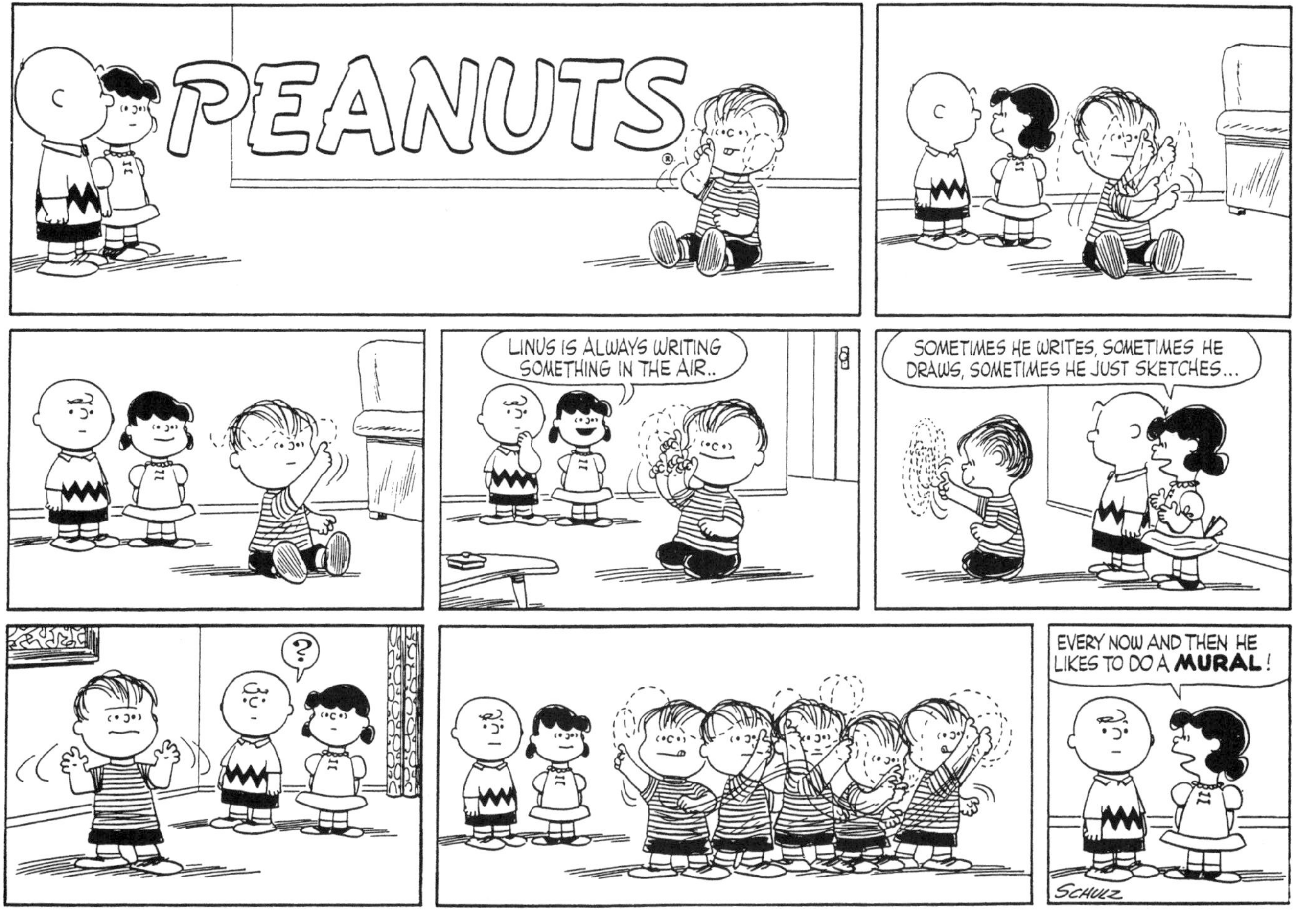

PEANUTS
LINUS IS ALWAYS WRITING SOMETHING IN THE AIR..
SOMETIMES HE WRITES, SOMETIMES HE DRAWS, SOMETIMES HE JUST SKETCHES...
?
EVERY NOW AND THEN HE LIKES TO DO A **MURAL**!
SCHULZ

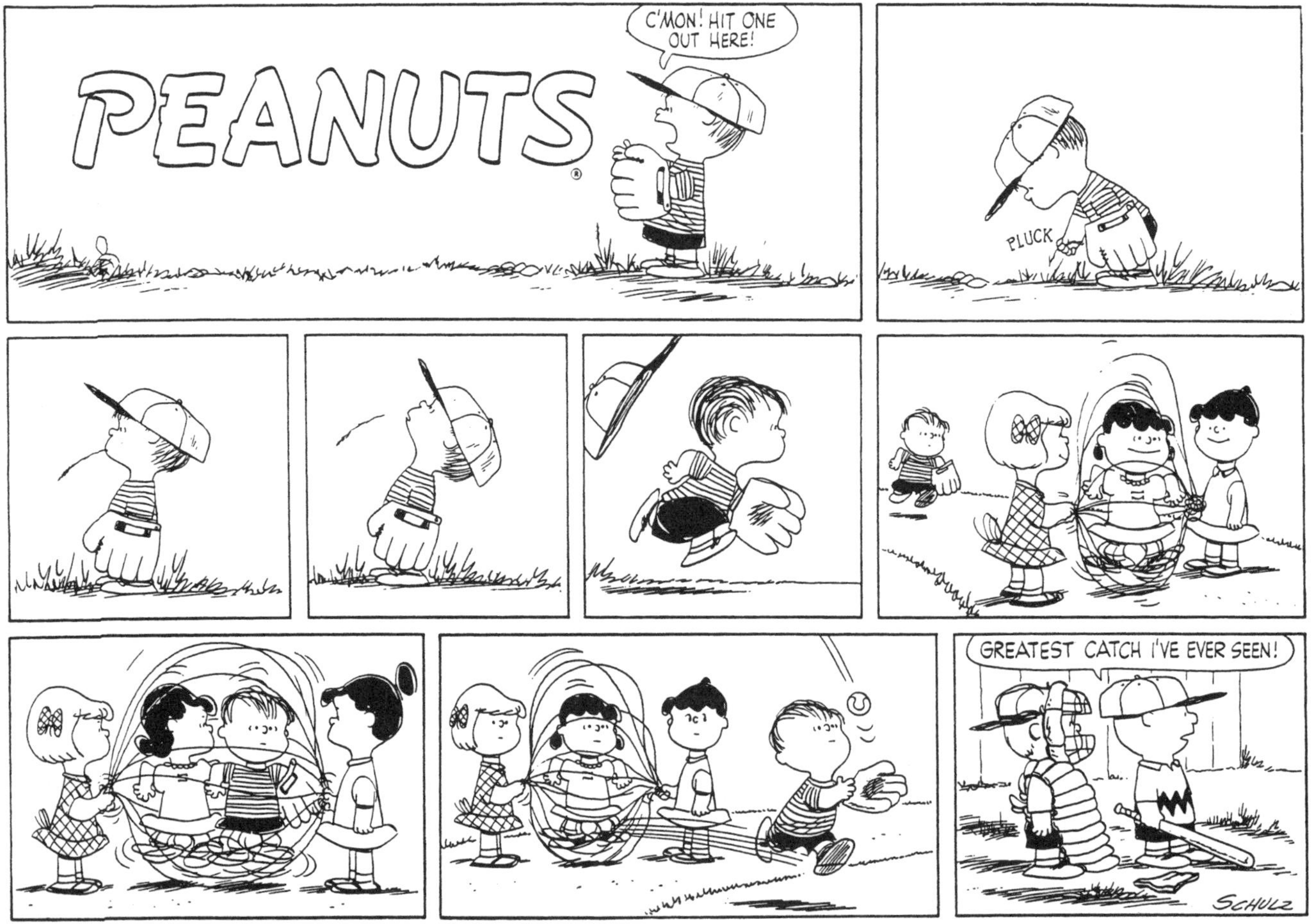
PEANUTS
C'MON! HIT ONE OUT HERE!
PLUCK
GREATEST CATCH I'VE EVER SEEN!
SCHULZ

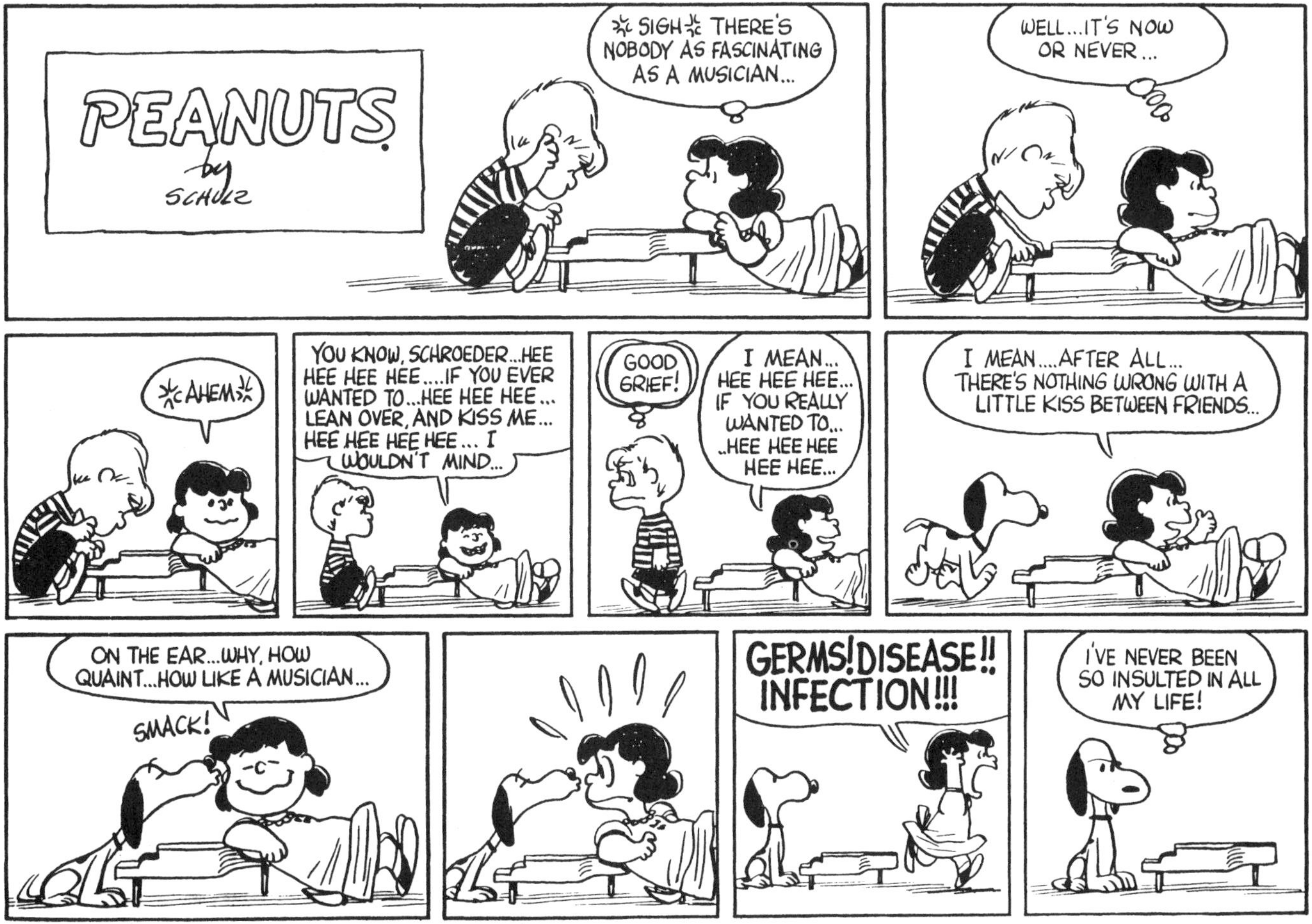
PEANUTS
by SCHULZ
SIGH THERE'S NOBODY AS FASCINATING AS A MUSICIAN...
WELL...IT'S NOW OR NEVER...
AHEM
YOU KNOW, SCHROEDER...HEE HEE HEE HEE.....IF YOU EVER WANTED TO...HEE HEE HEE... LEAN OVER, AND KISS ME... HEE HEE HEE HEE... I WOULDN'T MIND...
GOOD GRIEF!
I MEAN... HEE HEE HEE... IF YOU REALLY WANTED TO... ..HEE HEE HEE HEE HEE...
I MEAN.....AFTER ALL... THERE'S NOTHING WRONG WITH A LITTLE KISS BETWEEN FRIENDS...
ON THE EAR...WHY, HOW QUAINT...HOW LIKE A MUSICIAN...
SMACK!
GERMS! DISEASE!! INFECTION!!!
I'VE NEVER BEEN SO INSULTED IN ALL MY LIFE!

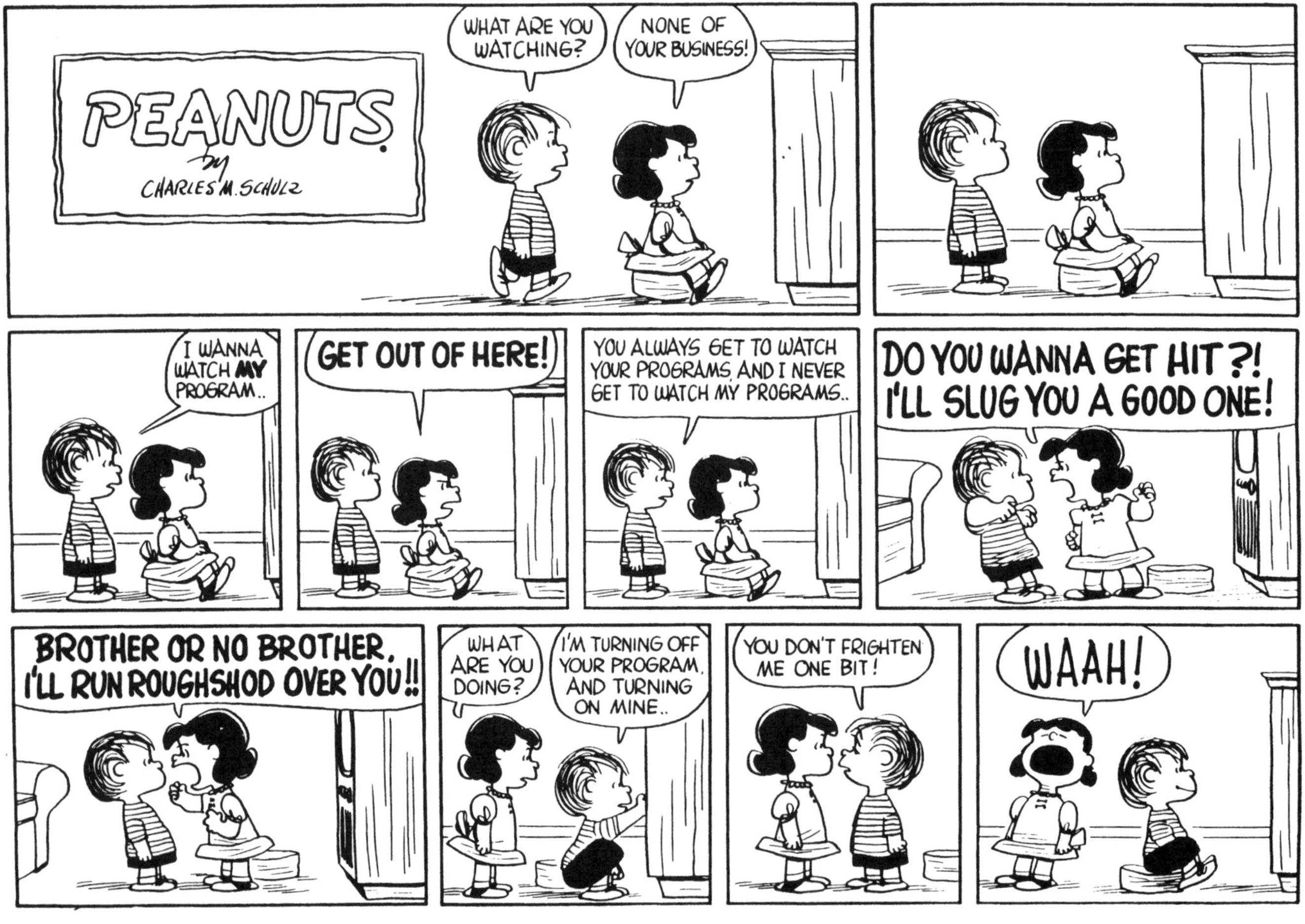
PEANUTS
by
CHARLES M. SCHULZ
WHAT ARE YOU WATCHING?
NONE OF YOUR BUSINESS!
I WANNA WATCH **MY** PROGRAM..
GET OUT OF HERE!
YOU ALWAYS GET TO WATCH YOUR PROGRAMS, AND I NEVER GET TO WATCH MY PROGRAMS..
DO YOU WANNA GET HIT?! I'LL SLUG YOU A GOOD ONE!
BROTHER OR NO BROTHER, I'LL RUN ROUGHSHOD OVER YOU!!
WHAT ARE YOU DOING?
I'M TURNING OFF YOUR PROGRAM, AND TURNING ON MINE..
YOU DON'T FRIGHTEN ME ONE BIT!
WAAH!

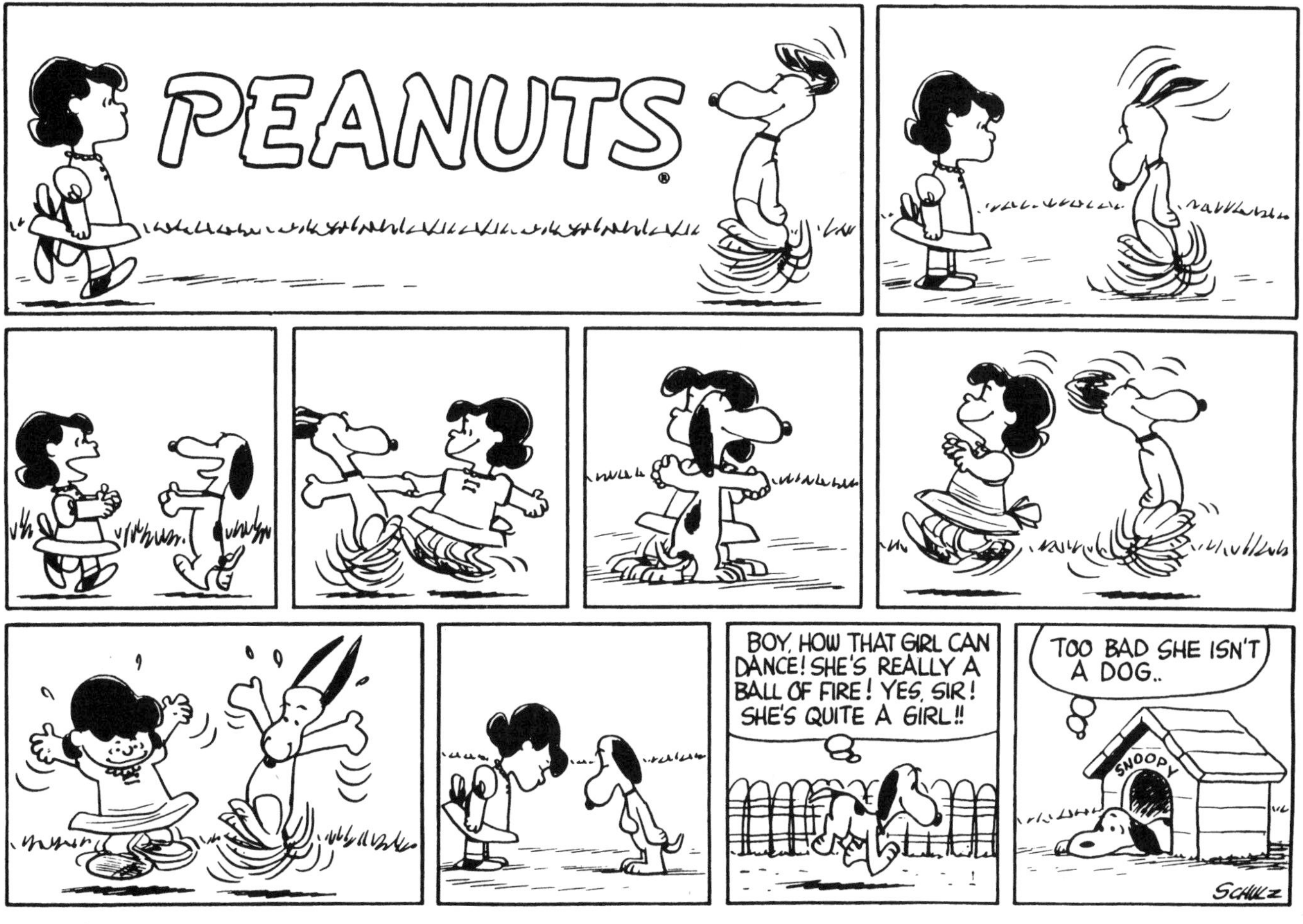
PEANUTS
BOY, HOW THAT GIRL CAN DANCE! SHE'S REALLY A BALL OF FIRE! YES, SIR! SHE'S QUITE A GIRL!!
TOO BAD SHE ISN'T A DOG..
SNOOPY
SCHULZ

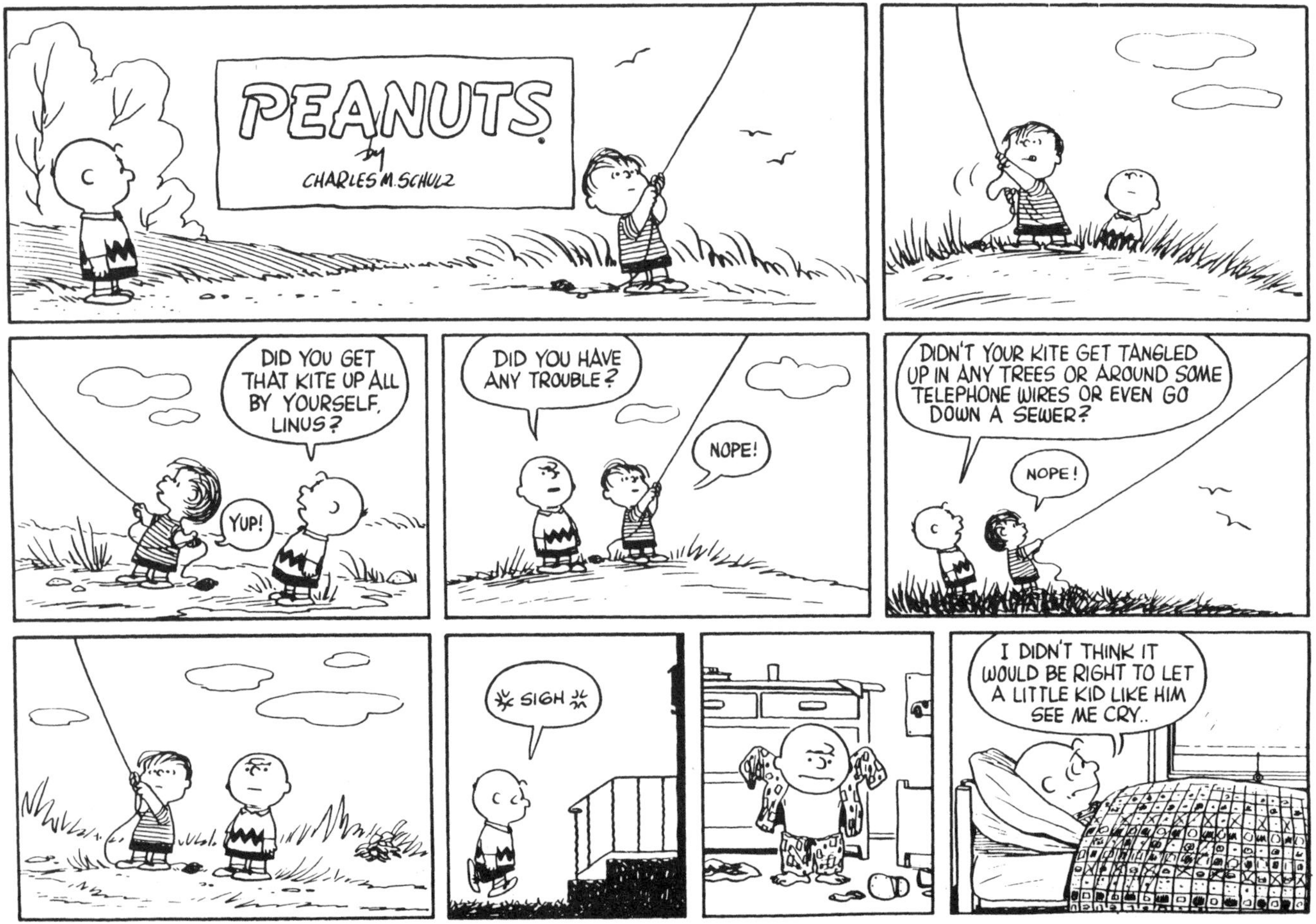
PEANUTS
by
CHARLES M. SCHULZ
DID YOU GET THAT KITE UP ALL BY YOURSELF, LINUS?
YUP!
DID YOU HAVE ANY TROUBLE?
NOPE!
DIDN'T YOUR KITE GET TANGLED UP IN ANY TREES OR AROUND SOME TELEPHONE WIRES OR EVEN GO DOWN A SEWER?
NOPE!
SIGH
I DIDN'T THINK IT WOULD BE RIGHT TO LET A LITTLE KID LIKE HIM SEE ME CRY..

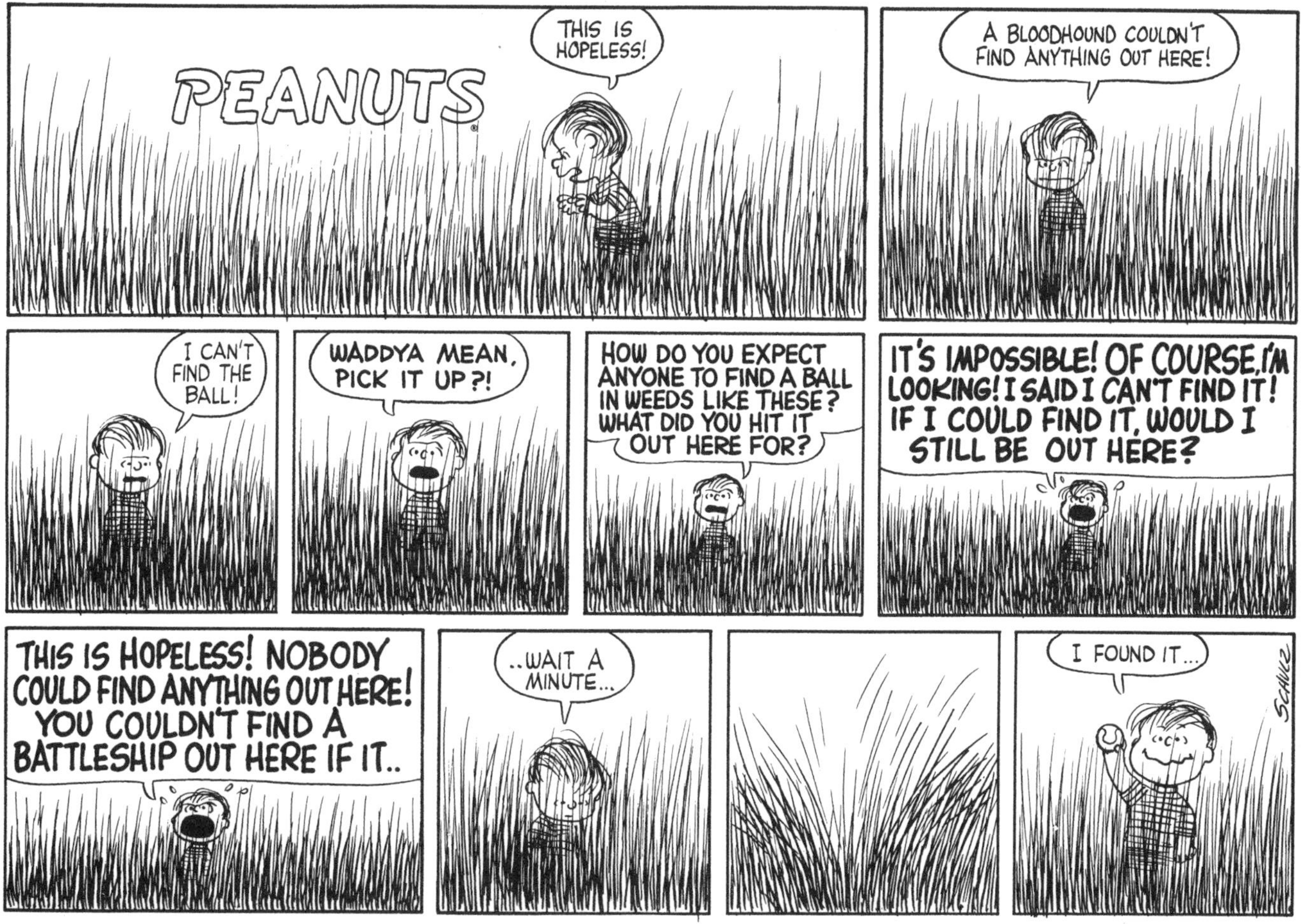
PEANUTS
THIS IS HOPELESS!
A BLOODHOUND COULDN'T FIND ANYTHING OUT HERE!
I CAN'T FIND THE BALL!
WADDYA MEAN, PICK IT UP?!
HOW DO YOU EXPECT ANYONE TO FIND A BALL IN WEEDS LIKE THESE? WHAT DID YOU HIT IT OUT HERE FOR?
IT'S IMPOSSIBLE! OF COURSE, I'M LOOKING! I SAID I CAN'T FIND IT! IF I COULD FIND IT, WOULD I STILL BE OUT HERE?
THIS IS HOPELESS! NOBODY COULD FIND ANYTHING OUT HERE! YOU COULDN'T FIND A BATTLESHIP OUT HERE IF IT..
..WAIT A MINUTE...
I FOUND IT...
SCHULZ

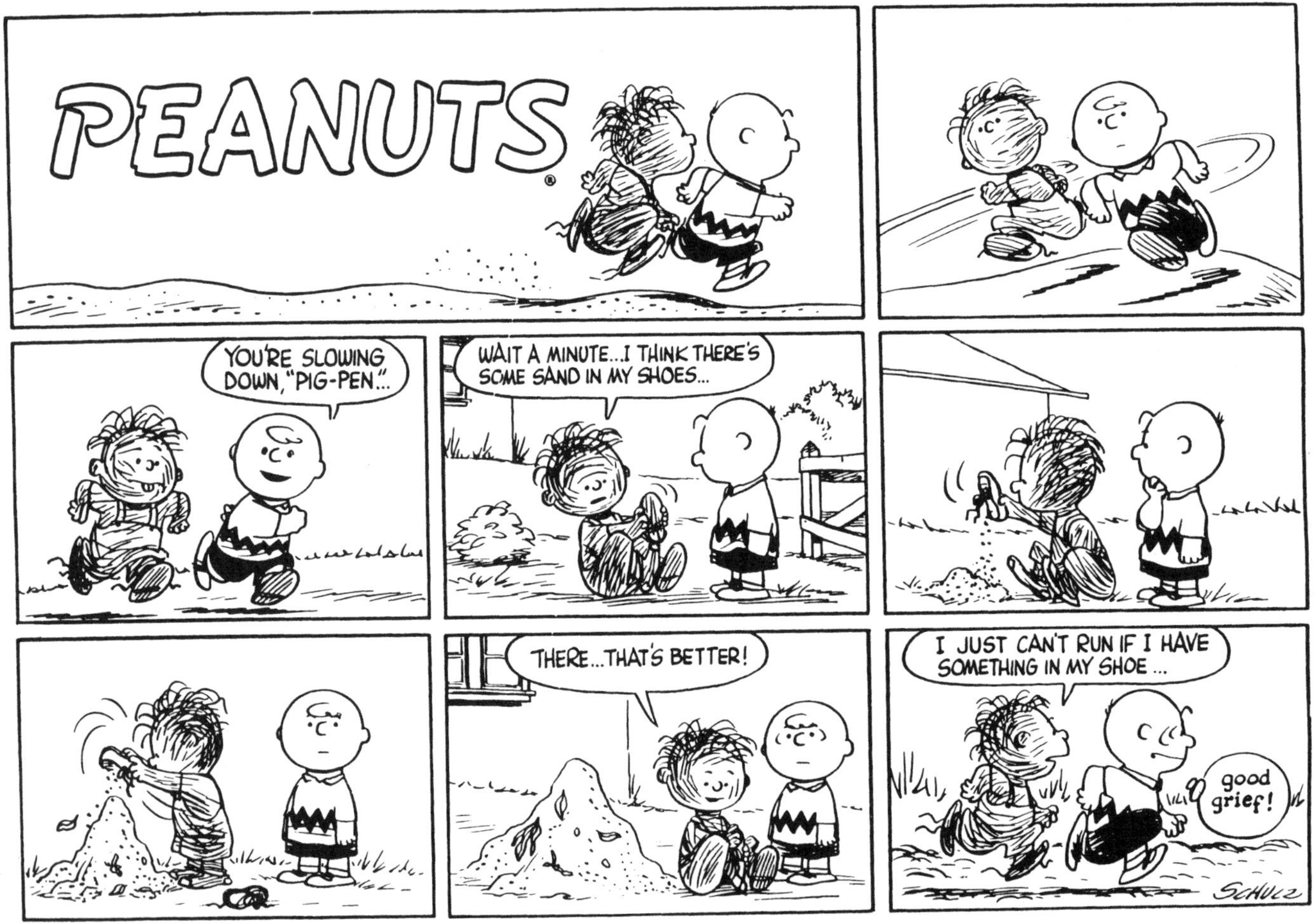
PEANUTS®
YOU'RE SLOWING DOWN, "PIG-PEN"...
WAIT A MINUTE...I THINK THERE'S SOME SAND IN MY SHOES...
THERE...THAT'S BETTER!
I JUST CAN'T RUN IF I HAVE SOMETHING IN MY SHOE...
good grief!
SCHULZ

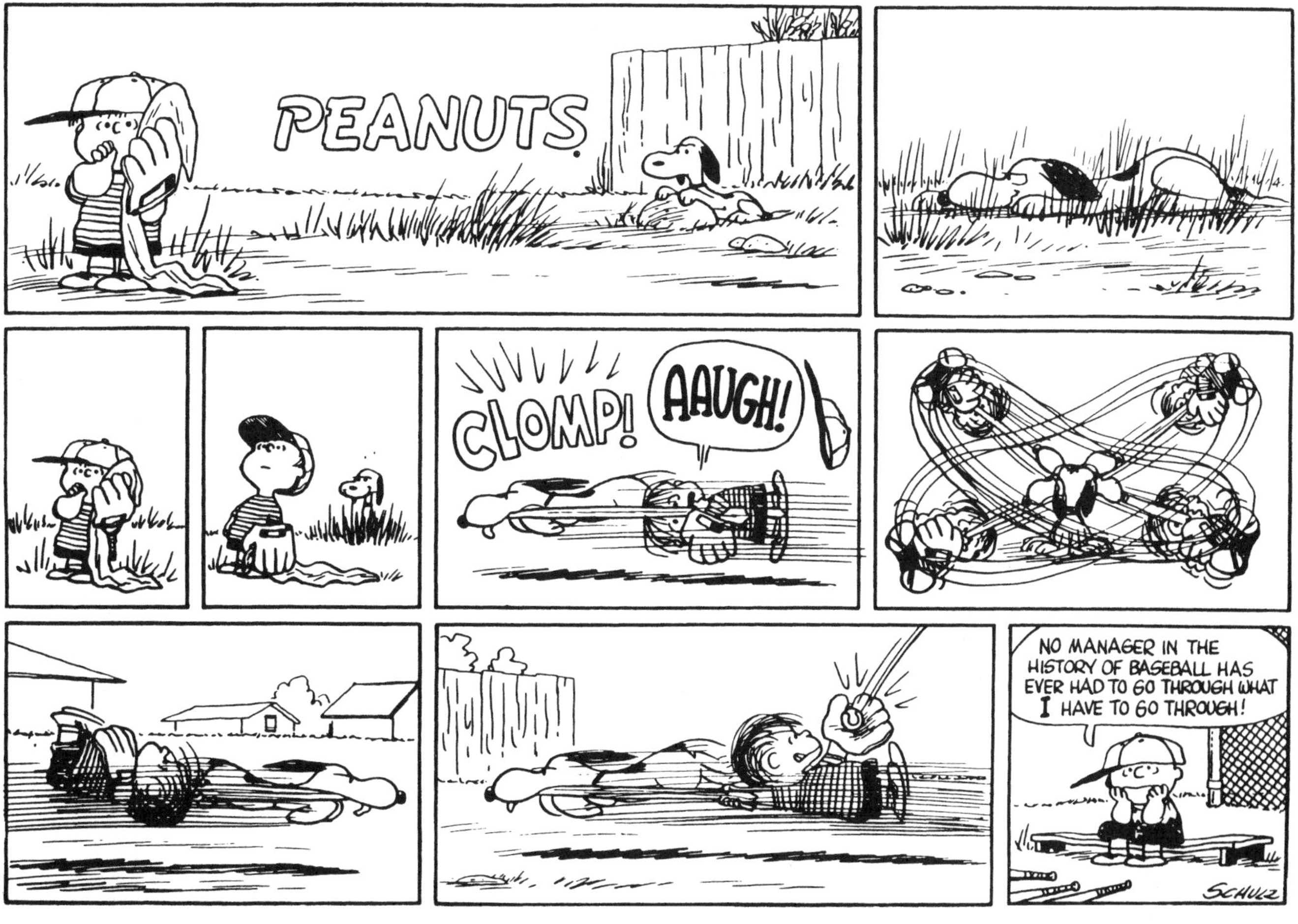
PEANUTS
CLOMP!
AAUGH!
NO MANAGER IN THE HISTORY OF BASEBALL HAS EVER HAD TO GO THROUGH WHAT I HAVE TO GO THROUGH!
SCHULZ

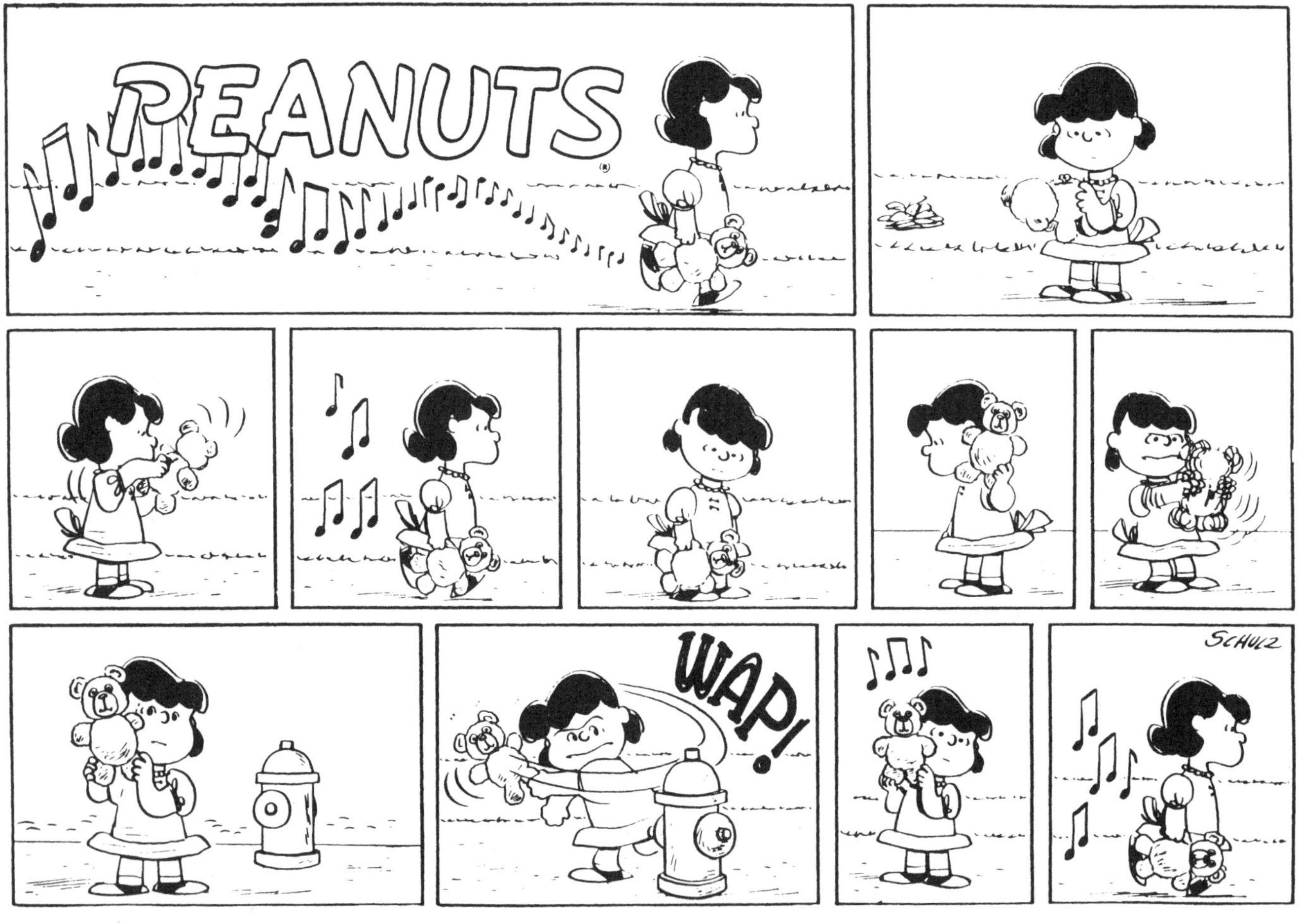

PEANUTS
WAP!
SCHULZ

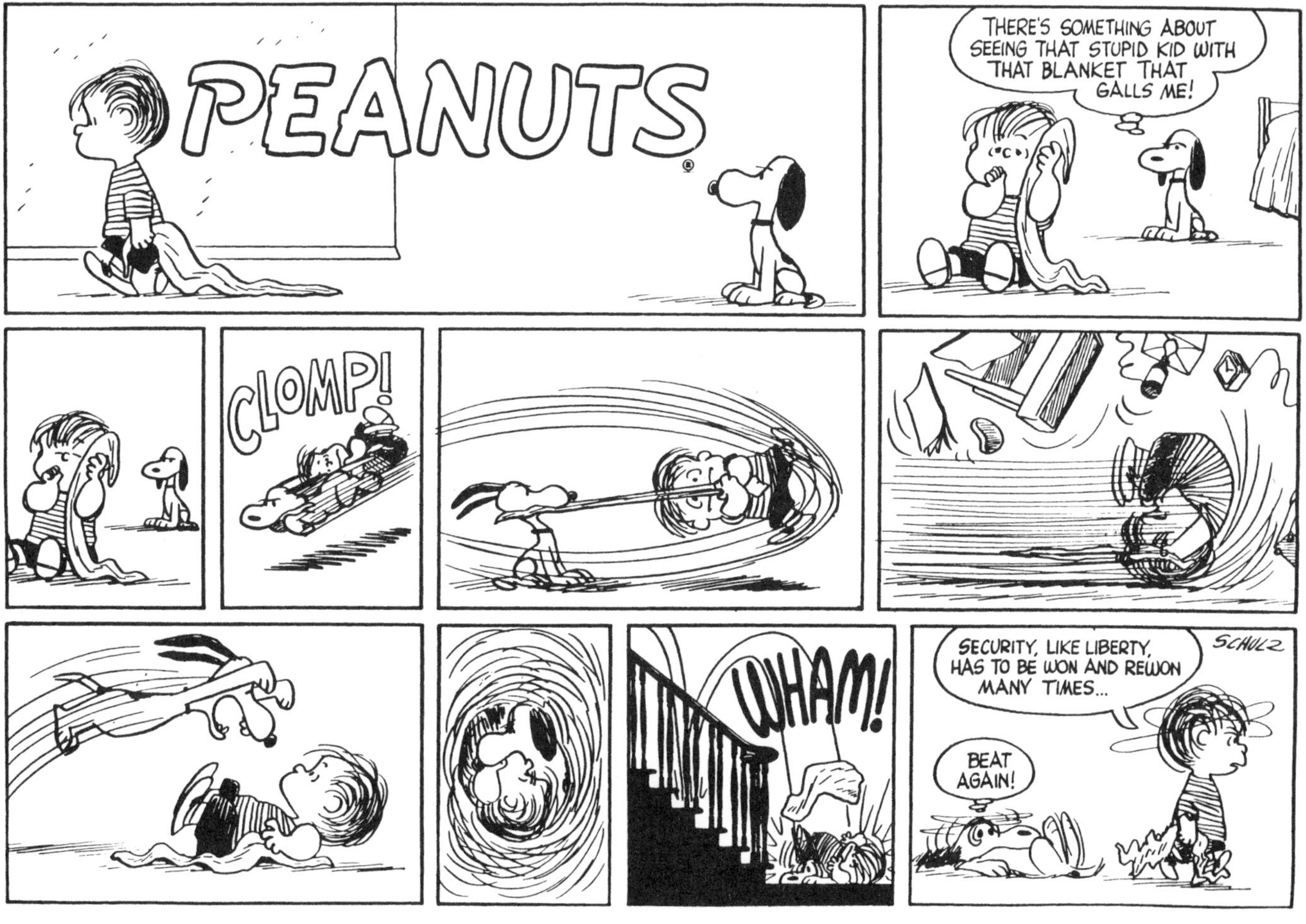
PEANUTS
THERE'S SOMETHING ABOUT SEEING THAT STUPID KID WITH THAT BLANKET THAT GALLS ME!
CLOMP!
WHAM!
SECURITY, LIKE LIBERTY, HAS TO BE WON AND REWON MANY TIMES...
BEAT AGAIN!
SCHULZ

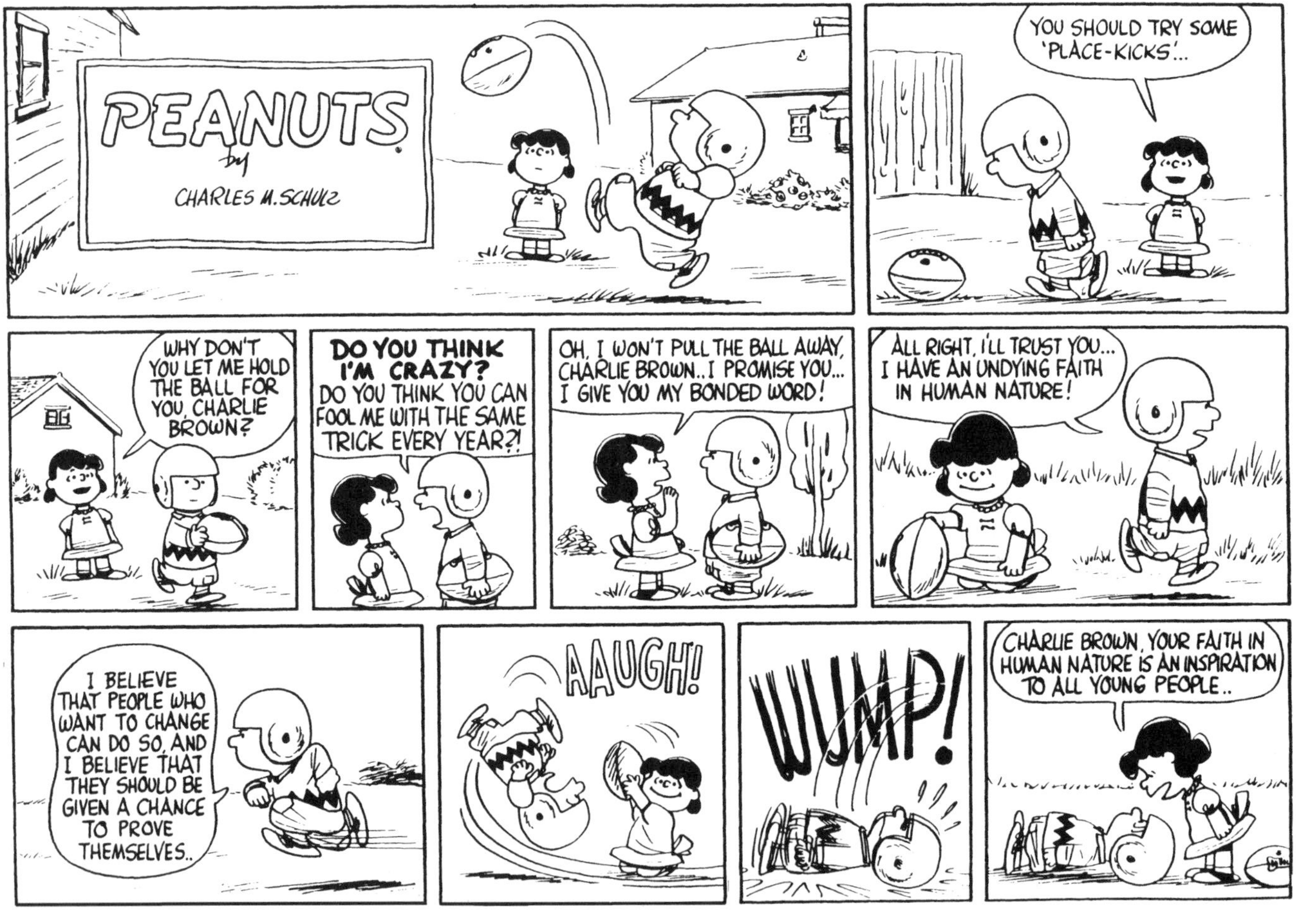
PEANUTS
by
CHARLES M. SCHULZ
YOU SHOULD TRY SOME 'PLACE-KICKS'...
WHY DON'T YOU LET ME HOLD THE BALL FOR YOU, CHARLIE BROWN?
DO YOU THINK I'M CRAZY? DO YOU THINK YOU CAN FOOL ME WITH THE SAME TRICK EVERY YEAR?!
OH, I WON'T PULL THE BALL AWAY, CHARLIE BROWN..I PROMISE YOU... I GIVE YOU MY BONDED WORD!
ALL RIGHT, I'LL TRUST YOU... I HAVE AN UNDYING FAITH IN HUMAN NATURE!
I BELIEVE THAT PEOPLE WHO WANT TO CHANGE CAN DO SO, AND I BELIEVE THAT THEY SHOULD BE GIVEN A CHANCE TO PROVE THEMSELVES..
AAUGH!
WUMP!
CHARLIE BROWN, YOUR FAITH IN HUMAN NATURE IS AN INSPIRATION TO ALL YOUNG PEOPLE..